Principles of

Bible Study

Donald McCluskey
Ancient Words Ministries

Contents

Preface v

Part One–The Foundation for Study 1

Chapter 1–Why Study the Bible? 3

Chapter 2–Influences on Our Understanding 17

Chapter 3–Start with the Scriptures 29

Chapter 4–A Well-Founded Approach 41

Chapter 5–Studying in the Spirit 69

Chapter 6–Principles for Applying the Scriptures 85

Part Two–Setting the Stage for Your Passage 113

Chapter 7–Selecting a Bible 117

Chapter 8–The Concept of Context 135

Chapter 9–Behind the Scenes 151

Chapter 10–Figures of Speech in the Bible 171

Chapter 11–More Figures of Speech 201

Part Three–The Simple Machines of Bible Study 229

Chapter 12–Paragraph by Paragraph 233

Chapter 13–Meditation and Reflection 239

Chapter 14–Reading Basics 247

Chapter 15–Worthy of Note 259

Chapter 16–Exploring Through Questioning 265

Chapter 17–Clarifying the Terms 273

Chapter 18–Follow the Weaver 289

Chapter 19–Dare to Juxtapose! 301

Chapter 20–Articulating Your Learning............................305

Chapter 21–Onward! 319

Appendix A–Progressive Revelation Examples 321

Appendix B–Common Idioms in the Bible 327

Appendix C–Guidance for Identifying Contextual Boundaries 335

Appendix D–Sample Questions.....................................349

Appendix E–Researching a Word....................................357

Appendix F–Juxtaposing Matthew 18:1–14......................365

Glossary..369

Bibliography 381

Index of Illustrations 383

Preface

When I was a young adult, I decided to take a journey through my Bible to review the notes and highlights that I had made over the years. As I made my way through the pages, it became apparent that many of my notes were simply clichés or memory aids with very few indications that I had truly understood the substance of God's Word. Even worse, my notes were not representative of the things that I had studied, but were summations of the lessons and messages of others.

As I reflected on these things, I distinctly remember feeling shallow and empty—even somewhat embarrassed. But as I look back, I see very clearly that my guide for that journey was none other than the Spirit of God. He not only revealed my lack of maturity and understanding, but also led me to consider the true nature of the Word and untethered me from the dependence on others for my understanding.

The years that followed were filled with further reflections about that journey and how I should respond—how I should approach a study of the Word and how to assess my current understanding by its light. The things I learned were rich and exciting. I was once groping in a dark mineshaft, seeking to find something of value, but as I learned how to study God's Word, it was as if someone turned on a light and I was dazzled by gemstones of all sizes and colors, sparkling up from the floor and embedded in the walls and ceiling! Their brilliance called me to consider how they reflected the glories of the One who placed them there.

The words of this book are my attempt to explain some of the things I've learned about studying God's Word that helped turn on the light. I have written from the perspective of a mentor—someone who has already been down the road that you're traveling. In this book, we explore subjects that are subtle, yet fundamental to an accurate understanding of the Word.

I invite you to join me on this journey into God's Word. You will learn more than study skills—you will learn a mindset for study, along with a common sense approach. This book is not a Bible study in itself. It does not tell you what to think, rather it teaches you how to think— how to approach God's Word and how to assimilate it into your mind, heart, and lifestyle. If you immerse yourself in God's Word by the principles of this book, you will truly become conformed to the image of God's Son.

I must make one more point before opening the door and escorting you into Chapter 1. Reading this book and learning its principles will not help you improve your life unless you actually engage in Bible study. Knowing these principles is like knowing how to drive a car. If you get behind the wheel and follow the driving principles, you will go places, but if you never get behind the wheel, then the principles are merely academic. In a similar manner, if you do not actually study the Bible, then your knowledge will not be of any benefit to you. Make it so. Open your Bible and immerse yourself in the Word of God and expect knowledge, wisdom, understanding, and blessing to follow.

Don

Part One

The Foundation for Study

*Give a boy a fish and
he will eat for a day;*

*Teach a boy to fish and
he will eat for a lifetime.*

1
Why Study the Bible?

The Bible is no ordinary book. The fact that it is a unified message of writings of about 40 authors of differing backgrounds over a span of 1,500 years is astounding. But when it is understood at face value as the message of God, the maker of the universe and all life, it takes on an aura that is unparalleled. If someone were to give you a book that contained secrets and truths about life and our world, would you want to open it to see what is inside? The Bible is that book, but the quandary exists in knowing how to understand its truths.

The purpose of this book is to teach believers how to understand the Bible, to interpret and apply it to their daily lives so they can tap into the vine of Truth and not have to rely on others to provide their spiritual nourishment. It's the same idea as the old proverb, "Give a boy a fish and he will eat for a day; teach a boy to fish and he will eat for a lifetime." Our goal is to teach believers how to harvest the living truths from God's Word so they can find spiritual nourishment for their souls and guidance in their daily lives.

Why Should We Study the Bible?
We study the Bible because we believe it is a message from God. But, it is far more than a simple communique or a cryptic transmission from somewhere in the universe. It is truth. It is an offer of peace from the heavens, a message of forgiveness and acquittal from the Judge we fear meeting after death, the plea of a loving Father for his straying sons and daughters to return to Him, the notification that an enormous inheritance awaits those who return, and the answer to the deepest mysteries and quandaries that run through the hearts of man. It is also an invitation that comes with an ultimatum—you may

live forever in paradise or face eternal condemnation for rejecting this extraordinary offer from the Divine King.

The message of the Bible addresses all of these matters and many more. So, when asked if it is worthy of our time and devotion, let me respond with the words of Jesus, "... what will it profit a man if he gains the whole world and forfeits his soul? Or what will a man give in exchange for his soul?" Truly, there are no other words that lead to eternal life and no other study that is more worthy of our attention than the teachings of the Bible.

An *accurate* understanding of the Word of God provides guidance and direction for living in this world. Like an owner's manual for life, God's Word leads to harmony in earthly relationships and proper regard for our Maker through worship, honor, and love. His ways are not intuitive to man, but when tested, they result in joy and hope in this life. Cultures that seek to accurately live out the words of God are hallmarked by true justice and mercy in society, food and shelter for the poor, hospitals for the sick, education for the masses, richness in relationships, an elevated esteem of human life, and a profound reverence for Truth.

A living understanding of God's righteousness as revealed in the Bible also produces something that the world cannot emulate: an internal, ever-present awareness that we must one day answer to God for our thoughts and actions on this earth. The result? Integrity in the hearts of believers that produces honesty and goodwill in all human relationships, including marital, family, friendship, neighbor, business, community, church, and government. What could be a greater deterrent to crime and social ills and a greater motivation for goodwill toward others than people who are motivated from their hearts to live honorably because they know they will give an account to God?

Why is there such a vast difference between the ideal that is established by God's Word and the reality of this imperfect world? It is, of course, because man was not designed to coexist with the knowledge of good and evil, and is therefore, incapable of living out God's perfect design. There will come a day, however, when God will rewire the hearts of men so we will have a natural desire and hunger to please Him and enjoy rich relationships with Him and each other.

The Bible teaches us that there is so much to gain and so much to lose in life. By following God's ways, there is great joy and hope to be found in this life and in the life to come. On the other hand, there is so much joy and hope to forfeit in this life and in the next if we do not learn and heed His ways. It quickly becomes apparent that we must learn how to study this message in a way that will lead us to an accurate understanding of its truths. We certainly cannot be content with a casual understanding that produces a partial truth, but misses the heart of His message. After all, a partial truth that is set forth as the whole truth is false. Therefore, a full and accurate study of God's Word is the only reasonable course of action for every person who desires life and Truth.

We have based this study on the assumption that God's Word was meant to be understood. His Word certainly contains some mysterious and cryptic passages, but the vast majority of them can be understood by an adult reader. We must say, however, that even though the words and sentences may be easy to understand, the concepts therein can be very difficult to comprehend and accept. Rather than being deterred by this, we can take comfort in it. The thoughts and ways of our Father in Heaven, the God of Creation, are higher than our ways and thoughts as the heavens are above the earth. If the ways of God were simplistic and intuitive, it would not be necessary to seek Him, but because He is the infinite Sovereign of the universe, His ways are profound, and thoughtful meditation is necessary to understand Him.

How Should We View the Scriptures?

The Scriptures should be approached with the utmost reverence and caution. They should be regarded as the words of the holy Creator who will give eternal life to some and judge others. With so much to gain and so much to lose, we dare not approach them in a flippant or casual manner. We will attempt to understand God's meaning in each passage and determine how we should respond. We honor God by honoring His Word, and we demonstrate this best through our humble obedience to Him.

It has been said that every person has his own interpretation of reality, whether he is aware of it or not. It has also been said that the Bible is God's interpretation of reality, but here I must disagree. The Bible is not God's interpretation of reality; it is His **declaration** of reality.

This is more than a matter of quibbling over words, since it describes the essence of the Scriptures, acknowledging that God is the Designer, Creator, and true Sovereign. In His Word, God has revealed and declared His design of the entire cosmos, which is much higher than a simple interpretation of reality. The value of everything is measured against God's declaration in His Word. Thus, it is of the greatest importance that we study the Scriptures with the intent of understanding the Designer's declaration, rather than manipulating His words to fit into our much smaller understanding. This is the only way to find Truth.

A View of Life from God's Perspective

God reveals His perspective through His Word. Historical events that we deem important, He may deem insignificant and therefore not include in His Word. On the other hand, events that may seem trivial to us, may be of such great importance to Him that He chose to record them in His Scriptures for our instruction.

An example of this is seen in the life of King Ahab of Israel. In 853 B.C., King Ahab, along with some allied armies, met the powerful Assyrian King Shalmaneser III in battle. During the course of the battle 10,000 Israelites lost their lives, but the Bible is completely silent about this important historical fact. However, during the same year, King Ahab's wife, Queen Jezebel of Israel, devised a plot to kill an unknown man so her husband could take possession of his vineyard.

The story of Naboth's vineyard in 1 Kings 21 may, at first reading, seem like an insignificant event. But we learn that it was very significant in the eyes of God because He dedicated a large portion of the Scriptures to the story. Comparing these two historical facts in the life of King Ahab teaches us that the Scriptures give insights about the things that are important to God, although they may not seem important to man. As we begin to understand God's heart and affections, we can adapt ours to become more like His.

There is much we can learn about the character of God by studying His Word and musing on these stories. Many stories in the Bible do not have the commentary of a prophet or narrator like the story of Naboth, but, we can learn about the character of God by musing on the stories in His Word and comparing them to His ways, which He makes known through the Scriptures. As we become increasingly familiar with the Scriptures we will naturally become increasingly familiar with the person of God.

Another example of God's perspective is found in Judges 18. Here we read the pathetic words of a man named Micah, "… you have taken the gods that I made and the priest … and what do I have besides [these]?" The Scriptures make no direct comment about his words, but through irony they reveal the folly of worshiping lifeless gods that cannot speak and must be defended by their makers. In contrast, the Scriptures declare the magnificence of the immortal, invisible God, Who needs no defense, and is the defender of those who serve Him. Once again, we see God's perspective through the words of the Bible, and hear His quiet voice that is only heard when we carefully study and muse on His Word.

The Bible is abundant with stories, decrees, and commentaries that reveal God's perspective regarding His design of man and His world. In His Word, we gain understanding about the things that bring Him delight or evoke His wrath. He speaks directly, telling us that He is holy and should be treated as such,[1] that justice is one of His key perfections,[2] and that He is a God of tender compassion and kindness to thousands.[3] In His Word, we learn that truth is paramount with

---

[1] "But the LORD said to Moses and Aaron, 'Because you have not believed Me, to treat Me as holy in the sight of the sons of Israel, therefore you shall not bring this assembly into the land which I have given them.'" Numbers 20:12

[2] "Justice, and only justice, you shall pursue, that you may live and possess the land which the LORD your God is giving you." Deuteronomy 16:20

[3] "Then the LORD passed by in front of him and proclaimed, 'The LORD, the LORD God, compassionate and gracious, slow to anger, and abounding in lovingkindness and truth; who keeps lovingkindness for thousands, who forgives iniquity, transgression and sin; yet He will by no means leave the

Him; God is always dealing in truth and seeking those who will worship Him in truth, [4] even to the extent that the Son of God is truth personified.[5]

Need I say more about how the Scriptures reveal God's perspective and character? His Word is packed with insights that are mined through prayerful meditation. As you muse on His Word, His intimations become visible like priceless jewels of eternal value; truths that are transcendent, yet immanent, from the Creator of the cosmos, just waiting to be discovered.

The Treasure Belongs to You

One of the greatest joys of studying the Bible directly, rather than relying on other teachers, is that you will gain ownership in your learning. What do we mean by ownership? We mean that you will become familiar with the exact text and context of the Scriptures and be able to assess and understand them for yourself. You will be able to confidently interact with others as you discuss God's Word and respond to those who quote a passage out of context or distort its meaning. Rather than quoting others, you will know and be able to quote directly from the source of truth.

On a personal note, it is the ownership aspect that has become one of my greatest joys and motivations for studying God's Word. There was a time when I focused on reading and listening to authors and

---

guilty unpunished, visiting the iniquity of fathers on the children and on the grandchildren to the third and fourth generations.'" Exodus 34:6–7
[4] "But an hour is coming, and now is, when the true worshipers will worship the Father in spirit and truth; for such people the Father seeks to be His worshipers." John 4:23
[5] "Jesus said to him, 'I am the way, and the truth, and the life; no one comes to the Father but through Me.'" John 14:6

speakers. I found myself adopting the views of the most persuasive or likable, but I seldom took time to verify their teachings. After several humiliating discussions, I finally realized that I had placed myself on thin ice as I defended the teachings of human authors rather than taking my stand on the solid rock of God's Word. As you develop your knowledge and skill in wielding the sword of God's Word, you will daily increase your share in this treasure of wisdom and Truth.

Once you arrive at a solid understanding of a passage, you will find that it will shed light on other parts of the Scriptures. Your understanding will extend from passage to passage and you will form connections between words, phrases, thoughts, and teachings in different parts of the Bible. Your perspectives will become more unified and you will gradually adopt the Scriptures' perspectives, becoming conformed to the image of Christ.[6]

Perhaps one of the most beautiful aspects of studying God's Word is that it is actually a form of worship. Whether through a casual reading or an intensive study, the very act of turning your attention to the Scriptures is worship of God. He desires our attention, appreciation, and adoration. The joy and praise that well up within our hearts as we meditate on His Word is not unnoticed by Him. It is a most sincere form of worship to become aware of His presence, magnificence, and immensity as you learn from His Spirit. Keep this in mind the next time you feel that Bible reading has simply become an item on your daily checklist. You can take joy in knowing that you are worshiping and honoring God as you honor His Word.

---

[6] 2 Corinthians 3:18 "But we all, with unveiled face, beholding as in a mirror the glory of the Lord, are being transformed into the same image from glory to glory, just as from the Lord, the Spirit."

Our Goal in Studying the Scriptures

What should be our goal as we study and interpret the Scriptures? Briefly stated, our goal is to understand the point of the speaker or writer of each passage. As we study Jesus' parables or His sermon on the mount, for example, we must strive to understand each point and the entire message that He is conveying. The same is true of the apostles and other writers of the Scriptures—our goal must be to understand their message.

Before I am accused of setting a short-sighted goal, I must explain that there are multiple goals in this endeavor. A study of the Scripture with the sole purpose of gaining knowledge or understanding is truly an incomplete goal.

Many would argue that we should study the Scriptures for the sole purpose of applying them to our lives. I do not disagree with this, but we must always pause to make sure that we have correctly interpreted a passage before we proceed to apply what we *think* we know. It is certainly possible to commit serious error if we take action without correctly understanding the instructions.

We do not need to search very far to find tragic examples of people applying an incorrect interpretation of God's Word. History records hideous acts of mankind that were done in the name of God, not because their actions were taught or ordained by Him, but because they grossly misinterpreted His instruction by misinterpreting His Word. Misapplication is often the direct result of misinterpretation.

Misapplications of God's Word are not only found at the macro level of history, but are also abundant in the everyday lives and relationships of His children. Such errors are frequently the basis for overlooking sin in our personal lives, and seemingly insignificant sins that are not confessed and addressed can become destructive causes of stumbling that harm the body of Christ. Jesus' principle is certainly true: "He who is faithful in a very little thing is faithful also in much; and he who is unrighteous in a very little thing is unrighteous also in much."[7]

Secret lusts, for example, are often the seeds that spawn addiction to pornography and can grow into indulgence and sinful relationships. Anger that begins as simple gasps of frustration can evolve into hatred and a desire to harm others. Grumbling that begins as whispers of discontent can breed gossip that alienates brothers and sisters in Christ and even divides churches. An unloving heart can evolve from ignorance of the plight of the hungry, thirsty, and unsheltered to despising their pleas for help. Assuming that these *seed* sins are insignificant can be the source of far greater problems for believers.

Accurately interpreting the Scriptures leads to clear direction from the Holy Spirit. From Paul's words in Ephesians 6:17 we learn that God's Word is the sword of the Spirit. As we sharpen our understanding of His Word, His Spirit is able to wield it in our hearts to improve us and to move others toward His purposes. The Spirit uses this sword as a weapon against the forces of darkness, including the darkness of our own hearts. He can also use it like a surgical scalpel to bring healing to our hearts.

As we follow this metaphor, a sword with a jagged, dull, or barely existent edge is not nearly as effective as one that is sharpened, well-defined, oiled, and polished. Sharpening our understanding of God's

---

[7] Luke 16:10

Word gives definition to our knowledge and discernment in our walk. Although it can be a laborious effort, studying God's Word is a required task that must be done by each follower of Christ. Relying on the studies and research of others cannot replace a direct study of the Word. Every person must engage in this task to the extent that he is able. The Word of God is the only book that is the sword of the Spirit. Unlike the writings of your favorite author, only the Bible has this power and it should, therefore, be the focus of every believer.

I realize that I am placing a great emphasis on the need to study the Word so it can be interpreted accurately, but the reasons become clear with a little thought. If a person designed a house and gave the blueprints to a builder, there would be an expectation that the builder would carefully study the plans before beginning the work. Without giving careful attention to the details, the final product could be very different from the intended design. The same is true of God's Word; He expects us to do our best to correctly interpret His message. We should not assume that we will learn it by being casually acquainted with the Word. Our understanding and subsequent lifestyle should be clearly representative of God's design for His creatures in this world.

It would, of course, be absurd to suggest that a person should not try to apply the Scriptures until he or she has a thorough understanding of them. We must apply them to our daily lives to the best of our ability, and we must also be committed to refining our understanding as we are given more light from the Holy Spirit and from mature believers. Spiritual maturity of believers is based on a commitment to understand the Word of God and adapt our understanding and lifestyles as its truths are illuminated for us.

What's Your Deadline?

It's strange how we sometimes feel that Bible study is a burdensome, time consuming effort. I must admit that it was once difficult for me to engage in detailed studies of God's Word for that very reason. But the question once occurred to me, "What is your deadline?" Did God ever imply that we need to complete our meditations on His Word by a certain date? On the contrary, there is no rush or deadline for completing our personal studies of the Word. It seems that the emphasis of the Scriptures is on the richness of learning as a time of worship and honoring God, the greatest honor being hearts that respond as He leads. This type of study and response are seldom found if we remove our attention from a passage before God's Spirit has had the opportunity to use it to move our hearts.

The study of God's Word must be viewed as a life-long endeavor, rather than a daily glance. I have not found a passage in the Bible that suggests that rewards or points will be given in heaven for the number of times we blaze through a reading or study of God's Word. On the other hand, great reward is promised to the one "who hears the word and understands it; who indeed bears fruit and brings forth, some a hundredfold, some sixty, and some thirty."[8] Ask the Sower about His desire for the Word that lands on the soil of your heart. He will tell you it is to grow to maturity in conformance to the message of the Word. Growing to maturity is not possible in shallow soil. It is not possible to rush the process of maturing or gaining wisdom. So, let's take our time and enjoy the journey as we explore principles of Bible study.

---

[8] Matthew 13:23

Chapter 1—Think About It ...

1. Why do you think there is such a vast difference between the ideal for mankind that is established by God's Word and the reality of this broken world?

   _____

   _____

   _____

   _____

   _____

   _____

2. Explain why the Scriptures are God's declaration of reality, rather than His interpretation of it.

   _____

   _____

   _____

   _____

   _____

   _____

3. Explain how the Scriptures reveal God's perspective and character.

   _____

   _____

   _____

   _____

   _____

   _____

4. Explain the benefits of knowing God's Word through your own studies, as compared to knowing it from the studies of others.

_____

_____

_____

_____

_____

_____

5. How would you describe our goals for studying the Scriptures?

_____

_____

_____

_____

_____

_____

6. Do you feel that believers should apply the Scriptures to their lives if they do not fully understand them? Explain your answer.

_____

_____

_____

_____

_____

_____

2
Influences on Our Understanding

Let's begin our study about studying by answering a question that is very common among critics of Christianity and even among Christians; it is a question that deserves a sincere and thoughtful answer. You are probably familiar with it or perhaps you have asked it yourself. It goes something like this: *If the Bible is true and does not contradict itself, then why are there different branches of Christianity and so many denominations?* Or, *If the Bible is God's Word, why do so many Christians disagree about its meaning?*

The answer? There are many factors that result in differences of understanding. The differences develop from the various influences on our approach to studying God's Word. Some of the influences are obvious, while others are subtle and sometimes barely discernible. In this chapter we will shine a spotlight on some of the more subtle influences and offer tips to increase our awareness of them.

The Sway of Assumptions and Presuppositions
Perhaps the most common influence on our interpretation of Scripture is found within our own assumptions about what the Bible teaches. An assumption or presupposition is simply a thought or idea that a person *believes* the Scriptures teach, before he or she studies them. Assumptions and presuppositions can have a profound impact on the outcome of a study, since we tend to interpret and subsequently understand the Scriptures in ways that fit our biases.

For example, if we assume the Scriptures teach about a God of love who only seeks the goodness and well-being of mankind, then Scripture passages that speak of God's anger or wrath might be allegorized or modified to match our assumptions about God's love. If we approach the Scriptures from the perspective that man is the center of God's affections, then we will likely not understand the many passages about the sovereignty and glory of God. If we presuppose that the Bible is not inspired by God, then we will be prone to viewing paradoxes as contradictions and discard the more obscure and difficult truths that lay before us.

You may have heard the term *exegesis*. It is a term from the ivory towers of academia that describes an approach to study. Exegesis means to *lead out*. In other words, allow the text to lead your learning; allow it to speak for itself. That's a good thing! As we study the Word, we need to be exegetical in our approach.

On the other end of the spectrum, we find an approach that is called *eisegesis* (pronounced *ahy-si-jee-sis*). Eisegesis is an approach wherein a person presupposes the meaning of a passage and proceeds to explain the passage in a way that supports his or her idea. Obviously, eisegesis is not the way to find the intended meaning of the writer or speaker. But I would like to make an important point about eisegesis. Although we may believe it is a philosophy that reigns in the schools of unbelievers who want to dilute the Faith, in reality, it is unwittingly practiced by many Christians on a regular basis as they study God's Word. As we study the Word, we must constantly ask ourselves if we are allowing it to speak for itself or if we might be twisting it to conform to our own presuppositions.

Let's take a look at some specific assumptions and presuppositions that may influence our understanding.

The Influence of Theological Systems

Perhaps one of the most subtle presuppositions is found in the realm of theological systems. Theological systems are abundant in the modern church, and although they can have a positive, stabilizing effect, they can also hide truths of the Word by predetermining a student's interpretation of passages.

In general, every Christian denomination represents a theological system by which it derives its understanding of truth and interpretation of the Scriptures. I want to make it very clear that I am not judging the truth or validity of these systems—I am only making the point that they can affect a person's judgment and interpretation of the Scriptures.

We must always be mindful that theological systems are man-made creations, and by that fact alone are of a much smaller and limited perspective than the words of God. A blind commitment to a theological system places human limits on our understanding of God's Word.

Theological systems can have a profound impact on our understanding of the truth. One possible negative effect of theological systems—even good theological systems—is that they can cause us to betray a pure interpretation of the Scriptures. Most Christians belong to a church body that embraces a theological system, and although commitment to a local church is healthy and beneficial, believers should be aware of the potential influence of such systems on their interpretation of the Word of God. It is essential that we give preference to the good and pure interpretation when differences arise.

The Influence of Experience

Most of us have heard people say they cannot believe the Bible or something in it because they have seen or felt something contrary to it in their own experience. For example, most of us have wondered how a God of love could allow innocent children to starve or suffer the ravages of war, or how a loving God could condemn people who have never had the chance to hear the name of Christ. Or, how a just God could allow the wicked to prosper while the innocent suffer, or why God would condemn people who engage in *victimless* sins when both parties consent. And of course, there is the classic, "How can something be wrong when it feels so right?"

As a result of personal experiences and feelings, people tend to approach the Scriptures from a self-righteous perspective that causes them to prejudge God and His Word before seeking to understand what He has to say. Judging God is never a good idea. We must always approach Him with reverence and concede that any shortcoming is on our part, not His. The wise will sit quietly and listen—they will ponder and ultimately adopt His ways, rather than rendering a judgment against Him.

When life is confusing, frustrating, and difficult to understand, we must remember that we should not lean on our own understanding, but instead trust the Lord; we should not be wise in our own eyes, but honor the Lord in our assessment of truth. To state it another way, we must interpret our experience by the Scriptures—not interpret the Scriptures by our experience. The way of disciples is to follow the teaching of their Master.

Stumbling Over Our Current Understanding

Another subtle roadblock that can keep believers from accurate interpretation is the assumption that they already understand a passage. Nothing can cause a person to miss the truth of a passage faster than assuming he already understands it.

This phenomenon is very common, and the solution is to regularly study the Word with an honest and good heart, asking ourselves if there may be another possible interpretation. You may have already had this experience and been enlightened through reevaluating a passage with a fresh look.

I am not suggesting that you should be suspicious of your understanding of every passage, or that you should be reluctant to take a stand on the things you've learned. However, you should be willing to revisit your interpretation when it doesn't seem to fit with the context or flow of a passage, or with newly gained understanding.

The Error of Incorrect Emphasis

The error of incorrect emphasis can be one of the most subtle obstacles in the pathway to accurate interpretation. As the term suggests, an incorrect emphasis is a tendency to either overemphasize or underemphasize a teaching or concept in the Scriptures. In many cases, the subject that is being unduly emphasized may not be a bad subject—it may actually be a very good subject—but the incorrect emphasis causes a bias that results in a skewed interpretation of the Word.

For example, a person who believes that spiritual gifts are the most important aspect of the Christian life might have a tendency to interpret distantly related or unrelated passages in light of spiritual gifts. In a similar manner, a person who places an undue emphasis on the prosperity of believers may tend to interpret distantly related passages as proof of this assumption. Other topics that are often unduly emphasized include nationalism, social agendas, and family.

So how do we determine the **correct** emphasis of the Scriptures? We approach them with an honest and good heart, and our understanding is refined as we become increasingly familiar with their teachings.

In order to avoid the error of incorrect emphasis, students should take an approach that is similar to dealing with assumptions. They should first acknowledge their affinity for certain subjects and the tendency to interpret passages with such a bias. It may also be helpful to study with others who have a more balanced understanding of the Word. Simply being aware of this subtle tendency is one of the first steps toward dealing with it. A good rule of thumb is to strive to place the same amount of emphasis on subjects as the Scriptures place on them. The Scriptures offer multiple perspectives on each subject, and we should seek to balance our understanding with all of them.

Proof-Texting or Contextomy
As students of the Word, we must make every effort to understand passages of Scripture within their context, with the goal of understanding the writer's or speaker's intended meaning. When a passage is extracted from its context and used to develop doctrine or prove a point that does not reflect the original intent of the writer or speaker, it is referred to as a proof-texting or contextomy.

Proof-texting is a blatant violation of the spirit of hermeneutics. The purpose of hermeneutics is to provide guidelines to help readers understand the intended meaning of the writer or speaker, while proof-texting has no such respect and frequently produces quotes or teachings that are very different from—even contrary to—the author's intended purpose.

Sadly, proof-texting is a common error among many Christians. Passages of the Bible are often extracted from their context by sincere believers and used in a manner not intended by the writer. Reasons for proof-texting are usually not mischievous or malicious, but stem from an ignorance of sound Biblical interpretation principles. Although believers may be sincere in their erroneous use of the Scriptures, the results of such misuse does not save their conclusions from falling into the realm of false teaching.

It is especially important to watch for proof-texting when dealing with cults. If teachings or statements are taken out of context or based on difficult or obscure passages that do not reflect the intended meaning of the author, then red flags should wave fervidly in your mind.

Truth is paramount in the Scriptures, and it must also be paramount for the children of God. Jesus told us that He is the Truth[9] and that He would send the Spirit of Truth who proceeds from the Father (see John 15:26).[10] Since Truth is a perfection of the Father, the Son, and the Spirit, then it should certainly be our pursuit as we study God's Word. Handling the Word accurately in an attempt to know the Truth clearly involves honoring the context as part of understanding the Author's intent.

Although proof-texting should be avoided at all costs, we should mention that it is permissible to quote a passage of the Bible without having to quote its entire context. What is the difference between an acceptable quote and proof-texting? Quoting is permissible if it is done within the spirit of the context, being used as the author

---

[9] John 14:6 "… I am the way, and the truth, and the life; no one comes to the Father but through Me."
[10] John 15:26 "… the Spirit of truth who proceeds from the Father …"

intended. It is not legitimate if the quoted text differs from the author's intended usage. There is a clear distinction between a legitimate quote and a proof-text. Do not feel that you must quote an entire chapter when making a point with a small passage. Using a passage as the author intended is perfectly legitimate.

Believers

There is another factor that profoundly influences a person's response to the Word. It is very simply that some people believe and others do not.[11] The outcome of their understanding and response is as different as light and darkness, and as different as the church and the world. Is a person's faith ordained by God or does it stem from some inner light within man? Regardless of its source, a person's faith or belief in the Word will have a great influence on his or her understanding and lifestyle.

Are you a believer? I suspect that you are or perhaps you are reading this book because there is a glimmer of hope in your mind that the words of the Bible contain something you desire. If you need strength for a failing faith, then take comfort—you have come to the right place. The Lord of the Scriptures—your Maker—is tender and merciful and will bring you along in your journey with Him. Isaiah says, "A bruised reed He will not break and a dimly burning wick He will not extinguish."[12] So follow the path of Christ with an honest and good heart and follow Him where He leads. Lean on Him and learn from Him and you will find rest for your soul.[13]

---

[11] "For indeed we have had good news preached to us, just as they also; but the word they heard did not profit them, because it was not united by faith in those who heard." Hebrews 4:2

[12] Isaiah 42:3

[13] Matthew 11:29

An Honest and Good Heart

Let's consider another fundamental ingredient for arriving at an accurate interpretation of the Scriptures. In Luke's account of the parable of the Sower, Jesus refers to the good soil as those who have "heard the word in an honest and good heart and hold it fast and bear fruit with perseverance"[14]. As we read our Bibles, the seed of the Word falls on the soil of our hearts and produces fruit as our soil permits. If we ask for the guidance of God's Spirit and truly strive to understand the Word with an honest and good heart, then fruit will be borne in our lives—it **will** happen if those conditions exist.

What does it mean to have an honest and good heart? I believe it simply refers to our efforts to understand the Word without any agendas, allowing God's Word to speak for itself as it was given. This means we must not interject interpretations or ideas for the purpose of proving our points or overlooking the portions that convict our hearts. The honest and good heart will make every effort to understand the meaning of the writer or speaker and respond in a way that will align itself with the Word. In this parable, Jesus used the metaphor of fruit to describe this process. In non-figurative language, we would refer to fruit as obedience or conformity to God's Word.

So, with an honest and good heart, let's do away with our assumptions, presuppositions, and agendas, and be nourished by the pure milk of the Word, allowing it to transform us into men and women who truly reflect the image of God. This will be our goal as we study God's Word.

---

[14] Luke 8:15

Chapter 2—Think About It ...

1. In a few sentences, explain how people's assumptions and presuppositions about God and the Bible can affect their interpretation of the Bible.

    _____

    _____

    _____

    _____

2. How can holding to a theological system influence a person's interpretation of a passage? Give an example, if you know of one.

    _____

    _____

    _____

    _____

3. Give an example of a teaching that resulted from an incorrect emphasis of a subject.

    _____

    _____

    _____

    _____

4. Explain what it means to study the Scriptures with an honest and good heart.

    _____

    _____

    _____

    _____

3
Start with the Scriptures

Let's take a break from the academic world for a few moments and just relax and clear our minds. Imagine that you decided to take a fresh look at understanding the Scriptures and you were considering how to interpret them accurately. If you were to ignore the lofty words of theologians and scholars, you would probably develop a simple and practical approach. For example, you might ask yourself how the people of the Bible interpreted and understood God's Word, and I would commend you for such a simple, practical idea!

Learning how Jesus, James, Peter, Paul, and other apostles, in addition to the prophets of old, interpreted the Scriptures provides extremely valuable keys to help us view and interpret God's Word as they did. Certainly, the Son of God interpreted the Scriptures as God intended, as did those He sent to record the Word. So, how did Jesus interpret the Scriptures? What can we learn from His use of the Scriptures as He quoted, applied, and appealed to their authority?

When we follow the example of Jesus, the apostles, and the prophets, we are actually applying a very important principle, which is to use the Scriptures as their own commentary. In other words, we must look to the Scriptures for insights about interpreting other Scripture passages. Let's explore some of these insightful passages from the Bible.

Jesus' Comments and Usage of the Scriptures
When Jesus preached His sermon on the mount (found in Matthew chapters 5–7), He made it very clear that the Law (i.e. the Law of

Moses[15]) was fully relevant to Himself and would be fulfilled in its entirety. In two sentences, He made some profound statements about the Law, its permanence, its subject (He is the subject!), its level of detail, and God's promise to fulfill it. Let's take a look.

Matthew 5:17

"Do not think that I came to abolish the Law or the Prophets; I did not come to abolish but to fulfill. For truly I say to you, until heaven and earth pass away, **not the smallest letter or stroke shall pass from the Law until all is accomplished.**" [*emphasis added*]

What can we learn about Bible interpretation from this statement?

- The Law of Moses applied to Jesus, so it should, at the very least, be worthy of our study in order to learn more about Him.
- The Word that God gave in His law had many details and He will assure that every one of them is accomplished, with no exceptions.
- Every single word and letter of the Law was ordained by God; even the seemingly insignificant elements of the Law have eternal meaning and God-given importance.
- We can trust God to follow through on His words, promises, and judgments, wherever they are found—in the law, the historical books, the psalms, or the prophets. His Word is unalterable and unfailing.

Jesus' parable of the Sower is recorded in three of the four gospels. Immediately after presenting the parable, He explained *privately* that

---

[15] The Law of Moses is recorded in the first five books of the Bible: Genesis, Exodus, Leviticus, Numbers, and Deuteronomy. These books are often referred to as "The Law" or as the Pentateuch.

His reason for speaking in parables was to prevent people from
understanding the mysteries of the kingdom, thus fulfilling the
prophecy of Isaiah 6:9–10. Let's see what we can learn from His use of
the Scriptures:

Matthew 13:13–15

"Therefore I speak to them in parables; because while seeing they
do not see, and while hearing they do not hear, nor do they
understand. In their case the prophecy of Isaiah is being fulfilled,
which says,

'YOU WILL KEEP ON HEARING, BUT WILL NOT UNDERSTAND;
YOU WILL KEEP ON SEEING, BUT WILL NOT PERCEIVE;
FOR THE HEART OF THIS PEOPLE HAS BECOME DULL,
WITH THEIR EARS THEY SCARCELY HEAR,
AND THEY HAVE CLOSED THEIR EYES,
OTHERWISE THEY WOULD SEE WITH THEIR EYES,
HEAR WITH THEIR EARS,
AND UNDERSTAND WITH THEIR HEART AND RETURN,
AND I WOULD HEAL THEM.'"

What can we learn about Bible interpretation from this statement?
- In this passage, Jesus teaches that the words of the prophets
  could be taken literally, to the extent that He did exactly as they
  said in order to fulfill them.
- We can infer that Jesus understood that **He** was fulfilling this
  prophecy.

When we consider Jesus' quotes of the Law and prophets, it becomes
very clear that we are to interpret their stories as being literal
historical facts. As He appealed to the Scriptures, He affirmed the

factuality of some of the mightiest miracles of the Bible, including the following.

Jonah and the great fish
Matthew 12:40

"… for just as JONAH WAS THREE DAYS AND THREE NIGHTS IN THE BELLY OF THE SEA MONSTER, so will the Son of Man be three days and three nights in the heart of the earth."

Noah and the great flood
Luke 17:26–27

"And just as it happened in the days of Noah, so it will be also in the days of the Son of Man: they were eating, they were drinking, they were marrying, they were being given in marriage, until the day that Noah entered the ark, and the flood came and destroyed them all."

The destruction of Sodom and Gomorrah
Luke 17:28–29

"It was the same as happened in the days of Lot: they were eating, they were drinking, they were buying, they were selling, they were planting, they were building; but on the day that Lot went out from Sodom it rained fire and brimstone from heaven and destroyed them all."

Peter's Teaching About the Scriptures

Peter was part of the inner circle of Jesus' disciples (*Peter, John, and James*). The letters he wrote clearly show that he spent a great deal of time with Jesus and learned and understood His teaching. Through Peter's letters, we get glimpses of Jesus' teaching that were not recorded in the gospels. Let's take a look at some insights from the apostle Peter.

2 Peter 1:20-21

"But know this first of all, that **no prophecy of Scripture is *a matter* of one's own interpretation**, for no prophecy was ever made by an act of human will, but men moved by the Holy Spirit spoke from God." [*Emphasis Added*]

What can we learn about Bible interpretation from Peter's words?

- Peter clearly teaches that the message of the prophets is God's message. We can infer that anyone who interjects or contrives an interpretation that is different from God's message is teaching the doctrines and precepts of men.

- We learn that the prophets of old spoke from God, being *moved* by the Holy Spirit.

- We can infer that the inspiration of the Scriptures was accomplished by the Holy Spirit moving men to speak God's message.

- We learn that the Scriptures were not written because humans decided to compose a message on God's behalf. On the contrary, they were written because the Holy Spirit initiated and oversaw the transmission of God's message to humans.

2 Peter 3:15–17

"... and regard the patience of our Lord *as* salvation; just as also our beloved brother Paul, according to the **wisdom given him**, wrote to you, as also in all *his* letters, speaking in them of these things, in which are some things hard to understand, which the untaught and unstable distort, as *they do* also the **rest of the Scriptures**, to their own destruction. You therefore, beloved, knowing this beforehand, be on your guard so that you are not carried away by the error of unprincipled men and fall from your own steadfastness ..." [*Emphasis Added*]

What can we learn about Bible interpretation from these words of Peter?

- Peter affirmed Paul's authority and placed his writings on the level of the rest of the Scriptures.
- He describes Paul's words as "wisdom given him"—things hard to understand.
- He warns us about distorting the Scriptures, whether from ignorance (untaught) or from mischievous (unprincipled) motives.

Paul's Teaching About the Scriptures

2 Tim 3:16-17

"All Scripture is inspired by God and profitable for teaching, for reproof, for correction, for training in righteousness; so that the man of God may be adequate, equipped for every good work."

What can we learn about Bible interpretation from these words of Paul?

- Paul declares the authority of the Scriptures over believers, which implies that we must bring our lives into alignment with them, rather than allow the message of the Scriptures to be softened to accommodate our natural desires.
- We learn that an accurate understanding of the Scriptures is able to train in righteousness.
- The Scriptures carry authority for reproving and correcting believers.
- It is possible for the man of God to be adequate in the work of God—this is an amazing statement, since it attests to the completeness of the Scriptures.
- That good works seem to be one of the goals or the *fruit* of the inspired Scriptures.

- We can infer that it is necessary for the man of God to know the Scriptures (i.e. study them) in order to gain the benefits that Paul describes.

Galatians 3:16

"Now the promises were spoken to Abraham and to his seed. He does not say, 'And to **seeds**,' as *referring* to many, but *rather* to one, 'And to your **seed**,' that is, Christ." [*Emphasis Added*]

What can we learn about the inspiration of the Scriptures from these words of Paul?

- Notice Paul's confidence in the smallest details of the Scriptures. His understanding of inspiration is in line with that of Jesus', down to *the smallest letter or stroke* of the script, in this case to the level of the singularity of a word versus being plural.
- As we follow Jesus and Paul's understandings of this micro-fine level of inspiration, we should also strive for precision in our interpretation of God's Word by examining its words with the greatest care and interpreting it with the utmost honesty of heart.

1 Corinthians 14:37–38

"If anyone thinks he is a prophet or spiritual, let him recognize that the things which I write to you are the Lord's commandment. But if anyone does not recognize *this*, he is not recognized."

What can we learn about Paul's understanding of his own words in his letters?

- Paul considered the words of his own writings to be "the Lord's commandment." This is very strong language! Recall that Peter also affirmed that Paul's writings are on par with the Scriptures (2 Peter 3:15–17).

- Paul very clearly stated that those who do not recognize this should not be recognized (probably referring to their authority for teaching, speaking, or being heard in the church).

David and the Ark

David was a man who deeply loved the Lord and cherished His Word, but he was certainly not perfect. Nonetheless, God used some of David's blunders to instruct believers of the following generations. The story of David moving the Ark of the Covenant provides profound insight into how God intended His Word to be understood and followed.

As the story is told in 2 Samuel 6:1–15, David ordered the ark of God be moved to Jerusalem from Baale-judah. To do so, the ark was placed on a new cart and moved with great celebration and music played on all kinds of instruments. At one point in the journey, however, the oxen nearly upset the cart and a man named Uzzah reached out and took hold of the ark to prevent it from falling, but because of his irreverent action, God struck him and he died.

Obviously, this brought a halt to the journey and celebration, and David's joy was turned to anger because of the Lord's outburst against Uzzah. As a temporary measure, David had the ark taken to the nearby home of Obed-edom until he could devise a plan to move it to Jerusalem; three months passed before the ark was moved.

In the very next verse, 2 Samuel 6:12, we are told that the Lord had blessed the house of Obed-edom on account of the ark of God. Then, without explanation, David went and brought the ark to Jerusalem with gladness and celebration. But we must ask ourselves what was different that made this trip a resounding success. One small insight is found in verse 13, which says there were *bearers of the ark* and they also offered a sacrifice after the ark had gone six paces. But was there more?

The answer is found in 1 Chronicles 15:1–15, which is a parallel account of the story in 2 Samuel. In verses 11–15 of this chapter, we learn that David did his homework by studying the statutes that Moses had commanded according to the word of the Lord. In this chapter we read:

> "Then David called for Zadok and Abiathar the priests, and for the Levites, for Uriel, Asaiah, Joel, Shemaiah, Eliel and Amminadab, and said to them, *"You are the heads of the fathers' households of the <u>Levites</u>; consecrate yourselves both you and your relatives, that you may bring up the ark of the LORD God of Israel to the place that I have prepared for it. 'Because you did not carry it at the first, the LORD our God made an outburst on us, <u>for we did not seek Him according to the ordinance.</u>'* So the priests and the Levites consecrated themselves to bring up the ark of the LORD God of Israel. **The sons of the Levites carried the ark of God on their shoulders with the poles thereon**, as Moses had commanded **according to the word of the LORD.**"
>
> *[Emphasis added]*

What should we learn from this story of David and the ark?
- We learn that God intended His ordinances to be continually honored.
- The details of His law are significant and not to be altered or ignored for the sake of convenience.
- We can infer that customs and teachings in the entire Bible can be explained through a greater understanding of the Laws and Prophets.

- The details of the Word are important to God and for that reason they should be important to us.
- Reverence for God is an axiom and He is eternally worthy of honor.

Clearly, the characters of the Bible did not allegorize the Scriptures or dismiss them as being irrelevant. The individuals in these Biblical accounts regarded the Scriptures as a sacred message from God that should be honored and revered. We look to the people of the Bible for our example as we seek to approach the Scriptures as they did, reverently accepting them as God's Word, wholly inspired by the Holy Spirit and, therefore, true, reliable, authoritative, without error, fully relevant and essential for those who desire to worship God.

Our Assumptions about the Scriptures
Now that we have briefly considered how the personalities of the Bible regarded and interpreted the Scriptures, it is a good time to consider our own assumptions to see how they align with theirs. As you consider them, you will no doubt see how most were derived from the Biblical perspectives that we just explored.

Everyone has assumptions and presuppositions about the Bible – some are healthy and others are not. We have our own set of assumptions and presuppositions about the Bible and how to interpret it. Most of them were developed by honest scholars throughout the centuries and were refined by other godly scholars and theologians. Many were formed by the Bible's teaching and by Biblical characters as they quoted the Scriptures and commented on their origin. The following is our list of *healthy* assumptions about God's Word:

1) The Bible is fully God's Word—it does not merely *contain* God's Word.

2) The Bible was inspired by God through the individual personalities of human authors (Divinely inspired as contrasted with the more common artistic or intellectual inspiration of man).

3) The Holy Spirit ensured the accuracy of the inspired writings down to the minutest detail.

4) The Holy Spirit was involved in the selection of words and thoughts by the writers.

5) The manuscripts that resulted were entirely without error; they were inerrant and flawless.

6) The Bible is God's message and He intended it to be understood by mankind—it is not merely a collection of cryptic writings with hidden messages.

7) The Bible is not a collection of allegories and cryptic sayings, although it does contain such.

8) The Bible is the authoritative source of truth—its truth trumps every other teaching and revelation.

9) The Bible is applicable to the lives of all people, whether they accept it or not.

10) Through the Scriptures, we can learn about the character, will, and mysteries of God. Without this special revelation from God, we could know about Him, but we would not know the details of His character, creation, and providence.

We have been referring to the above statements as our assumptions, but over the years they have also become our assessment of God's Word due to their unparalleled origin, development, and reliability. In light of our assessment of this treasure, we must be diligent to use the greatest care as we attempt to interpret its meaning so we may receive the greatest understanding and blessing from the Author.

4
A Well-Founded Approach

"I have great respect for orthodoxy, but my reverence for inspiration is far greater. I would sooner a hundred times over appear to be inconsistent with myself than be inconsistent with the word of God."

C.H. Spurgeon—*Metropolitan Tabernacle Pulpit,* 26: 49–52

The Truth

I would like to lay the groundwork for our approach to Bible study by exploring the concept of Truth. Pursuing, knowing, and living by Truth should be the norm, not just for seekers of God, but for every human being. After all, what long-term profit can be gained by ordering our lives on baseless assumptions that only lead to false hopes and unfounded fears? In reality, it's like living in a fairytale world with imaginings that will never come true, while denying dangers that will one day become a horrifying reality.

Ignorance may be bliss for a time, but the wise diligently seek the truth so they can prepare for reality. Who wants to live a life of being deceived? Who would want to stand before God on that day as one who did not diligently pursue truth, completely unprepared for that meeting? Sometimes the truth can be cold and hard and not what we want, but we must nonetheless accept it so we can come to terms with it and be prepared for the reality to come.

As worshipers of God and seekers of eternal life, pursuing a crisp, clear understanding of the Truth is of supreme importance. Truth is paramount in the realm of theology since there are few signposts outside of the Scriptures. Our eternal well-being stands in the balance and no one can afford to be flippant or casual in the pursuit.

Theology is not a matter of forming a religion or manufacturing a personal god based on what seems right or feels good. We cannot change the character and nature of God any more than we can change the character and nature of our galaxy. God has clearly declared who He is, and He will not be morphed by our imaginations, regardless of how much we would like Him to be something other than what He has already declared. It is because of this that we seek Him, rather than seeking to shape Him. We seek with the intent of worshiping the Deity we encounter—not with the intent of denying or shunning Whom we find.

As seekers of God, we must pay close attention to the message of His Word. It is for this reason we are emphasizing interpretation principles that will act as guideposts to keep us on safe ground as we interpret His Word and encounter the only true God Whom everyone will stand before on that great day to come. We seek the precious element of truth because only the truth will make us free.

Hermeneutic Principles and Rules

For thousands of years, philosophers, scholars, and theologians have sought insights and methods for accurately understanding the writings and sayings of others. This area of study is called Hermeneutics. The modern state of hermeneutics is an attempt to capture the best of these thoughts so they can be applied to any textual or verbal communication. The principles of hermeneutics are guidelines that help the reader understand the speaker or writer's intended meaning.

By adhering to the principles of hermeneutics, we establish ground rules that help us maintain a consistent approach to interpreting and understanding God's Word. It is important that we approach our study of the Scriptures in an organized manner. Henry Thiessen wisely observed that, "the man who has no organized system of thought is at the mercy of the one who has such a system."[16] Our goal is to approach our study of the Scriptures in an organized manner so we will not be at the mercy of our own carelessness, nor at the mercy of those who intentionally or unintentionally distort the Scriptures.

As we begin our discussion of hermeneutics, we need to clarify the difference between principles and rules. It is tempting to devise a list of hermeneutic *rules* that could be applied to each type of Scripture passage, or perhaps create some software that could scan a Scripture passage and produce an interpretation. It would be great to have a clear-cut, mechanical procedure for interpreting the Scriptures that is based on a crisp, rule-based methodology. But the truth is that hermeneutics is better described and implemented as a set of principles rather than rules. So what is the difference between a principle and a rule? Briefly, a principle describes a goal or purpose, whereas a rule is a concrete, black-and-white directive that is based on a principle.

For example, parents make rules for their children—do not play in the street, do not play with matches, do not swim alone, etc. But these rules are based on the principle "Be safe." Since young children do

---

[16] (Thiessen 1949, 28)

not understand every potential hazard in the world, it is necessary to protect them by creating specific rules that relate to their lives.

If parents were to simply teach the principles "be safe" or "be kind", then a naïve child would be completely unaware of the potential danger that might be lurking if he or she were to show kindness to a stranger who tried to allure him or her with a gift. Wouldn't it be great if we could just tell children the principle—to be safe—and not have to burden them with a suffocating list of dos and don'ts? As we mature and become familiar with the different realms in which we live, the need for rules can be gradually replaced with an understanding of principles. The concept of rules versus principles is similar to the letter of the law versus the spirit of the law.

We have chosen to relay the hermeneutic concepts at the *principle* level, rather than at the *rule* level. Perhaps you will be relieved to know that there is no authoritative list of hermeneutic rules or principles that govern the interpretation process. That is because there are too many possible interpretation scenarios to manage. Furthermore, it would be an endless and tedious task to search for the specific set of rules that would apply to each passage of the Bible. By providing a smaller, more manageable set of principles, you will be able to understand the goal of interpretation, as well as have an understanding of the tasks that must be completed in order to arrive at a solid interpretation of a Scripture passage.

By way of example, Jesus gave us two broad principles that act as guideposts as we seek to understand the Scriptures and apply them to our lives. They are the greatest and second greatest commandments of the law.

"And He said to him,

'YOU SHALL LOVE THE LORD YOUR GOD
WITH ALL YOUR HEART, AND WITH ALL YOUR SOUL, AND WITH ALL YOUR
MIND.
This is the great and foremost commandment.

The second is like it,
YOU SHALL LOVE YOUR NEIGHBOR AS YOURSELF.
On these two commandments depend the whole Law and the
Prophets.'"

Matthew 22:37–40

These two principles form the foundation of God's desire for us, the priorities that should govern all of our decisions. It is obedience from a heart of love for God and our fellow man. When uncertainty arises about the interpretation of any given passage, we can look to these guideposts to see where the great, overriding emphasis should be as we seek to obey the God of love.

Hermeneutics: Principles for Interpretation

Hermeneutic Principle #1
The Scriptures are our source of authoritative truth.
The teachings of the Scriptures supersede tradition, experience, emotion, and human understanding. To use philosophical terms, the Word of God is absolute truth. In our modern world, some people maintain that there are no absolutes, but we strongly reject that notion, graciously reminding them that such a statement is an absolute statement in itself. Of course, we remind ourselves that the absolute truth of the Scriptures is found by accurately interpreting them.

How does this statement, which is also one of our healthy assumptions, give us a principle for interpreting the Scriptures?

Esteeming the Scriptures as authoritative truth means that their truths must be given priority over all of our assumptions, presuppositions, desires, existing world views, personal agendas, and the popular agendas of this world. We must understand our world and order our priorities according to the truths of God's Word.

Hermeneutic Principle #2
There are no contradictions within the Scriptures.

The Scriptures were given by the same Spirit; He did not insert any contradictory teachings in the Bible. The Scriptures were not casually penned by men at their own desire. Instead, the Holy Spirit inspired and moved the prophets and apostles to relay His message as God desired.

Because God's Spirit was overseeing the inspiration process, there are no errors, mistakes, or contradictions in the Scriptures. No message of the Lord will contradict the whole counsel of the Scriptures. If a message that is contrary to the Scriptures is presented to you, be assured that it is not from the Lord.

The Scriptures do, however, contain teachings that *seem* to be contradictory, but when we study them carefully, we realize they are paradoxical in nature and fully reconcilable. Seeking the relationship between paradoxical statements often brings great insight into our understanding of the Lord. There is no truth that contradicts another truth. God's Spirit, Who Jesus referred to as *the Spirit of truth*, maintained perfect harmony within the Scriptures, and we must approach them with that confidence.

Take, for example, the following passages. These can be somewhat difficult to understand because they seem to contradict the more well-known passages that teach us that God loves the world (ref. John 3:16) and desires none to perish (ref. 2 Peter 3:9).

a. Luke 8:10 "And He said, 'To you it has been granted to know the mysteries of the kingdom of God, but to the rest it is in parables, so that SEEING THEY MAY NOT SEE, AND HEARING THEY MAY NOT UNDERSTAND.'"

b. Romans 9:13 "Just as it is written, 'JACOB I LOVED, BUT ESAU I HATED.'"

c. Romans 11:7–8 "… but those who were chosen obtained it, and the rest were hardened; just as it is written, GOD GAVE THEM A SPIRIT OF STUPOR, EYES TO SEE NOT AND EARS TO HEAR NOT, DOWN TO THIS VERY DAY.'"

d. 1 Samuel 2:25 (regarding Eli's sons) "… But they would not listen to the voice of their father, for the LORD desired to put them to death."

e. 1 Kings 22:21-22 (read the entire story in 1 Kings 22:1–40) "Then a spirit came forward and stood before the LORD and said, 'I will entice him.' The LORD said to him, 'How?' And he said, 'I will go out and be a deceiving spirit in the mouth of all his prophets.' Then He said, 'You are to entice him and also prevail. Go and do so.'"

As we study the Scriptures, we will, at times, have to concede that we just do not understand how to interpret a certain passage. We may, sometimes, be tempted to accept an interpretation that doesn't quite fit the various contexts and flow of the passage, but it is of fundamental importance that we do not force an interpretation that just doesn't quite fit.

It's okay to simply accept that fact and admit that we just don't know. It is not a disgrace to not know everything; after all, we are human and not divine. But living with an "I don't know" is usually just a temporary state. When we encounter a difficult passage, rather than force fitting an interpretation, we should simply flag it in our minds and notes, and be on the lookout for other Scriptural teachings that answer the question.

The discipline of not force-fitting an interpretation helps us keep our minds open to the true solution when it comes along. If we accept an interpretation that just doesn't fit, then we will not be on the lookout for the correct one and we may miss it when it is revealed to us if we have stopped watching for it. Trusting that the Scriptures do not contain contradictions, and waiting and watching for the right interpretation, is a discipline that students of the Word must take seriously. Our Teacher, the Holy Spirit, desires that we mature in our understanding, but He will teach us as we seek and as we are able to receive the meatier portions that He serves.

Hermeneutic Principle #3
The Scriptures are their own best commentary.
As we search for insights and understanding about the correct interpretation of a Scripture passage, the best place to begin is with the Scriptures themselves. Rather than initially referring to a commentary from a human author, asking a friend, or accepting the view point of your favorite speaker or scholar, you should first consult the teaching of God's Word for insights. The Scriptures were inspired from a unified voice—the Holy Spirit—and the message of each passage clarifies and reinforces the messages of other passages.

After you have thoroughly studied a passage and referred to related Scriptures for additional insight, you will be ready to explore the learning and conclusions of other scholars who have commented on it as well. At this point, you will be equipped to follow their reasoning and recognize their accuracies and inaccuracies.

Hermeneutic Principle #4
God revealed His Word in a progressive manner.

As the Scriptures were given by God throughout the centuries, new information and insights were revealed that shed light on His previous revelations. The newer revelations provide additional information about matters that were previously revealed, which enlarges the picture and our understanding. This phenomenon is referred to as **progressive revelation**. It is important to understand that progressive revelation does not contradict or nullify prior revelation; it simply augments it to enlarge the overall picture.

Perhaps the theme that is most commonly revealed in this progressive manner is that of God's Anointed One. You are no doubt familiar with the Hebrew word for anointed one, which is Messiah. Its Greek equivalent is Christ, which is probably even more familiar to you. In the same way that we refer to our Lord as Jesus Christ, it would be equally legitimate and respectful to refer to Him as Jesus Messiah or Jesus the Anointed One. The Scriptures boldly proclaim God's message of the Messiah as the hope of Israel and the light of the Gentiles because of the salvation that is found in Him.

It is interesting, however, that this supremely important message is not majestically announced at the beginning of the Bible. On the contrary, it is quietly intimated in the beginning and slowly unfolds throughout the 1,500-year revealing of the Scriptures in a *progressive* fashion; it is a progressive revelation.

The first hint about the Anointed One is found in the opening pages of the Bible in Genesis 3:15, which records the curse that God pronounced upon the serpent:

> "And I will put enmity between you and the woman, and between your seed and her seed; He shall bruise you on the head, and you shall bruise him on the heel."

These cryptic words indicate that the serpent is going to inflict a non-fatal injury on the seed or offspring of the woman. On the other hand, the offspring of the woman will, one day, inflict a death-blow to the head of the serpent.

When a person first reads these words, it is easy to completely overlook the prophetic significance of the message. How could a student of God's Word know that this passage is actually a prophecy about God's Anointed One? Honestly, it would be difficult to prove without the aid of subsequent passages that progressively shed additional light on this one. But, a diligent study of God's unfolding revelation in the Bible clearly reveals that the final judgment and destruction of the serpent (i.e. Satan) is one of the mighty acts of the Messiah.

Take a moment to study the verses in Appendix A—Progressive Revelation Examples. As you consider the verses in the table, you will get a glimpse of how the Scriptures *progressively* reveal God's message in the Bible. The verses in the table teach about the Messiah and ultimately reveal that Jesus is the Christ (Messiah). After reading the latter verses in the table, it becomes apparent that the earlier verses are truly early intimations of a much larger prophetic picture.

Progressive Revelation and Hermeneutics

Having an awareness of Progressive Revelation can help students of the Word gain deeper insight into passages that would otherwise be difficult to understand. For example, Psalm 118:22–23 is clearly a Messianic psalm[17] since Jesus referred to it in His dialogue with the chief priests and elders in Matthew 22:42.

Psalm 118

22 The stone which the builders rejected
    Has become the chief corner stone.
23 This is the LORD'S doing;
    It is marvelous in our eyes.

Jesus' quote of Psalm 118 only included verses 22 & 23, but when we turn to the psalm and look into the verses that immediately follow, it becomes obvious that they are also referring to the work of the Messiah through his sacrificial death:

Psalm 118

24 This is the day which the LORD has made;
    Let us rejoice and be glad in it.
25 O LORD, do save, we beseech You;
    O LORD, we beseech You, do send prosperity!
26 Blessed is the one who comes in the name of the LORD;
    We have blessed you from the house of the LORD.
27 The LORD is God, and He has given us light;
    Bind the festival sacrifice with cords to the horns of the altar.
28 You are my God, and I give thanks to You;

---

[17] A *Messianic* psalm is a psalm that refers to the Messiah. It is not necessary for the psalm to include the term Messiah, as long as its content refers to some aspect of the Messiah or His work.

> You are my God, I extol You.
> 29 Give thanks to the LORD, for He is good;
>   For His lovingkindness is everlasting.

In these verses we find a treasure of teaching about the Messiah. For example:

- The *day which the Lord has made* (v24) is probably referring to the Passover (Aviv 14), rather than just any day or any Sabbath day.
- "Blessed is the one who comes in the name of the LORD" is another Messianic verse that Jesus ascribes to Himself (Matt 21:9, 23:39, Mark 11:9, Luke 13:35, & John 12:13).
- "Bind the festival sacrifice with cords to the horns of the altar" is no doubt a reference to Jesus, rather than just a Passover lamb—recall that Jesus is our Passover (1 Corinthians 5:7) which means He is the Sacrificial Lamb for our sins.
- Notice the joy, praise, and thanksgiving of the psalmist. Although the death of the Lamb might seem like a somber event, it is in reality the ultimate source of joy, praise, and thanksgiving, since, through His work, the Messiah obtained eternal redemption for all who believe.

Hermeneutic Principle #5
Scripture passages must be evaluated in light of their literary styles.
The Scriptures contain a variety of literary styles, which include narratives, parables, epistles (i.e. personal letters), poetry, wisdom and proverbs, laws/rules/exhortations, and prophecy. Each literary style requires a slightly different approach to its interpretation, so we

must be able to recognize the various genres in order to interpret each passage accordingly.

For example, if we were to buy a book of poetry from a bookstore, we would naturally view its grammar and style differently from that of a novel or a self-help book, interpreting the words and sentences in a manner appropriate to the genre we are reading. As students of God's Word, we need to be watchful for changes in genre and interpret as the writer or speaker intended.

Hermeneutic Principle #6
A Scripture passage should be evaluated within the flow of its textual context.

As we explain this hermeneutic principle, it is important to emphasize that different types of contexts exist. This principle addresses the *textual* context, which refers to the words, sentences, and paragraphs (i.e. the text) that surround our passage. The World Dictionary says the word "context" stems from the Latin word "contextus", which carries the idea of putting together by interweaving. From a literary standpoint, we will be tracing the threads that the writer or speaker wove throughout our passage—how ideas and logic were introduced and interconnected.

Understanding the weave of the context is of the greatest importance for gaining an accurate understanding of the message, since our goal is to understand the speaker or writer's intended meaning. Our interpretation should attempt to find a natural fit for the passage within the logical flow of the words and thoughts that precede and follow it. The Scriptures were written in a very logical style with well-developed themes; it is very unusual to encounter a random thought that is unrelated to its context. Students must take time to study and muse on each passage to understand how it blends with its textual context.

You have probably heard someone say that a passage was "used out of context," which implies that it was not used as the speaker or writer intended. In order to help you honor the textual context of a passage, Chapter 8 explains how to determine the *contextual boundaries*. Once the boundaries have been identified, we may proceed with the interpretation process. It is sometimes difficult to determine where the contextual boundaries begin and end, but it is a skill that can be developed with practice.

Hermeneutic Principle #7
Each Scripture passage should be evaluated in light of its environmental contexts.
In addition to understanding a passage as part of its textual context, it is also important to account for the influences of the environment in which it was written. The environmental contexts include:

+ Historical
+ Cultural/Social
+ Geographical
+ Political/Governmental
+ Religious
+ Military

For the sake of simplicity, we will refer to these environmental contexts as the *Big-6* and we will elaborate on them in Chapter 9.

It is important to be aware of the influences of the Big-6 environmental contexts since they can have a subtle and unspoken impact on a correct interpretation of a passage. It is very common for writers of the Scriptures to assume the reader already has an understanding of some of these influences, and not explain them in their writings. For example, the gospel writers seldom explain the historical background of the Roman occupation of Israel; they assume the reader is aware of the situation. Furthermore, the New Testament writers frequently assume the reader has an understanding of the place of the Mosaic Law in Judaism and, subsequently, on the church, so they relay their stories and teachings with little or no explanation.

As you gain familiarity with the various environmental contexts, the intended meaning of the writer will become more apparent. In many cases, the same environmental contexts will apply to an entire book of the Bible, as is the case with the four gospels. In other cases, however, there will be multiple layers of the Big-6 as the stories unfold. For example, the book of Daniel opens with Daniel serving in the courts of the Babylonians, but chapter 5 closes with the kingdom being received by Darius the Mede, and the book closes as he serves Cyrus the Persian (see Daniel 1:21 and 6:28). When studying the book of Daniel, it is helpful to understand the related environmental contexts of these kingdoms in addition to understanding the historical context of Judah's exile to Babylon.

Hermeneutic Principle #8
Figures of speech should be understood through the eyes of the Biblical writer.
God's Spirit used the hearts and minds of human writers to relay His Word as He inspired it through their personalities and experience, rather than by means of dictation. As a result, the Scriptures contain figures of speech, illustrations, and expressions that were familiar to each writer. For example, people who live in an agricultural community would naturally use expressions about planting, growing, harvesting, and livestock and their illustrations might be expressed

through metaphors that were familiar to them. Because of this, we see the metaphors of sheep and shepherds which depict the people, their leaders, and even God.

As we read the Scriptures, we must be aware that they are rich with figures of speech and we must learn when to interpret them as figures versus literal statements. The decision can sometimes be challenging, but we must make the effort to understand the writer/speaker's intended usage. Interpreting a figure of speech as if it were a literal statement is every bit as erroneous as interpreting a literal statement with a figurative meaning. Because of this, we must proceed cautiously as we study the Word. We will discuss figures of speech at length in Part Two of this book, and provide guidelines for determining whether an interpretation should be literal or figurative.

Hermeneutic Principle #9
Use the clear to interpret the unclear.
As we interpret the Scriptures, passages that are difficult to understand should be understood in light of those which are clear and easily understood. In other words, use the clear to interpret the unclear – do not skew the meanings of clear passages with weak interpretations of passages that are not easily understood.

Someone recently asked about the meaning of Jeremiah 31:22, which says, "... For the Lord has created a new thing in the earth—A woman will encompass a man." The person who asked the question explained that she was approached by a member of a cult who used this *unclear* verse to *prove* that the Messiah was going to return as a woman, and she just happened to be the leader of her cultic church. This is a clear example of distorting the well-established teachings of the Scriptures about the Messiah and distorting them with the unclear passages of the Scriptures.

Many cults and false teachers intentionally ignore this key hermeneutic principle of as they seek to advance agendas that are in line with their own desires, but outside the truth of God's Word.

Hermeneutic Principle #10
Clarify the terms as you explore a passage.
One of the most fundamental elements of communication is to have a concise understanding of the terminology that is being used. If the speaker and listener are using a word differently, then all sorts of misunderstandings can result. Because of this, it is essential that words and terms are clarified as they arise in discussion or in written material. As you can imagine, this principle is of the utmost importance as we interpret the Scriptures.

The Spirit of God chose to inspire His Word through the personalities of men who lived in eras and cultures that are far removed from our own. It is because of their long-ago, far-away perspective that we must give special attention to understanding their usages. As part of this effort, we must investigate the meanings of the words in their original languages and cultures and consult the expertise of language scholars to help us gain this understanding.

Words and Terms
You have probably noticed that we have mentioned both *words* and *terms*. A term is a word or group of words that describe a concept or an idea. Learning the meanings of a word in the original language is not necessarily the end of our investigation. Although this may seem like a trivial concept, it actually has some profound implications in our studies.

For example, as we consider the "fear of the Lord," how should we understand the word *fear*? Some interpreters feel it means reverence, while others feel that it carries the idea of a type of respect that is characterized by a healthy anxiety or terror. Once again, it is essential that we understand the terminology before we attempt to interpret a passage, since it will ultimately affect our understanding and lifestyle.

In later chapters, we will explore words and groups of words that we refer to as figures of speech. When evaluating figures of speech, it usually does not make sense to place a great deal of weight on the individual meanings of words that makeup a figure, since they are intentionally not used in their natural sense. In the case of a figure, the *term* may actually refer to an entire phrase that embodies the concept that the figure conveys. For example, In Ecclesiastes 2:12, Solomon says, "The wise man's eyes are in his head, but the fool walks in darkness." In this case, the figure "eyes are in his head" may be considered to be a *term* that suggests that the wise man considers the outcome of his ways. We will explore the procedure for clarifying the terms in Chapter 17.

Hermeneutic Principle #11
Only the explicit teaching of a passage may be understood as having the full authority of the Scriptures.
As we study the Scriptures, our goal is to understand the intended meaning of the original writers or speakers. As part of this process, we meditate on their words and seek to understand their *immediate* meaning, but in the process we also develop *inferences* that are based on our interpretation and reasoning. It is of great importance, however, that we distinguish between the immediate teachings of a passage versus the secondary teachings that are based on our inferences.

Interpretation is the process of determining—to the best of our ability—the intended meaning of a passage of God's Word. An accurate interpretation of a passage embodies the full authority of God's Word. On the other hand, our inferences or *secondary interpretations* do not carry the same weight of authority as the primary interpretation.

As an example, Exodus 20:13 says, "You shall not murder". Some might consider this a prohibition against all categories of taking the life of a human being, and therefore conclude that military action, capital punishment, and even self-defense fall into the category of murder and accordingly make their own rules and decrees. We must, however, be mindful that such conclusions are inferred by the reader and not explicitly prohibited in the Scriptures. A proper understanding of "You shall not murder" must be tempered by a correct interpretation of the whole body of the Scriptures.

Some teachings of the Scriptures are quite clear and easily applied universally. But, we must be very careful when we elevate our secondary interpretation to the level of carrying the full authority of the Scriptures. Although we may be convinced that our inferences are Scriptural, we cannot rightly say that everyone should view them as having the full authority of the Scriptures.

Prohibitions against gambling, consuming alcohol, and dancing, are statutes that people sometimes find in the Scriptures through inferences. Although there may be some wisdom in following these guidelines, we must be mindful that they are not explicitly taught in the Scriptures and are, therefore, man-made inferences that do not carry the full authority of the Scriptures. Once again, we must strive for a pure, undiluted interpretation of the Word.

Hermeneutic Principle #12
Honor the Book.

As we study any given book of the Bible, there is a tendency to look to other books of the Bible to gain insight into the current book. Although this cross-referencing is an essential ingredient for accurately understanding the whole of Scripture, it is important to first make an effort to understand the teaching within each book as it was given. Once we have applied adequate, disciplined study to the current book of study, we may – *rather we must* – refer to other books of the Bible for the purpose of gaining a comprehensive understanding of God's Word. Adhering to each book in this manner is referred to as honoring the book.

You might ask how it would make a difference if we were to study a book independently of other books versus studying them together. We can trace this back to our simple discipline of striving to understand the words of a writer or speaker in their original context, so we can make sure that we understand them as intended. If we allow the writer or speaker's words to be influenced by words in another book, perhaps from a different context, then we may interpret the teaching in the current book in a way that was not intended. We must study each book, within its context, before allowing it to be influenced by the teachings of other parts of the Scriptures.

I was recently studying Matthew 17:24-27 with a friend and I made the comment that it looks like Jesus was suggesting that sons of the kingdom are not required to pay taxes. My friend immediately quoted Jesus words in Matthew 22:21, "... render to Caesar the things that are Caesar's; and to God the things that are God's." and declared that we are, indeed, required to pay taxes. Although I agree with the statement, I responded that we must *honor the book* and first understand the immediate lesson before coloring it with teaching from other passages. In the case of Matthew 17:26 & 27, we can learn some very interesting things about the kingdom and our place in it, when we honor the book and seek to understand Jesus' intimations without external influences, even if they are from the same book.

Once we have fully studied a book of the Bible, cross references should *first* come from other books of the same author or speaker, *secondly*, from other books of the same testament (Old or New), *thirdly*, from anywhere in the Bible, and *finally* from extra-Biblical sources. The discipline of honoring the book may sound like a small issue, but it can have a profound impact on a final interpretation of the Word.

Hermeneutic Principle #13
In general, there is only one correct interpretation of any given Scripture passage.

Have you ever heard someone read a passage of Scripture and follow it with the question *"What does it mean to you?"* Although this question might simply be an invitation for discussion, it also represents a common misunderstanding about the nature of the Scriptures. The misunderstanding is that any given passage of Scripture can have many meanings that are determined by the situation, mindset, or need of each reader. The truth is, however, that nothing could be farther from the truth. As the Holy Spirit inspired the Scriptures, He did so with a very specific purpose for each passage. Each passage, therefore, contains one, and only one, correct interpretation—God's truths are not determined by anyone's current situation or existential insights.

Once we have thoroughly studied a passage and arrived at the correct interpretation, we should ask "How does it *apply* to my life?" And therein is the principle: Each passage of Scripture has one, and only one, correct interpretation, although it may hold many *applications*. In other words, there are many principles and parallels that the Holy Spirit can bring to mind as He leads us to respond to a correct interpretation of the Word. How does this work? Chapters 5 and 6 of this book will bring this concept to light as we explore *Studying in the Spirit* and *Principles for Applying the Scriptures*.

Is it ever possible for a passage to have multiple interpretations? This question has been the subject of much debate over the years with godly people on both sides of the issue. It is often referred to as "The Principle of Double Fulfillment in Interpreting Prophecy." Briefly, it describes the belief of some Biblical scholars that certain *prophecies* can have both *near-term* and Messianic fulfillments.

For example, Daniel 11:31 refers to an *abomination of desolation*, who would arise, desecrate the sanctuary fortress, do away with the regular sacrifice, and "set up the abomination of desolation." This prophecy speaks of a man who would desecrate the temple, as did the Greek King Antiochus IV Epiphanes who persecuted the Jews in Jerusalem and instituted the worship of Jupiter in the Temple of God[18] in 167 BC.

If Daniel's words are, indeed, a reference to this event, then Jesus' reference, 200 years later to an *abomination of desolation* who is yet

---

[18] 2 Maccabees 6:1–11

to come, refers to yet another fulfillment of Daniel's prophecy. "Therefore when you see the ABOMINATION OF DESOLATION which was spoken of through Daniel the prophet, standing in the holy place (let the reader understand),"[19] So the interpreter must ask, "Is this a double fulfillment of prophecy?"

With the exception of prophecy, we should approach the Biblical text as if it has only one correct interpretation. On the other hand, God's Spirit can *apply* His truths to our lives in a myriad of different ways. Thus, we have one correct interpretation for each passage, but many possible applications.

Hermeneutic Principle #14
Interpret each passage in the natural, intended sense of the writer or speaker.
People sometimes have a tendency to read Bible passages as if they were written exclusively to themselves, completely ignoring the original intention of the writer or speaker. For example, a well-intentioned friend of mine explained his interpretation of the parable of the Prodigal Son as an allegory of his personal family situation. He believed the relationship of the father to the younger son was identical to his own, and the relationships of the older brother also mirrored his family experience. It is possible that similarities exist, but such an interpretation is not consistent with Jesus' purpose for the parable, nor does it blend with the textual context or the Big-6 contexts.

In other instances, people have interpreted the Word with the assumption that it is to be spiritualized or allegorized to find a deeper or more universal meaning. Interpreters of medieval times believed

---

[19] Matthew 24:15

that a literal (i.e. normal) interpretation of the Scriptures was not useful. They proceeded to develop various levels of interpretation, teaching that each verse of the Bible contained a moral teaching, a practical teaching, and an allegorical principle. These interpreters "would view the story of the fall, for instance, merely as a picture of the present sinful condition of each man, and that of the virgin birth as merely expressing the thoughts of Christ's superhuman character."[20]

As we saw in Chapter 3, however, the godly characters of the Bible did not dilute the intended meanings of the writers of the Scriptures in such a way. Without question, Jesus, David, Peter, and Paul understood them in their natural intended sense. Even though allegorical and other figurative meanings are occasionally taught, their overall interpretation approach is to accept the natural intended meaning of the writer or speaker.

In like manner, as this principle states, we must seek to understand the Scriptures as the writers and speakers intended their words to be understood. Once we arrive at an accurate interpretation from their perspective, we must work with God's Spirit to apply them to our lives as He leads. Chapter 6 is dedicated to exploring how to apply the Scriptures to our lives.

Hermeneutic Principle #15
Study a passage thoroughly on your own before seeking assistance from others.
In Chapter 2, we highlighted some influences on our understanding as we study God's Word. These influences include our assumptions and presuppositions, the influence of theological systems, our own

---

[20] (Packer 1958, 101–114)

experience and those of others, and our current understanding. Our point is that we must approach our study of the Scriptures with as little bias as possible.

In like manner, our study and conclusions can be influenced by commentaries and friends, so we must discipline ourselves to first study passages on our own with the assistance of the Holy Spirit, *before* subjecting ourselves to other influences. As we mentioned, these influences may not be bad in themselves, but they can make it difficult for us to read and view the Scriptures from an objective perspective.

Because of this, Hermeneutic Principle 15 advises us to *first* study the Scriptures from an unbiased perspective before allowing ourselves to be influenced by people and resources that can sway our objectivity. Once you have thoroughly studied a passage on your own, we strongly recommend that you consult friends, advisors, and commentaries to enlarge your perspective and perhaps, refine your understanding.

Conclusion

The hermeneutic principles that we've listed address the great majority of interpretation concerns for studying the Bible. As mentioned earlier, the study of hermeneutics is designed for both sacred and non-sacred literature. Principles 5 through 10, for example, can be applied to almost any text if the words "Scripture" and "Biblical" were removed. The principles of hermeneutics are guidelines that help the reader understand the writer's intended meaning, but we must always be mindful that studying with an honest and good heart is the spirit that drives our study methodology.

We will be referring to this list of hermeneutic principles throughout this book. In order to easily refer to them, we have assigned a number to each. The numbers do not represent a defined convention of hermeneutic principles that have been established by some world-wide body of standards—they are simply numbers that we've assigned for the purpose of easy reference. It would probably be a good idea to bookmark this page or remember the page numbers because you'll be returning here soon!

Hermeneutics: Principles for Interpretation

1) The Scriptures are our source of authoritative truth.
2) There are no contradictions within the Scriptures.
3) The Scriptures are their own best commentary.
4) God revealed His Word in a progressive manner.
5) Scripture passages must be evaluated in light of their literary styles.
6) A Scripture passage should be evaluated within the flow of its textual context.
7) Each Scripture passage should be evaluated in light of its environmental contexts.
8) Figures of speech should be understood through the eyes of the Biblical writer.
9) Use the clear to interpret the unclear.
10) Clarify the terms as you explore a passage.
11) Only the explicit teaching of a passage may be understood as having the full authority of the Scriptures.
12) Honor the Book.
13) In general, there is only one correct interpretation of any given Scripture passage.
14) Interpret each passage in the natural, intended sense of the writer or speaker.
15) Study a passage thoroughly on your own before seeking assistance from others.

Chapter 4—Think About It ...

1. What does it mean to live by the truth and why is it of
    fundamental importance?

    _____

    _____

    _____

    _____

2. Why is it important to know the Big-6 Contextual information of a
    passage? Where would you research the Big-6 information about
    a passage?

    _____

    _____

    _____

3. In your own words, explain the meaning of Hermeneutic Principle
    #9: Use the clear to interpret the unclear.

    _____

    _____

    _____

    _____

4. What is the purpose of Hermeneutic Principle #12: Honor the
    Book?

    _____

    _____

    _____

    _____

5
Studying in the Spirit

In a lecture at The Pastor's College in London, Charles Spurgeon, *the prince of preachers*, chided those who felt they were self-sufficient in their study of the Word, saying, "It seems odd, that certain men who talk so much of what the Holy Spirit reveals to themselves, should think so little of what he has revealed to  others.... A respectable acquaintance with the opinions of the giants of the past, might have saved many an erratic thinker from the wild interpretations and outrageous inferences."[21]

Spurgeon's point was that students of the Word should be willing to learn from holy men who are taught by God and are mighty in the Scriptures, rather than looking to themselves as being islands unto themselves for their understanding. Like Spurgeon, we also encourage students to study the writings of others who have studied God's Word with the Holy Spirit, with an honest and good heart. But, we must also emphasize that there is a correct order for our study — we must **first** study the Scriptures with the help of the Spirit, and **then** consult the learning of others. As we explained in Chapter 2, approaching the Scriptures with a bias can skew a pure interpretation of the Word, including the bias of godly scholars, who may or may not have arrived at thorough or correct conclusions.

---

[21] (Spurgeon, 2010) Lecture 1

What Does it Mean to "Study in the Spirit?"

The idea of studying in the Spirit might sound strange in some ways, but it should be the common experience for all Christians. Studying in the Spirit does not imply assuming a trance-like state and waiting to be overtaken by another personality, nor is it a matter of diminishing our intellectual skills and waiting for random thoughts to consume our minds. Studying in the Spirit does not imply speaking in tongues or manifesting any other spiritual gift. Studying in the Spirit is simply a humble, silent interaction between you and the Spirit of God, asking for His guidance, sensing His prodding and expecting His illumination. It is a matter of allowing the Spirit to become a part of our intellectual thought processes and watching for insights that come from Him.

The Holy Spirit is given to every Christian as a gift from God when they come to faith in Christ. This is not a small or insignificant gift—it is magnificent! He is forever present in the life of each believer in Christ. Our spiritual strength is not a matter of needing more of the Holy Spirit, but rather a matter of appropriating what God has already given to us. The implications of having the Spirit of God living within us, guiding us in His gentle, quiet manner are profound. Believers need to be willing to recognize His quiet voice and practice interacting with Him.

Before we explore the idea of studying in the Spirit, it is important to emphasize that we are referring to studying in the Spirit of God, rather than some sort of inspiration of our own spirits. You have probably heard a musician or poet say they were inspired as they wrote a new work, which is usually referring to their own heightened creativity, whether with or without the assistance of another spiritual being. As we study in the Holy Spirit, we are indeed studying and thinking with the assistance of another spiritual being—the Spirit of the eternal God.

Our interaction with the Spirit takes place through casual, sincere conversation that is very real. We shouldn't necessarily expect to hear a voice responding to our questions. Instead, we should follow the prodding and thoughts He places within us.

What does this look like? Obviously, it will differ for different people. It is not a formal, rigid interaction, but a warm and friendly conversation. You might ask, for example, *"Lord, please teach me with your Spirit—please give me understanding of this passage and how it fits with the other teachings of your Word. Can it really mean this? Am I understanding this as You meant it? Look at the cross-referenced verse? Look into the original language's meaning for that word? Should the emphasis of the sentence be on this word instead of this one? Revisit the paragraphs that precede this passage? Consider this passage in light of the passage that follows ... how does it temper its meaning?* As we ask questions of the Spirit, we expect answers and trust the thoughts and prodding that we receive through prayerful study.

The Spirit's Role in Teaching Believers

The Scriptures contain some interesting passages that teach how the Spirit moves us. For example, Paul tells us, "The Spirit Himself testifies with our spirit that we are children of God,"[22] which suggests that the Spirit of God is interacting with our spirits. In the book of Acts, the apostles and elders sent a letter to the church at Antioch, saying, "For it seemed good to the Holy Spirit and to us to lay upon you no greater

---

[22] Romans 8:16

burden than these essentials …"[23] How did the apostles and elders know that it seemed good to the Holy Spirit? There was clearly a supernatural moving within their hearts that let them know the mind of the Spirit. The Holy Spirit moves by silently prodding so we can know and understand as He directs.

Paul affirms the Spirit's influence on our learning—"Now we have received, not the spirit of the world, but the Spirit Who is from God, *so that we may know* the things freely given to us by God, which things we also speak, not in words taught by human wisdom, *but in those taught by the Spirit, combining spiritual thoughts with spiritual words.*"[24] [italics added for emphasis] It is these spiritual thoughts and words that we must learn to appropriate as we study God's Word.

In 1 John 2:20–21, & 27, the apostle John speaks of an anointing from the Holy One, which teaches the truths of God to believers:

> "But **you have an anointing from the Holy One**, and you all know. I have not written to you because you do not know the truth, but because you do know it, and because no lie is of the truth....
> As for you, **the anointing which you received from Him abides in you, and you have no need for anyone to teach you; but as His anointing teaches you about all things, and is true and is not a lie, and just as it has taught you, you abide in Him.**" [Emphasis added]

Other passages in the Scriptures teach about the working of God's Spirit in our lives, specifically in relation to His guiding, leading, and teaching us. The purpose of this chapter is not to prove our position

---

[23] Acts 15:28
[24] 1 Corinthians 2:12–13

about the Spirit's role in teaching us. Instead, we confidently assert that the Scriptures support this view and leave it to the reader to decide whether the Scriptures should be studied with or without the assistance of the Holy Spirit.

Prayer Is Essential for Studying in the Holy Spirit

Studying God's Word without interacting with the Holy Spirit is little more than an academic effort of the flesh. We see many unbelieving scholars studying the Bible as an academic pursuit without believing it is God's Word, and without the assistance of the Holy Spirit. On the other hand, there have been many unbelievers whom the Spirit has brought to faith in Christ as they've looked into the Word, regardless of whether their motives were sincere or skeptical when they began. But, unfortunately, many unbelievers will close their Bibles when their studies have concluded, with their hearts as dark as when they began.

The situation is not as grim when believers study the Word of God without prayer or the assistance of the Spirit, since the Spirit lives within and will enlighten them to the truth as they read and study. In all cases of reading and studying the Scriptures, whether the reader is a believer or unbeliever, we can be confident that God's Word will not return to Him without accomplishing His desire.[25] Furthermore, Paul tells us, "... a natural man does not accept the things of the Spirit of God, for they are foolishness to him; and he cannot understand them, because they are spiritually appraised. But he who is spiritual appraises all things, yet he himself is appraised by no one. For WHO HAS KNOWN THE MIND OF THE LORD, THAT HE WILL INSTRUCT HIM? But we have the mind of Christ."[26] Thus, the regenerated mind that we've

---

[25] Isaiah 55:11
[26] 1 Corinthians 2:14–16

been given in Christ truly gives us added insight into the Scriptures. Although we strongly recommend prayerful study, the Spirit is fully able to wield His Word in believers who simply read it.

The believer who seeks understanding and guidance from the Spirit of God is much more likely to receive illumination, simply because God answers our prayers when we seek Him. Prayer is an expression of humility before God, acknowledging that we do not have the answers or understanding within ourselves. Instead, we rely on God to guide and illumine us through His Word. Before and during our study, we should pray that He will teach us and influence our minds and hearts as we study, asking Him to make us sensitive to His leading, directing us as we read, study, and meditate on the Word. Our goal is for Him to fashion our hearts with an accurate understanding of His truth and perfect us as Christ is perfect.

When the Spirit leads us into an understanding of a passage, we say that He has *illumined* us. In other words, the light has come on in our minds and hearts about a passage. Illumination is the work of the Spirit leading us to understanding and giving insight into His Word by showing us how to apply it. In my experience, I have found the more I pray for understanding, the more I receive His illumination—I believe it's safe to say there is a direct correlation between prayer and illumination.

The Leading of the Spirit
At one time or another in your life, you probably prayed that God would give you some sort of insight, so you closed your eyes and opened your Bible to some random page and pointed to a verse with your finger to learn the message He had for you. What? You've never done that? It's true that this is probably not the best approach to

seeking God's direction, but it's funny that we've all done it at one time or another in their lives … myself included!

We must ask, however, does God's Spirit ever lead us to a passage that He wants to use to teach us something? Absolutely! Does having the gift of God's Spirit mean that we do not have to be as careful or disciplined in our study of the Word, since He is our Teacher? Absolutely **not**! The Scriptures have much to say about commending people who are skilled in their work, disciplined in their craft, and accurately handle the word of truth. We must apply our best skill and attention to learning God's Word, especially if we will be teaching and guiding others by what we learn.

As we study God's Word, we must be sensitive to His prodding, detours, and sudden inspirations as we follow His leading. But, we must ask, how do we know if these directions are from the Spirit or from ourselves or another source? How can we know if we are studying in God's Spirit? The first question to ask yourself is, "Have I prayed for the Spirit's assistance?" If so, you can be confident that He will assist you. At the same time, you must also consider whether you may be distracted by other things that would keep you from discerning His leading.

Secondly, you can be confident that God's Spirit will not lead you to an interpretation, application, or conclusion that is contrary to the teaching of the whole Word of God. If you find the results of your study leading you to approve of thoughts, behaviors or lifestyles that are forbidden by the clear teaching of the Word, then you can be confident that God's Spirit did not lead you there. If your lifestyle is a pattern of indulging in sinful behavior with the intent of simply asking forgiveness afterward, then you can be confident it was not God's

Spirit that led you there. If you find yourself adopting views with emphases that are not in accordance with the rest of the Scriptures, then you should carefully reevaluate them and prayerfully ask for the Spirit's guidance.

What can get in the way of Studying in the Spirit?
We have already seen how it is possible to grieve the Holy Spirit by our actions. Peter also tells us that certain behaviors may cause our prayers to be hindered[27] that could impede His leading in our study of the Word.

Many believers are familiar with Jesus' words, "… know the truth and the truth will make you free." His words must be understood in light of their context which teach us that obeying Him (i.e. "continue in My word") is the prerequisite for knowing the truth:

> "So Jesus was saying to those Jews who had believed Him,
> **'If you continue in My word**,
> *then* you are truly disciples of Mine;
> **<u>and</u> you will know the truth**,
> and the truth will make you free.'" [28]
>
> [Emphasis Added]

From these passages, we can conclude that sin and sinful attitudes in our lives can become a hindrance to gaining illumination and understanding.

---

[27] 1 Peter 3:7—the context is not honoring wives or esteeming them as fellow heirs of the grace of life
[28] John 8:31–32

Clearly, assumptions can also prevent us from hearing the leading of God's Spirit as we study since there is a tendency to not look beyond what we *think* we know or *want* to believe. Similarly, we've seen that people sometimes study the Scriptures with the intent of justifying their position, rather than studying to learn. A mentality of not facing the truths of the Scriptures as they are presented can also prevent the illumination of the Spirit. Another factor that inhibits the Spirit's leading is pride in the heart, which not only affects our sensitivity, but it is an abomination to God. He will not honor a prideful heart.

Finally, as we learn from the Spirit, we must give credit where credit is due. When we study and ask for the Holy Spirit's assistance, we should acknowledge His help and thank Him and give credit to Him for teaching us the things we've learned. For example, when we talk with others, we might say, "I really believe that God's Spirit showed me this truth from the Scriptures as I studied this passage this week." Or, "I've really been praying for illumination about this and I think God has given me understanding of this passage."

We must be very careful, however, that crediting God's Spirit does not become a cloak for personal arrogance. To assert that we have received a word from the Lord and thus demand the attention and compliance of others, places us on the same level as a prophets of old, who are subject to being stoned if their word does not come true. Such assertions should be accompanied by accountability from others, and if the track record is not 100% accurate, the speaker would probably do well to evaluate their own heart and not speak in the name of the Lord.

What Should We Expect When We Study in the Spirit?
When we ask for the guidance of God's Spirit, we should study *expecting* Him to lead us and guide us into His truth. He desires that

we know His truth, assured us He would guide us, and told us that we should be led by the Spirit. We should expect:

- To see truths we have not seen before, even if we have known the passage for years.
- To gain insight and understanding of how certain passages relate to other passages.
- To have our understanding of Scripture passages sharpened beyond our previous understanding.
- To get closer and closer to an accurate understanding of our passage of study.
- Our ability to discern truth to be sharpened if we study faithfully from an honest and good heart, knowing that discernment is a gift of the Spirit and a product of practice. "... Solid food is for the mature, who because of practice have their senses trained to discern good and evil."[29]
- We should expect the Spirit to convict us of sin, truth, and our need for action.

We should be aware that discernment is a gift of the Spirit given in differing quantities to people as He desires. "... and to another the effecting of miracles, and to another prophecy, and to another the distinguishing of spirits ..."[30] Because of this, you may find that some people in the church seem to grasp spiritual concepts more quickly and easily than you do. This should not be a discouragement to you; God's Spirit equips the body of Christ with spiritual gifts as He determines is best. Regardless of how the Spirit has gifted you, every

---

[29] Hebrews 5:14
[30] 1 Corinthians 12:10

Christian should faithfully study the Scriptures to the best of his or her ability.

We should not necessarily expect to understand every passage immediately. Some parts of God's Word require years of study to understand how they relate to other passages in the Bible. A lifetime of study and understanding is one of the greatest gifts and legacies that can be passed on to future generations. Each generation of believers can be established and enriched because of the faithful study of believers who preceded them and we should strive to pass-on a legacy of rich learning from God's Spirit to those who follow after us in this world.

Meditation—The Fountainhead of Understanding

What do we mean by *meditation*? What do the Scriptures mean when they speak of meditation? There is much confusion about meditation, and it is often accompanied with some fear and suspicion. But the Scriptures strongly encourage us to meditate on the words of God, so we must conclude that Scriptural meditation is an exercise that the Lord wants us to embrace. Consider some of the teaching of Psalm 119:

> **Psalm 119:**
> 15 "I will meditate on Your precepts and regard your ways."
>
> 23 "Even though princes sit and talk against me, your servant meditates on Your statutes."
>
> 27 "Make me understand the way of Your precepts, so I will meditate on Your wonders."
>
> 48 "And I shall lift up my hands to Your commandments, which I love; and I will meditate on Your statutes."

78 "May the arrogant be ashamed, for they subvert me with a lie; But I shall meditate on Your precepts."

97 "O how I love Your law! It is my meditation all the day."

99 "I have more insight than all my teachers, for Your testimonies are my meditation."

148 "My eyes anticipate the night watches, that I may meditate on Your word."

Let's return to our question—What do the Scriptures mean when they speak of meditation? In contrast to the meditation of other religions, which teach a meditation that clears the mind of all thoughts and influences, the meditation of the Bible has a very clear object with an intellectual and spiritual focus. Rather than disengaging his intellectual faculties, the Psalmist directed his gaze on the Lord's precepts and ways, upon His statutes, wonders, commandments, law, testimonies, and word. His meditation was characterized by love and affection for the Word, with a desire to learn from it and understand. It was not an attempt to adapt the Word to his own ways and presuppositions. Is this type of meditation a normal activity in your life? It should be.

Let me try to bring the meaning of Scriptural meditation a little closer to home. I would guess that you have meditated on something at one time or another in your life; you probably do it more often than you realize. For example, if a man decided to design and build a piece of furniture, he would probably consider different features of the item; he would consider a preferred style and the type of wood that would be used for the project. He would then take the steps a little deeper, considering the dimensions of the wood to be cut, the method of joining the edges, the design of the drawers and hardware, and the desired finish. The process might go a little deeper as he actually cuts and shapes the wood, and finishes it to create the final product.

Although we would probably not say that our friend has meditated on the furniture project, meditation is exactly what he has done. In a similar way, followers of Christ meditate on the Scriptures by considering them, carefully weighing their meaning, and prayerfully deciding how they can implement them in their lives—how they can adapt their hearts to the words on the pages to bring them to reality in their lives. It is this process the writer of the 119th Psalm described and cherished. This type of meditation should be the normal routine of every believer.

Memorization

Is there a difference between meditation and memorization? Yes, the two are actually completely different processes and they produce very different results. Memorization is the intellectual activity of storing information in your mind so you can recall it later. Does memorization have the same outcome as meditation? Certainly not! You might consider memorization to be analogous to placing a book on a bookshelf to retrieve later, while meditation would be like studying the book. Memorization produces recall, but meditation produces understanding.

It is certainly possible for a person to memorize a portion of Scripture without understanding it; the understanding would result from the meditation. A friend once asked, "How can a person meditate on the Scriptures if they have not memorized them?" The response was simply, "I just have the book on my lap!" Memorization is not a prerequisite for meditation, although meditation may inadvertently produce memorization.

Another long-time *teacher*-friend of mine constantly chided me about my emphasis on meditation over memorization. I must admit that I would respond with friendly chides about his emphasis of memorization over meditation. But one time, as I was sitting under his teaching, the value of meditation over memorization became very clear. As he was quoting a verse to the class, he forgot a key word in the verse—the key word was "not," which changed its entire meaning. Because I had meditated on the verse, I had become familiar with its thrust and direction, and immediately knew there was error in the air. He and I had some more fun bantering about our methods of learning, but his little misquote revealed a fundamental advantage of meditation over memorization. Understanding will help you remain in the *spirit* of a passages' teaching and will even help with your memorization. Memorization does not have this built-in safeguard for staying in the truth.

Please do not quote me as saying that memorization is not good—it is an excellent exercise for Christians. Memorization enables us to meditate on the Word when the book is not in our laps. My point is that meditation is an essential exercise that will lead students of the Word to understanding, which is our desired result.

We should meditate as we attempt to interpret the Word and as we attempt to apply it. It is best accomplished through interaction with the Holy Spirit, asking Him to instruct us, enlighten us, and show us how to apply the Scriptures to our hearts and lives. Scriptural meditation is one of the key ingredients for integrating God's Word into our hearts and leading us to conformity to the image of God's Son.

Conclusion

The concept of studying in the Spirit is difficult to describe since the Scriptures do not seem to provide instructions for doing so. Understanding the concept is a matter of compiling the related teachings in the Scriptures that address the concept, and considering how we might implement them in our lives. In other words, it seems that we simply meditated on the Scriptures and arrived at this understanding of studying in the Spirit—I encourage you to do the same!

Chapter 5—Think About It ...

1. How would you describe the Holy Spirit's role in teaching us as we study God's Word?

   _____

   _____

   _____

   _____

2. What should we expect when we study in the Spirit?

   _____

   _____

   _____

   _____

3. How would you describe *Scriptural* meditation?

   _____

   _____

   _____

   _____

   _____

4. What is the difference between meditation and memorization? How would you describe the result of each?

   _____

   _____

   _____

   _____

   _____

6
Principles for Applying the Scriptures

We often talk about the need to *apply* the Scriptures to our lives, but what does that really mean? Many would say, *"Just do it,"* but there is much more to spiritual growth than simply mimicking a behavior, although we certainly do not minimize the need for behavior modification! We must practice a type of application that is more than a simple "Read it, Do it." or "What does that mean to me?" response. Application of God's Word is the essence of discipleship and must be approached thoughtfully.

As we gain understanding of the Scriptures, we must work toward assimilating the Word of God into our hearts. One of the highest goals of studying His Word is to bring our understanding into alignment with His truth, to adopt His perspectives as our own, and to conform our ways to His. Jesus made it very clear that whatever is in the heart will become a person's words and actions. Thus the most effective principles for application are those which operate on the heart. Our brother Paul told us to "... be transformed by the renewing of your mind ..."[31] This statement describes the essence of *applying* the Scriptures, since the heart is a component of the mind.

Application Before Interpretation?
At this point, you might be wondering why we would begin exploring principles for applying the Scriptures when we have not yet discussed the interpretation process. Let me commend you for asking another excellent question! It is certainly possible that a person might apply a

---

[31] Romans 12:2

85

concept that is based on an incorrect interpretation that could result in error, so your point is well taken.

In response, I would say that each passage of Scripture contains multiple lessons and truths and we must be careful that we do not miss these smaller treasures by overlooking them during our study of a larger passage. It is easy for these *smaller* gems of the Scriptures to be eclipsed by the main theme of a passage, so it is appropriate and of great value to explore them and seek to learn from them during your study. As the message of the larger passage becomes clear, your understanding of the smaller passages will also be refined and sharpened and help you apply them correctly.

Allow me to illustrate with an example from a small section of Jesus' Sermon on the Mount. In Matthew 7:1-5, we find some fascinating insights about hypocrisy and making sure we are without fault before judging others. Even though the primary thrust of the passage is hypocrisy and judging, Jesus gave us a principle along the way that should be ingrained in our minds as a fundamental part of our reasoning and being. That principle is found in Matthew 7:2, "For in the way you judge, you will be judged; and by your standard of measure, it will be measured to you." If our focus was on the overall teaching of the Sermon on the Mount, then it is quite possible that we would overlook this profound principle that should shape the perspective and behavior of every believer.

Reflective Questioning
It would be very easy to read this principle and even recite it without giving it the meditation and reflection it deserves. Throughout your study, you should pose questions to yourself in an attempt to ensure that your heart is fully aligned with the teachings of the Word. Why use questioning? We use questions because, unlike statements or

observations, questions will force you to muse on each point and force you to develop a response. Typical questions might be:

❖ Do I judge others? Whom do I judge? When do I judge? What are specific situations wherein I judge ... while driving? At work? In class? Among peers? When jealousy arises within me?

❖ What basis or standard do I use when I judge? Am I ever guilty of the offences that I judge in others? If so, do I judge with the same standard of measure, or do I find ways to dismiss the charges against myself? What is my standard of measure for the things I judge? Is it reasonable? Is it based in emotion, truth, or something else? Would I want God or others to use my standard of measure when judging me?

❖ What must I do to keep from being guilty of the same offense? Do I need to change my behavior or my standard of judgment? Do I need to grow in love and understanding regarding the weaknesses of others?

❖ Am I tolerant of certain sins of others because I tolerate the same sins in my life? Have my own standards of right and wrong been compromised as a result of my tolerance of the standards of others? What have I learned about my own obedience and/or sin from my judging others?

These are just sample questions that relate to Jesus' words in Matthew 7:2; there is no special order or methodology for composing them. Developing questions is a simple matter of considering a Scripture passage and asking how well your heart and life conform to its teaching and asking God's Spirit to lead you. As you ask the questions, you should answer them thoughtfully. It may take some time to weigh them and to prayerfully develop honest responses. You should set aside some private time that is dedicated to this activity. When you find deficiencies in your ways, your questions should explore the reasons and possible resolutions. Believe me, you **will** find a gap between the standard of the Scriptures and the state of your heart and life!

It is probably not necessary to write your questions and answers unless they spark some unusual insights or, perhaps, deserve further probing, or perhaps reveal your own guilt and or need for change. If you ask a question that reveals an important deficiency in your knowledge or understanding about the subject, it might be wise to write it so you can keep it in front of you and explore it further at another time. Remember, the purpose of these questions is to **apply** the Scriptures; you will develop an entirely different set of questions as you explore the meaning of a passage. It is important to use this time to examine your conformity to God's ways. This is *not* the time to examine the conformity of someone else's ways!

So many things can be learned by dwelling on the words of the Scriptures and reflecting on them through reflective questioning. The discipline of asking questions of ourselves carries the benefit of requiring that we answer them. You may already know the answers to many of your questions—on the other hand, a little more reflection might yield the answers you lack. Some questions will require soul-searching and honest evaluation of your heart, while others might evoke difficult or even painful thoughts.

At times, it can be very painful to relive and review events of the past, but the grace of God can help us accept them with supernatural peace and will give us the ability to love and forgive as Jesus taught us. Forgiveness is, perhaps, the greatest healer of the heart. As followers of Christ, we are not only required to forgive others from the heart, but we are freed from having to devise plans of spite and revenge, since God will deal with offenders.[32] Forgiveness and mercy are the chemo for bitterness; prayerfully addressing our condition and responding as the Word instructs, will lead to the peace of God, which is beyond all comprehension. We can take comfort knowing that the Spirit of God is tender, loving, and consoling, while at the same time, deeply convicting.

Interacting with the Spirit about His Word can reveal many things; things that we have never considered, things that we do not want to consider, and things that we do not want to address. As we ask and answer with an honest and good heart, the Spirit can freely convict us of sinful attitudes and behaviors, of injuries we've inflicted in others and our need to ask forgiveness. He can convict us of our need to forgive, whether we've been asked or not.

Planning Your Steps

In addition to posing questions about the past and present, you should also focus on the future. Consider your feelings and attitudes about the future; decisions you face and difficulties that you anticipate. Ask yourself, "How will I respond if a certain trial or temptation arises?" How should I respond? How can I assure that I will respond in a Christ-like manner? Am I hiding or ignoring a possibility for flirting with a temptation or indulging in a sin? Is there a fellow believer in whom I can confide, who will encourage and hold

---

[32] Romans 12:19 "Never take your own revenge, beloved, but leave room for the wrath of God, for it is written, 'Vengeance is Mine, I will repay,' says the Lord."

me accountable about a specific temptation? Have I been completely honest and forthcoming with my accountability partner(s) about the difficulties I'm facing?

This type of application is certainly not in the realm of academia. It is the submissive interaction with the Spirit of God that differentiates students from disciples. Every child of God must walk the path of a committed disciple. Remember that the goal of our study is not only to increase our understanding, but to learn from our Master on this journey and live by His words as faithful followers.

To some, the idea of discipleship can sound like a dehumanizing sacrifice of individuality. But as we consider God's Word, we should constantly be mindful that He is the Designer of this world—the One Who carefully and thoughtfully designed you as an individual. His Word holds the knowledge and understanding that you are looking for that will bring order and harmony to your life. Jesus' promise of joy and abundant life come with the guarantee that whoever believes in Him will not be disappointed.[33] Applying His ways may be difficult and painful at the beginning, but you will find that His wisdom and insights hold the keys that can liberate us from the bondage of sin and mature us as children of God.

Descriptions and Prescriptions

I'm sure you're excited to begin applying the Scriptures to your heart, but I need to caution you about something very important before you proceed. We have stressed that God and His Word are truth. But you should also be aware that His Word records some untruths—some lies. Genesis 3:4, for example, records the lie of the devil through the

---

[33] Romans 10:11 "For the Scripture says, 'WHOEVER BELIEVES IN HIM WILL NOT BE DISAPPOINTED.'"

serpent, "You surely will not die!" Is this truth? Yes, it really happened. Is it a lie? Yes, the man and the woman truly died *in some way* on the day they ate of the fruit. The Scriptures record many other lies, as well, but God is not the author of the lies; He recorded them in His Word for our instruction.

In addition to lies, the Scriptures also record evil deeds that were done by both wicked people and by the people of God. In many cases, the deeds are condemned by God, as He clearly declares His disapproval of them. On the other hand, the Scriptures also provide accounts of deeds that were done by God's own people, but it is left to the reader to determine if they are good examples for us to imitate or if they are bad examples that we should avoid. In other words, are they *prescriptions* from God for us to follow or are they simply *descriptions* of accounts that we should view as sinful and avoid?

The description-prescription questions are not always easy to answer. Examples include accounts of multiple wives and concubines; accounts of extreme treachery and torture of enemies; and accounts of slavery. Does the silence of the Scriptures about these subjects suggest that it's okay for followers of Christ to engage in such activities? It's not likely, since they probably violate the second greatest commandment, which is "Love your neighbor as yourself."[34] Our point, however, is that we should not necessarily adopt a passage into our lives, just because it's in the Bible. We must apply effort to determining if the concept was actually *prescribed* for us or if it is simply a *description* of misbehavior.

With this in mind, let's explore some of the different ways believers can apply the Scriptures to their hearts. In this chapter, we'll look into

---

[34] Leviticus 19:18, Matthew 22:39

reflection, values, fruit, and principles, in addition to some other ways we can interact with God's Spirit to understand and apply His Word to our lives.

Reflections

True transformation requires allowing God's Word to shape the heart. By this, we simply mean considering the truths you have learned from your study of the Word through quiet introspection and meditation with the help of the Holy Spirit to see specifically how it relates to yourself. As you muse on the things you've learned, ask God to lead you with His Spirit as you ask yourself questions like:

1) What are the teachings, exhortations, and commands in the passage? How do they relate directly to me?
2) What can I learn about God from this passage? What are the things He loves, hates, blesses, and curses? Are there things that He hates that I condone or even secretly love? Do I desire things that are an abomination to Him?
3) What perspectives of the writer or speaker are taught in the passage? How would it look if a person owned these perspectives and truly lived by them?
4) What does this passage teach that I must apply to my relationships with my spouse, parents, children, other relatives, friends, neighbors, acquaintances, and relationships at work?
5) What must I do to bring my relationships into conformity with God's Word? Do I need to apologize and reconcile with someone? Do I need to cease or begin a behavior in a relationship?
6) What principles are taught in the passage? In what way can I see the truth of the principles in my own experience and in

the world around me? How can I remember them and walk by them?

7) How can I incorporate this passage into my life and into my thoughts? How do I adopt its perspectives as my own? How should I evaluate my world in light of this passage? How can the things I've learned become part of my normal decision-making process?

8) What can I learn about God's perspective or declaration from this passage?

9) How should I respond? It's time for decision and action— what should I do? What problems will I encounter as I seek to follow what I've learned? How will I deal with the consequences? How can I thank God for His blessings?

10) What other questions might come to mind? Are there questions I'm avoiding because I don't want to hear the answer?

As you consider the things you've learned, allow God's Spirit to lead you to think of situations in your life that might require a response. Perhaps God is prompting you to ask for forgiveness from the Lord or from another person, perhaps to reconcile with someone, or make restitution, or perhaps to reach out to someone.

God's Spirit uses His Word to shape our understanding and our person. Although you might suggest some possible applications of a Scripture passage, do not limit the work of the Spirit by presuming that your applications are what He intends for another individual. Each person needs to pray and ask the Spirit to help integrate His teaching into his or her life. Humbly ask God to search and know your heart so there will not be anything that is offensive to Him. It is certainly possible to resist the Spirit's efforts to transform us, which

truly grieves Him. When we are convicted of something that needs to
change, but we ignore or refuse His prodding, we are actually
resisting God's Spirit and thus grieving Him, as Paul taught us in
Ephesians 4:30. [35]

Start With the Heart
Assimilating the Scriptures into our hearts will have a greater impact
on our behavior, obedience, and sanctification than the simple "Read
it. Do it." approach. The heart does not simply guide us, rather, the
heart is actually who we are. But no one can know its complexities
because of its twisted deceits; it even lies to itself.[36] The only way we
can assess the condition of a heart is by comparing it to the pure
Word of God. So, I will once again emphasize that true transformation
can only occur when application is directed at the heart. As the heart
is transformed, actions **will** follow. If actions do not follow, then the
heart has not been transformed. Words and behavior are simply a
barometer of the condition of the heart.

Is there ever an occasion when we should use the "Read it, do it."
method? Absolutely! One of the most inadequate excuses for
disobedient behavior is, "I didn't do it because my heart just wasn't
into it." We must always seek to obey God and follow His Word,
whether we feel like it or not. Jesus' Parable of the Two Sons[37] clearly
illustrates this concept.

It's interesting that obedience has the effect of spawning further
obedience. Once we form a habit of obeying, deterring from that path

---

[35] Ephesians 4:30 "Do not grieve the Holy Spirit of God, by whom you were
sealed for the day of redemption."
[36] Jeremiah 17:9
[37] Matthew 21:28–31 (the parable of the two sons)

feels awkward and wrong. This is especially true when raising children. In general, children are not born with an innate sense of compliance, which may be the understatement of the century. But as we teach them the outward ways of obedience, we are actually constructing forms around their lives that are like the wooden forms that shape a concrete foundation. Given enough time, the forms may be removed and the desired shape will remain.[38] It is easier for a person's heart to conform to obedience if the actions are already in alignment.

Jesus taught us that which fills the heart will proceed forth from the mouth. The same is true of our actions.[39] When our hearts are in conformity with the ways of Christ, our lives will be characterized by the fruit of the Spirit. This is the reason for developing a deep familiarity with God's Word and His ways and assimilating them into our hearts and lives.

Unsung Verses

There is the tendency to view our learning of the Scriptures as an academic pursuit that has a goal of taking our knowledge from point A to point B, but there is immeasurable merit in meditating on the information, reason, logic, insight, and illumination that are found on the journey from point A to point B. From these unsung teachings we find a wellspring of truth that yields understanding and leads us to maturity.

As we read the words of God and become familiar with His thought structures, logic, character, teachings, mysteries, conflicts, paradoxes, passions, and the wealth of other information He gave through the

---

[38] Robert Cross
[39] Mark 7:21–23

prophets and apostles, we begin to sense the rhythm of the heart of God Himself. There is so much we can learn from the unsung verses that lay between the doctrinal anthems of the Bible. These seemingly insignificant verses may not directly support a major doctrine or give light to our immediate footsteps, but they are jewels of knowledge and insight about our lives, our world, and how we fit into the story of God's love.

So don't feel like you must find a practical application in every phrase of the Bible. Sometimes it's enough just to know it because God wants us to know it; words of life from Him. There may never be an occasion to repeat the words to others, teach them in a class, or even receive a pat on the back for spending time with them. But, you will be surprised how these small tidbits of Scripture will come to life and give understanding of God's ways and character.

As we study and meditate, we can certainly find intimations that teach about God and His declaration of truth, but we walk on thin ice doctrinally when we attempt to find an application in every passage in the Bible. Such a pursuit can result in weakly founded, superfluous interpretations of the Scriptures. Forcing an application when it is not appropriate can also distort a pure interpretation of a passage.

On the other hand, we have an obligation to consider every passage, with the help of the Holy Spirit, asking what we can learn from it and how we might apply it to our lives. While musing on these passages you will find applications that relate to your own behavior, understanding, attitudes toward God and others, worship, and a myriad of other truths the Spirit might reveal.

Values

As we spend time with each phrase and thought in God's Word, we become increasingly familiar with His character, the things He loves and hates, and everything in between. It is our part to reflect on these revelations of His character—His values or *perfections*—so we can adopt them as our own, making His values our values.

What do we mean by values? Values are simply the moral or ethical perspectives that are meaningful or *valuable* in someone's heart and life. For example, the Scriptures are very clear that God places great value on human life, on reverence of His holy name, on moral purity, and on honoring elders, parents, masters, and rulers. On the other hand, we also learn about things that are not as important in life, as we observe God's perspective of them. We must always consider His values from the bigger picture of His Word, rather than by simply supporting our views with *proof texts*. As we grow in our understanding of our Father's loving concern for people and His creation, we become comfortable adopting His values as our own, knowing that they are truly good for us and for our world.

It's humorous that many people view this transformation of the heart as brainwashing. They use the term with a negative connotation, but clearly, the minds of humanity are in dire need of a good scrubbing— a thorough cleansing and reorientation. Therefore, I have no reservations about having my brain washed and transformed by the renewing of my mind so that I can know the will of God. The critics are reluctant to admit that everyone is being brainwashed by whatever influences they choose to adopt, whether it is the spin of news casts, teachers and professors, clergy, activists, friends, movies , television, internet influences, or even their own reasoning. Since we are able to select the soap for our brainwashing, it makes much greater sense to submit to an influence with values that transform us into gentle and quiet spirits, which are precious in the sight of God, and result in love, peace, respect, and harmony with others.

The majority of our application of the Scriptures should take place between our ears, internally, in the hidden person of the heart. As we meditate on the majestic passages and the seemingly insignificant phrases of the Scriptures, we should seek to apply the values we learn from God through His quiet voice. As we imitate His ways, our minds and hearts become conformed to His, our affections and desires become aligned with His, and our behaviors and lifestyles begin to please Him. This is the process of sanctification—modifying the control center of our behavior and setting ourselves apart to Him.

Is it enough for our application efforts to focus on the heart? You can be certain of this—a person's actions will be a clear reflection of the state of his or her heart. If you feel that your heart is right, and yet your actions and behaviors are not, perhaps it's time to focus your meditations on God's passion for the things He desires and the things He hates. His passions are often intimated in passages that speak of His desire to reward or the certainty of His judgment of certain actions or lifestyles.

For example, Matthew 25:31–46 paints a vivid picture of God's passion for the well-being of people and the abundant reward for those who carried-out His desire and the eternal punishment for those who did not. From musing on Galatians 5:18-24 we learn of the intensity of God's hatred for sinful lifestyles of the flesh and his love for the deeds of the Spirit. We learn that those who oppose His ways do so at the cost of inheriting the Kingdom of God—an enormous price to pay for the momentary pleasures of sin.

The Scriptures refer to this the transformation of our minds as sanctification. Sanctification or sanctify simply means to set something apart for a special use. In our case, we are to be set apart from our natural inclinations and desires, for the Lord's special use. It is these internal changes of the heart, the values that we hold, that fulfill the greatest commandment—to love the Lord your God with all your heart and with all your soul and with all your mind.

Fruit

Let's turn our thoughts to the subject of fruit—Biblical fruit. In John 15:8, Jesus tells us, "My Father is glorified by this, that you bear much fruit, and so prove to be My disciples," but there is much speculation about what Jesus meant by His metaphor of fruit. The answer becomes quite clear and concrete, however, through some meditation on the Word. In the sentence that precedes His statement, Jesus told the disciples they should abide in Him and in His words, which can be somewhat ambiguous, but can be understood as *living* in His words and teaching. Stated another way, living within the words of Christ will result in bearing fruit.

There is another passage of Scripture that gives more insight into the meaning of fruit. It is found in Jesus' parable of the Sower, as presented in Matthew 13, Mark 4, and Luke 8. It is obvious in this parable that the goal of the Sower is to bear fruit. But, "What is fruit?" Does it refer to good works, converts, obedience, or something else? By carefully comparing the symbols in the parable to Jesus' explanation, we learn that whatever this fruit may be, the seed that produced it is God's Word[40]. It follows then, that the fruit which

---

[40] Word of the Kingdom (Matthew 13:19), the Word (Mark 4:14), and the Word of God (Luke 8:11)

grows from this seed is a lifestyle of *living-out* the Word—conformity
to its teachings and exhortations.

Since the Father is glorified as His children bear fruit—as they are
conformed to the Word of God—we gain further insight into our
objective in studying His Word, the seed. In order to be conformed to
the Word of God and to the words of Jesus, to be transformed into
the image of Christ, and to have our minds renewed, it is necessary
for us to meditate on His truths with the full intention of agreeing
with them and adopting His ways and perspectives as our own. This is
how we become Christ-like. This is how we are conformed to the
image of God's Son[41]. We are changed by reading, studying, learning,
and meditating on His Word, by knowing Him and aligning our hearts,
thoughts, affections, delights, and perspectives with His.

For example, when we read about God's hatred of something (e.g.
fornication, lust, adultery, divorce), or His concern for the poor, His
love for the lost and for His children, His desire for our holiness, we
don't just echo the words and teach it or preach it while allowing the
offenses to exist in our lives. Instead, we agree with Him from the
heart and seek to understand how His way is truly right and how it
results in the greatest good for us and our world. In order to align
ourselves with His ways, we must deny ourselves the right to indulge
in disobedience, endeavoring to adopt His perspectives and
assimilate His ways into our hearts.

As His Spirit works in our hearts, we will become conformed to Christ
or *shaped* like Him and find ourselves responding as He would. We
will have joy when righteousness flourishes, righteous anger when
wickedness gains ground, and respond with action and word as Christ

---

[41] Romans 8:29

would. We truly become like our Father, sons of the living God, as we bear fruit from the seed of His Word This is the essence of Biblical fruit which, stated simply, is conformity to the Word of God, in the heart, producing a Christ-like lifestyle.

A Solo Act Before God

Imagine yourself alone on a stage before God with no one else around to see or hear—God is the only one in the audience. On this stage, your thought life and physical life play-out in His presence. Your thoughts, both the good and the utterly wicked, and every thought in between, are heard and observed by the Father. He hears your silent mutters and curses just as clearly as He hears your silent prayers. He knows your inner person, where your thoughts dwell, and the motives behind them better than you know yourself. This performance—your life—is truly the most important performance you will ever give.

As you grow in His Word, meditating on it, applying His truths, and conforming your ways and heart to His, your solo-act will become more enjoyable to Him and to you. Imagine yourself on stage. When that old temptation raises its head in your heart and you turn from it and ask Him for help to flee from it or overcome it. You might pray silently, *"How am I doing Lord? I'm trying—I'm resisting—I want to respond in a way that will please you."* Or if you're prone to outbursts when driving, as you get behind the wheel of your car, you whisper a prayer, telling the Lord that you want to respond to other drivers with His love—*"please help me in this... How am I doing Lord?"* Or discussing with Him how you might help someone whom He's brought to your mind... *"How can I help this person? Please help me as I consider different ways. Please open a door for me to do this. Please prepare the person with your Spirit before we meet."*

You can take comfort, knowing that our Father wants to see you succeed in this performance, on the private stage of your heart, so give Him the performance of your life!

Applications
As we learn from Hermeneutic Principle 13 there is generally only one correct interpretation of any given Scripture passage, although there may be many applications. Clearly, as followers of Christ, we should seek to apply the Scriptures, but we should also be very careful about the weight of authority that we place on our applications. Some applications are very clear and are direct teaching from the Scriptures, while others may be something we infer through reasoning.

Furthermore, we must clearly distinguish between interpretation and application. An interpretation is an assessment of what a passage is actually saying within its context, while an application is our response regarding how we should understand, think, feel, believe, and behave, based on its teaching.

We should always seek to obey the clear teachings of Scripture and encourage other believers to follow them, as well. But, it may not necessarily be right to require other believers to follow applications that are *inferred* from the Scriptures—that is, applications that are based on our own convictions, rather than the direct teaching of the Scriptures. In other words, we may create our own list of *Do's* and *Don'ts*, but we must not consider other Christians unspiritual if they do not hold the same convictions. On the other hand, we must certainly take a united stand with other believers to hold to the direct commandments of the Word.

Applying Principles
The Scriptures are full of principles that instruct us in the wisdom of God. As we meditate on each passage, we should look for underlying principles and consider how we might apply them to our lives, although we must be careful to not overlook the passage's immediate message.

Let's take a look at an example of a principle in the Scriptures. In His sermon on the mount, Jesus said, "But I say to you, do not resist an evil person...",[42] This verse contains a very clear principle, although it is easy to lose sight of it if we only focus on Jesus' examples of how it could be fulfilled. His examples include turning the other cheek when slapped, willingly giving more than required to people who sue you, and going two miles with those who force you to go one mile.

But as we examine this principle of not resisting an evil person, even to the extent of cooperating with them beyond their demands, we can find many applications for our own lives. We could simply relive the events of the previous day or week and find examples of situations we could have handled differently.

We would certainly be missing Jesus' point if we limited our obedience to His three examples. In our own lives, we have many opportunities to *not resist an evil person*. A twenty-first century example might be kindly allowing an aggressive driver to have the place in front of you. Or, perhaps, buying a cup of coffee for an unkind coworker, or responding with kind words to someone who insults you publically.

---

[42] Matthew 5:39

Another principle of Christ is to pray for those who persecute us—
that should be pretty easy, shouldn't it? How should we pray for
those who persecute us? I do not necessarily pray for God's blessing
on them, but I do pray that God will draw them to repentance and
enable them to turn from the sin that hurts both of us. But you can
probably think of other ways to pray for your persecutors... perhaps
that God would help them with a family difficulty or perhaps asking
the person if you could pray for them regarding something that you
know is hurting them.

Another principle is *blessed are the peacemakers*. As I have
considered my enemies in light of this principle, I have come to the
point of truly preferring that they repent and make peace with God
and side with Him, rather than facing judgment. This is the way of
sons of God and the mark of maturing believers. Forgiving others
from the heart[43], which is another principle, mending relationships,
and preparing ourselves and others for that sobering day to come[44],
are clearly requirements for loving our enemies, which is another
principle of Jesus. There are so many ways to fulfill the principles of
Christ, and with a little thoughtfulness, we can build bridges between
others and Christ.

What do we learn about the character of God through the principles
of the Scriptures? What type of person or character would be so
committed to loving that it would be extended to those who hate
Him and us? What do you learn about yourself as you consider how
you measure up to any given principle? Would others describe you as
a faithful follower of Christ based on the way you live out His
principles? God is fully aware of the atrocities and injustices that have

---

[43] Matthew 18:35
[44] Romans 14:10–12

been committed against His children—even against Him, yet His commands and principles should still govern our lives, regardless of the difficulties that we must face as we honor them.

Consider Jesus' words "love your enemies and pray for those who persecute you." How could the mind of man conceive of such a God? The answer is that man cannot and would not, which attests to the fact that their source is from a higher Being; a Being whose ways are most excellent and very different from the ways of man. No one has seen God at any time; the only begotten God who is in the bosom of the Father, He has explained Him.[45] As you consider the infinitely high ethic that is behind the principles of the Scriptures, remember that they come from God and give us a glimpse of His character that we are able to know because Jesus has explained Him.

As you become familiar with the Word, be on the lookout for its principles and be prepared to accept them and spend time integrating them into your life. Obviously, this type of introspection and meditation takes time. It is not something that comes from listening to a sermon or hearing a lesson. There is no substitute for meditating on God's Word in order to assimilate it into our lives and bring ourselves into conformity with His ways and desires. Be aware, however, that principles are not found in every passage of the Bible, so don't fabricate a principle if it's not there!

Teaching, Counseling, Parenting, Discipling, Mentoring
As we study the Scriptures, should we seek to apply them only to ourselves? That should definitely be our first priority since we don't want to be guilty of trying to remove a speck from someone's eye

---

[45] John 1:18

while having a log in our own[46]. It is of fundamental importance that we keep our focus on our own pure and accurate understanding of the Word and subsequent lifestyle, while always being on guard for any seed of hypocrisy that might take root within us. Nonetheless, the Scriptures also teach us that they are inspired by God and useful for reproof and correction.[47]

When the writer of Hebrews said "by this time you ought to be teachers..."[48] he was not suggesting that every believer will have the gift of teaching and should be teaching on stage in front of others. His point was that every Christian should understand the elementary points of the Faith and be able to confidently explain them to others.

Because of this, we want to be knowledgeable and equipped to carefully and skillfully help others. For example, in Matthew 18, Jesus gave us a model for how to restore a person who has strayed into sin. The goal of this process was not punishment or church discipline, but rather to restore the one trapped in sin. Those who are best equipped to carry-out such a task are those who have an understanding of God's Word, which implies that we must also be on the lookout for Scriptural truths and ways that can teach and help others.

God's Word applies to Christians and non-Christians alike, but we must meet each person where they are in their spiritual condition

---

[46] Matthew 7:4–5

[47] 2 Timothy 3:16 "All Scripture is inspired by God and profitable for **teaching**, for **reproof**, for **correction**, for **training** in righteousness; so that the man of God may be adequate, equipped for every good work." [Emphasis added]

[48] Hebrews 5:12

and rely on the Spirit to help us use His Word so He can wield it in the hearts of others. Our role is to help others apply God's truths to their lives, even if they know nothing about the Scriptures, and thereby enable them to understand and avoid the pit-falls of defiance against God. Whether we are evangelizing people who know nothing about God or teaching a group of mature believers, we can be confident that the Holy Spirit is the one Who produces the fruit of our labor.[49]

Conclusion

Applying the Scriptures to our lives, specifically to our hearts, should be one of the highest goals of our personal study of God's Word. It is difficult and often counterproductive to reduce our application of God's Word to a rigid set of steps or rules that we must follow, since we must be led by the Spirit. For this reason, we encourage believers to live by principles, rather than a rule-based, mechanical approach as they seek to apply the Scriptures.

I've come to believe that the deeds that I accomplish as a Christian are not as important as who I am in my heart. From God's Word, we sense that He is not as impressed with our works as He is with our motives for pursuing them. Paul said, "... if I give all my possessions to feed the poor, and if I surrender my body to be burned, but do not have love, it profits me nothing."[50] Why doesn't it profit Him? The most likely answer is because God's concern is based on what we are inside; He is not impressed by deeds done for pretense or hollow attempts to buy His favor.

Thus, it is not *what* you've done, but rather, what is inside of you that defines you and makes you who you are. God told us through Isaiah,

---

[49] 1 Corinthians 3:6 "... God was causing the growth."
[50] 1 Corinthians 13:3

"But to this one I will look, to him who is humble and contrite of spirit, and who trembles at My word."[51] It is because of God's emphasis on the quality of the inner man that our emphasis for applying the Scriptures is on the transformation of the heart.

Be certain, however, that a focus on applying the Scriptures to the heart does not release us from living-out the works of the Lord in our lives! On the contrary, we were created in Christ Jesus for good works, which God prepared beforehand so that we would walk in them.[52] It is this transformation of the *whole* person—heart, mind, soul, and strength[53]—that indisputably confirms that we are the workmanship of the Creator, Himself.

Our goal is to understand the words of God at a granular level—its truths should become organic in our lives. We are not suggesting that there is no place for the very detailed, disciplined mechanics of God's Word. We certainly believe such an approach is essential for an accurate interpretation, understanding, and application. Our point is that the believer's study must not stop at the interpretation level, nor should the application level be a simplistic "Read it. Do it." response. The goal should be to seek the desire and intent of God's heart so we can imitate and honor Him as His beloved children.[54]

Our goal is not to distill our knowledge of the Word of God down to clichés or simple phrases for the purpose of memorizing or navigating the Word, since much of the richness and truth is lost when we reduce a message or letter down to a summary statement. Our

---

[51] Isaiah 66:2b
[52] Ephesians 2:10
[53] Mark 12:30, Luke 10:27
[54] Ephesians 5:1 "Therefore be imitators of God, as beloved children;"

ultimate goal is to know the detailed thoughts of the teaching of God, so that we may begin to think, reason, and feel as He does. We want to see things from God's perspective and we want to adopt His perspectives as our own. We want to understand our world as He has taught us in His Word.

It is this type of application that will fuel the fire in the hearts of the church and transform God's Word into impassioned, intelligent action on the part of believers that will change our world. This type of application produces believers with hearts of wisdom, maturity, and understanding with love and compassion and a genuine desire to live in our world as salt and light, glorifying our Father who is in heaven.

When the Scriptures are applied in our hearts in this manner, the body of Christ will be known by its love, harmony, unity, and holiness, and the natural outflow to the world will be impassioned evangelism, feeding the poor, showing hospitality to the homeless, treating the sick, clothing the impoverished, and visiting the imprisoned. Then, on that great day, many surprised believers will hear the invitation of the King, "Come you blessed of my Father and inherit the kingdom that was prepared for you from the foundation of the world!"[55] Our end goal should always be to apply the Scriptures in a way that will produce joy for our King.

---

[55] Matthew 25:31–46

Chapter 6—Think About It ...

1. What advantages can reflective questioning offer beyond a normal study of the Word?

   _____

   _____

   _____

   _____

2. Describe the concepts of *Descriptive* and *Prescriptive* teachings and how they factor into applying the Scriptures

   _____

   _____

   _____

   _____

3. Explain the importance of focusing on the heart as we apply the Scriptures to our lives.

   _____

   _____

   _____

   _____

4. Explain how we should respond as we discern God's values or perfections in the Word.

   _____

   _____

   _____

   _____

5. What is the essence of *bearing fruit* in the context of applying the Scriptures?

    _____

    _____

    _____

    _____

    _____

    _____

    _____

6. Explain the difference between interpretation and application.

    _____

    _____

    _____

    _____

    _____

    _____

7. How would you describe the essence of applying the Scriptures?

    _____

    _____

    _____

    _____

    _____

    _____

Part Two

Setting the Stage for Your Passage

Setting the Stage for Your Passage
In Part One, we laid a foundation and built a framework for a sound approach to Bible study. In Part Two, we will continue building, teaching you how to set the stage for your study. When we talk about setting the stage, we are referring to the steps you will need to complete in order to fully understand your passage. You will find that Part Two is taught at a more granular level, as we take a hands-on approach to our exploration.

Part Two begins with a chapter that will help you understand how to select a Bible for your study. It provides information about different English versions of the Bible and is written to help you make an informed choice of a Bible version.

After you have selected your Bible, you will then select your passage of study. One of the most important steps of setting the stage is to determine the contextual boundaries of your passage by identifying the places in the text where the context begins and where it ends. The section within those boundaries is the section of Scripture that you will study. We will explore the concept of context in Chapter 8.

Once you have identified your contextual section, we will explore the background of the book, its author, and the various environmental contexts. Understanding the Big-6 environmental contexts will add color, culture, climate, and character to your passage.

The next step will take you into the realm of figures of speech of the Bible. Since figures of speech are so common in the Scriptures, we will explore them as part of setting the stage, in a way that is similar to researching the history or culture. It is better to introduce figures of speech at this point, rather than trying to explain them after you begin your study. Understanding the figures of the Bible will eliminate a common source of confusion and greatly increase your ability to interpret God's Word accurately.

These are some of the principles of Bible study. The skills are not difficult, but they do require effort. In addition to enhancing your personal study skills, one of the greatest benefits of this approach is that it will help you assess the quality and validity of the teaching of others, to protect yourself from false teaching. Is their teaching sound? Are they using a reliable version of the Bible? Did they consider the background of the book and honor the context of the passage? Are they correctly interpreting figures of speech and have they arrived at the most likely meaning of words? The chapters ahead will sharpen your ability to discern error and hone in on truth.

As you study the upcoming chapters, you will find that the approach tends to be of a free-form nature, rather than a regimented series of steps that must be followed. The reason is to leave room for the leading of God's Spirit as you study. It is very easy to exclude Him if we are overly concerned with following a system, as we may miss His prompting. This free-form approach gives you the liberty to follow His leading while observing principles that will keep you on the path and out of the woods of error.

Part Three explains a very simple approach for studying a passage and will equip you with some very powerful tools for study. For now, however, let's take a look at selecting a Bible.

7
Selecting a Bible

If you have ever walked through the Bible section of a Christian bookstore, you have probably been amazed at the great variety of Bibles on the shelves. In addition to numerous versions, there are also study Bibles for almost any phase and walk of  life that you can imagine, along with options for various bindings, colors, print size, study notes, maps, concordances, and cross-references. Selecting a Bible can be intimidating for even the informed buyer!

But it is important that we are informed about our selection of a Bible, because we must have highly reliable translations for our studies to lead us to a clear understanding of the original message. We have been blessed with many English translations of the Bible, and it is important that we understand how versions were developed and which would be most appropriate for our study. We need to know something about the translators' approach as they rendered the message in English. Did they produce a freeform paraphrase of the original or did they attempt to translate it as literally as possible? Or their version may be somewhere between a freeform paraphrase and a literal translation—perhaps they attempted to translate on a thought-for-thought basis.

In this chapter, we offer some guidelines for selecting a version of the Bible, along with the rationale behind our recommendation. Since the goal of our study is to understand the intended meaning of the original writer or speaker, then it seems that the obvious choice would be to select a version that renders the literal meaning of the original language. On the other hand, translators of literal versions also occasionally interject their interpretations when difficulties arise. If we were to create a word-for-word translation of the Bible, we would probably have difficulty understanding its meaning because of the many differences between languages. Someone may suggest then, that a paraphrased version might be the best option for our study. But we should ask what degree of paraphrasing is acceptable? Is a freeform paraphrase that does not accurately convey the small details of the Scriptures acceptable? Perhaps we would be more comfortable with a paraphrase that better adheres to the original message, while losing only a small portion of the detail.

There are generally four categories of translation types, which are listed and briefly described in Table 1 on page 119. Take a moment to study Table 1 and familiarize yourself with the name of each model and its translation approach.

Figure 1 – Bible Version Comparisons (page 120) illustrates how the translation approaches compare to each other. Notice that Figure 1 shows three of the categories, along with some well-known Bible versions and gives an indication of where they land on the translation spectrum. It is, however, unrealistic to suggest that a particular version is exclusively one translation type or another.

As you study Figure 1, notice that the original language is on the right and that the *exactness* of the versions decreases as they progress leftward toward the freeform paraphrase. This does not necessarily mean that the *accuracy* or *faithfulness* of the message decreases as we move toward the left—I am referring to the exactness of the wording and grammatical structure of the original language. There is certainly a point, however, where portions of the original message can be lost as the paraphrase approaches a freeform rendering.

Translation Approaches	
Word-for-Word	Attempts to translate each word of the original language into the target language. Due to the many differences between languages, the resulting translations can be difficult to understand.
Literal (*Formal Equivalence*)	Strives to reproduce the meanings of words and the grammatical structure of the original language. The focus is on maintaining the details of the original text, including original idioms and figures of speech.
Thought-for-Thought (*Dynamic Equivalence*)	Strives to convey the meaning of the original text so the target language readers (i.e. English readers) will understand the meaning in the same way that the readers of the original language would have understood it. Note that the *translators'* interpretation plays a large part, sometimes replacing idioms and figures of speech with phrases that are more familiar to the reader.
Paraphrase *Note: There are varying degrees of paraphrases, with "freeform" being the most extreme.*	A translation approach that seeks to clarify the original text by rephrasing it so it is easily understood by modern English readers. The focus is generally on clarity, rather than on the details of the original text. Note that the *translators'* interpretation plays a large part, frequently replacing idioms and figures of speech with more familiar phrases.

Table 1—Bible Translation Types

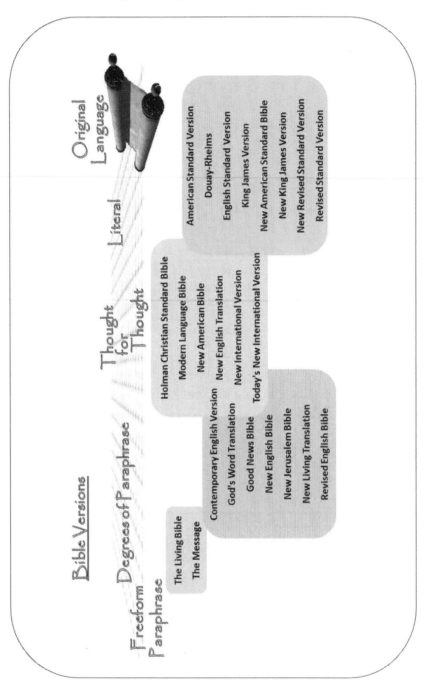

Figure 1 - Bible Version Comparison

Translation Teams

Sometimes we envision our Bibles to be the product of a single individual who faithfully labored by candlelight through late hours of the night to create a new version of the Bible. Although that may have been the case centuries ago, it is, fortunately, not the case in our modern world. Most modern Bible translations have been produced by teams of godly scholars, people highly acclaimed for their knowledge and understanding of the Biblical languages. Their translation decisions are not based on the opinion of a single individual. They are based on the honest collaboration of teams of learned scholars, which minimizes the possibility of an individual translator biasing the resulting translation—an accountability system that is at the heart of modern translation work.

These teams of experts are not small; they sometimes consist of scores of learned scholars who combine their expertise, resulting in outstanding scholarly achievements. For example:

- The Holman Christian Standard Bible (HCSB) translation team consisted of over 100 top conservative Christian scholars from various denominations.

- The English Standard Version (ESV) translation team was comprised of more than 100 leading evangelical scholars and pastors.

- The New English Translation (NET Bible) was completed by more than 25 scholars—experts in the original Biblical languages.

- The New American Standard Bible *Revision* or *Update* team (NASB-U) consisted of more than 20 scholars from a wide variety of denominations.

I am emphasizing the "teams of experts" aspect for a very important reason. As we study our English versions of the Bible, we need to have confidence that they are highly reliable. I emphasize this for your own comfort and confidence as you study. Many Christians tend to feel that their study of the English Bible is less than adequate and that they need to embark on a lifelong study of the Biblical languages in order to *arrive* at some sort of mystical understanding of God's Word. Please allow me to put your concerns at rest.

First of all, the New Testament makes it clear that God has gifted the church, equipping her to accomplish His work. I believe that He raised up godly scholars, who are gifted in their desire and ability to interpret the Biblical languages. The modern English translations are their gifts to the church. More importantly, they are God's gift to the church and we can fully enjoy them and rely upon them as we study.

Secondly, I believe it is unrealistic to expect the normal Christian to become fluent in the Biblical languages to the extent that they could read and study from them. This is not a matter of their ability—it is a simple matter of practicality. Very few people, who are holding full-time jobs and raising families, are able to attend classes and apply the study time that is necessary to master the Biblical languages. This very obvious fact was one of our primary motivations for writing this book!

What is the likelihood that a normal Christian would study the languages in a way that would elevate him or her to the level of a *gifted* language scholar or to the level of a *team* of collaborating language scholars? There would certainly be great benefit to learning the languages at a deeper level, but we must be mindful that our central focus must be on the actual message of God's Word. Is it possible that our time is better spent in reverent, meditative study of

reliable English versions, focusing on the message? I must say,
however, that even though it may not be necessary to become a
scholar of the Biblical languages, Biblical *word studies* are clearly
within reach of everyone. We will explain how to research words in
the *Clarify the Terms* chapter.

Finally, if you have a desire to study the Biblical languages and are
able to do so, then I strongly encourage you to pursue it. It is certainly
a rewarding and challenging endeavor, and you may be one whom
God has gifted to understand His Word to bless others with your
learning. For now, however, let's explore how we can better
understand the English Bibles that we've been given.

The Translator's Challenge
Imagine that you received a letter with the following characteristics:

+ Only capital letters
+ No spaces between words
+ No punctuation
+ No paragraph separation

Could you make sense of it? Would it be challenging to decipher its
meaning? Suppose Ephesians 1:13–14 were given to you in that form
in English as in Figure 2. How easy would it be to understand?

INHIMYOUALSOAFTERLISTENINGTOTHEMESSAGEOFTRUTHTHEGOSP
ELOFYOURSALVATIONHAVINGALSOBELIEVEDYOUWERESEALEDINHIM
WITHTHEHOLYSPIRITOFPROMISEWHOISGIVENASAPLEDGEOFOURINH

Figure 2—Ephesians 1:13–14

If you were already familiar with this passage, it may have been relatively easy to interpret. But consider the difficulties that are faced by scholars who must make translation decisions under much more challenging conditions, including deteriorated manuscripts, ancient languages that are no longer in use, in addition to having to understand the mindsets of past ages and cultures and Big-6 contexts that are very different from their own. The image in Figure 3 is an example of a Greek text that would present such challenges.

Figure 3—A portion of Papyrus 46.
The Earliest Manuscript from the Apostle Paul—*Public Domain – PD-1923*

You have, no doubt, noticed that your English Bible contains upper and lower case letters, spaces between words, punctuation, and separation between paragraphs. Where did these features come from and how were they included in our translations? The fact is that they were decided and provided by the highly skilled language scholars who laid the groundwork for modern translators. Most modern translation teams are not faced with all of these questions, since the majority of these concerns were addressed by scholars who compiled the ancient manuscripts into the concise Greek New Testaments that are widely available today and are commonly used for modern translation work.

One of the most commonly used Greek New Testaments is the Novum Testamentum Graece,[56] which is the basis for some modern English Bibles, including the ESV and the NASB. In addition to this resource, modern translators are also able to access electronic images of the Dead Sea Scrolls and other ancient manuscripts to shed light on uncertainties that arise.

Despite having this elevated platform, translators still face challenges that must be addressed. For example, a careful comparison of the ESV and NASB will reveal differences in their renderings—differences that were based on the opinions, philosophies, and convictions of the translation teams. Rather than viewing these as translational challenges, we view it as an opportunity to explore the varied opinions of experts, which may give insight into our passage of study. You will have the opportunity to see some of these differences in Chapter 19 as we explore juxtaposing.

Punctuation—Let's Ask Grandma

Is punctuation truly important? Let's ask grandma which of the following statements she prefers:

Let's eat grandma!
or
Let's eat, grandma!

---

[56] (The Institute for New Testament Textual Research, 2012) "Novum Testamentum Graece" by Tobias Aland—originally compiled and edited by a team of scholars, led by Eberhard Nestle and Kurt Aland.

Grandma had to lie down after she read the first statement, but I think she prefers the statement with the comma. This simple example illustrates the importance of punctuation, which is one of the many challenges that faced those who translated God's Word from the ancient texts. Scholars had to deliberate about the meaning of the original texts since they did not include punctuation. They had to make judgments about how words, phrases, and clauses should be grouped into sentences, and where punctuation should be added, in order to make them understandable to the English reader. Let's take a closer look at these details.

Words

It can sometimes be challenging to select the most appropriate English word that accurately conveys the meaning of a Greek or Hebrew word. In Chapter 17—Clarifying the Terms, we explain that there is a difference between words and terms. In other words, a word can have multiple meanings or terms, which we refer to as the *semantic range*. In some cases, the translators have chosen to provide marginal notes that tell the reader of an alternate word that would be acceptable. How do we determine the meaning of a word? In most cases, the answer is by its context, but we will explore this subject in more detail in Chapter 17—Clarifying the Terms.

Capitalized Words

Since the original Biblical languages did not differentiate between upper and lower case letters, the translators had to decide how to render words in English with cases. Perhaps you've noticed in your Bible that a word is capitalized in some places, but not in others— words like LORD, Lord, and lord; God and god; Spirit and spirit. In many cases, capitalizing is a matter of reverence for the proper name of God. The translators also capitalized the first word of each sentence to make them readable to the English reader. When you see a capitalized word in your English Bible, be careful about being overly emphatic about its meaning, since the decision came from the translators, rather than being part of the original text. Most Bibles explain their capitalization methodology in their preface.

Paragraphs

I would like to make a special point about the paragraphs in our English Bibles, since they are very useful in our studies. We have noted several times that the original Bible texts did not give any indication of where paragraphs began and ended—they were determined by the translators. In that light, if you were a translator, how would you determine how to group the words, phrases, clauses, and sentences into paragraphs? The answer goes back to the purpose of a paragraph, which is to group text that is devoted to one idea or related thoughts. When the message of the original text seemed to transition to a new idea, then the translators created a new paragraph, which they indicated by a new line or indentation.

Why do I emphasize this point? First of all, the fact that paragraphs represent a thought or idea is of great importance as we seek to determine where the context begins and ends. As you will learn in Chapter 8—The Concept of Context, the boundaries for contextual changes are usually found at the beginning or ending of a paragraph, making them relatively easy to find.

Secondly, since a paragraph is a section of text that is devoted to one idea, it provides a natural, bite-size portion of text that can be studied as a unit of thought. As we study a contextual section, we will trace the writer or speaker's flow, from paragraph to paragraph, using the *Follow the Weaver* tool. The paragraph-by-paragraph approach enables us to study a contextual section in its entirety, as a unit, and gives a comprehensive view of the overall message. We will explain the paragraph-by-paragraph approach further in Chapter 12.

Chapters, Verses, and Headings

We would be remiss if we did not mention the chapter and verse numbers, and section headings that are found in modern Bibles. The original Biblical texts and the subsequent copies did not contain chapter and verse numbers. After all, when was the last time you wrote a letter to someone and numbered each section and line? These features were added to the Bible more than a thousand years after the New Testament was completed. Although several attempts were made at organizing the Bible into chapter divisions, the one that remains in use today was created in A.D. 1205 by Stephen Langton, the Archbishop of Canterbury.

Even though the chapter and verse numbers of the Old and New Testaments contain some interesting and unexpected twists, few people, if any, claim that they were inspired by the Holy Spirit, as were the Scriptures; they were added as a convenience for studying and deliberating over the Scriptures.

In a similar way, the headings of books, chapters, and sections that are found throughout most Bibles are not found in the oldest manuscripts. They were added by translators, as they translated the Bible into other languages. In some cases, the headings can mislead the reader from the actual message of the original writer or speaker. Because of this, we recommend that students give little attention to the headings before studying the text. After their study is complete, they should return to the heading(s) and judge the accuracy for themselves. Even the best English translations contain headings, so don't let that keep you from using an otherwise excellent version.

Electronic Bibles

Electronic Bibles, whether computer software, mobile apps, or Internet-based, offer some tremendous advantages in our Bible study capabilities. There are, however, some advantages and disadvantages to both.

Perhaps the greatest advantage of electronic Bibles is found in their powerful search capabilities. Depending on the software, the ability to search for a word, name, or phrase can be focused on a specific section of the Bible or on the entire Bible; the results can be easily reviewed and copied. Perhaps the greatest advantage of electronic searches over hardcopy is the ability to search for a phrase or multiple words, which is very difficult when using a hardcopy concordance. We have listed some of the advantages and disadvantages of electronic and hardcopy Bibles in Table 2.

Electronic Bible	Hardcopy Bible
Searching is easy and thorough; easy for multiple search items.	Searching via hard copy can be very slow and difficult, especially for multiple search items.
Pages and passages can be difficult to remember because they are not hard and fast, changing visually due to scrolling, page-width, and device differences.	Pages and passages are easier to remember, since hardcopy Bibles do not change in appearance as do electronic Bibles.
Notes and comments can easily be lost with software or device upgrades. Cloud-based notes may be more secure. Notes can easily be shared with other users and can automatically transfer from device to device.	Notes and comments will always remain with this copy of the Bible, but they must be manually transferred when you replace it or they will be lost.

It is easy to become distracted with the attractions of electronic devices (apps, phone calls, text messages, advertisements, reminders, etc.)	Minimal distractions.
Battery requirements may be an issue when traveling or forgetting to charge, making the Bible inaccessible or unusable.	Batteries not required—external lighting may be required.
We recommend using both hardcopy and electronic Bibles.	

Table 2—Comparison of Electronic and Hardcopy Bibles

Which Should I Use?

At this point, you may still be asking, "Which version of the Bible should I use for my studies?" The better question would be, "Which **versions** of the Bible should I use for my studies?" In reality, the English reader can benefit from studying multiple literal versions. My personal preference is to study from two literal versions: The New American Standard Bible (NASB) and the English Standard Version (ESV). But I also refer to other versions as I study, including the New International Version (NIV), which is a thought-for-thought translation.

I believe there is more to be gained from starting with a study of literal versions, spending time reflecting on their meaning before consulting the interpretations of thought-by-thought or paraphrase versions. This approach allows us to muse on the literal wording and consider its meaning before being influenced by the interpretations of other students of the Word. As we will explain in a later chapter, using multiple version types can yield special insights as we view them side by side.

I also use an electronic Bible when I study, taking advantage of its powerful search and research capabilities. For my devotional time, however, I enjoy hiding away with an old-fashioned hardcopy Bible, which is free from distractions, so I can meditate and focus on the message of the Word. If I encounter something that needs research, I usually make a note of it and explore it at a later time.

I should also mention that my hardcopy Bible contains some helpful study features, including a small concordance in the back, maps, notes about literal meanings, and cross-references to related passages. As you decide on a hardcopy Bible, you may want to make sure that these features are included.

Modern English Bibles come in a full range of version types, including varying degrees of paraphrases, thought-for-thought, and literal translations. It is our belief that literal versions of the Bible provide the best view of the intended meaning of the original writer or speaker. But, it is important to realize that even the most literal translations contain a certain amount of interpretation of the translators, due to the difficulties of translating from one language to another. In other words, every English version of the Bible contains some degree of pre-interpretation by the translators.

Since our goal is to understand the intended meaning of the original writer or speaker, it seems that the best way to proceed would be to study from a literal version that keeps the interpretive aspect to a minimum, and discipline ourselves to use our own meditation and reflection to seek understanding. Once we have applied our best effort to understanding the passage, we should then refer to thought-for-thought or paraphrase translations to gain insights from others.

The subject of Bible versions is deep and it can be a very sensitive and emotional subject for some. Our goal in this chapter has been to introduce the subject and present a practical recommendation. Some excellent books have been written on this subject and we refer you to one in particular, *The Complete Guide to Bible Translations*[57] by Ron Rhodes, which is an excellent, comprehensive guide.

Things You Will Need for Studying the Bible
In order to be equipped to gain as much as possible from your study, there are some items that you **must have**. In addition to using old-fashioned paper, pens, highlighters, and hardcopy Bibles, we are going to take advantage of the technology of our era by using electronic study tools to expedite our work. You should try to obtain everything in the following list before you begin your study.

Required Items for Study

1) The most important requirement is a Bible; either an electronic or a hard copy is fine. A *literal* version of the Bible is preferable, such as the ESV, NASB, NKJV, or ASV.

2) You will also need a way to **print** a section of the Bible on paper. If you have a computer or other type of device (e.g. tablet, smartphone, etc.) that will allow you to do this, then that will be adequate. *It is very important that you are able to print the Bible text for your study!*

3) Unless you have access to a theological library, either electronic or hardcopy, it is helpful to have internet access so you can research the background of your passage and book of the Bible.

---

[57] (Rhodes, 2009)

4) You will need a pen or pencil and some paper for taking notes. Highlighters can also be very helpful for marking words, thoughts, ideas, themes, etc.

   - If you have a means of *electronically* annotating a text with comments, highlights, scribbles, drawings, etc., then feel free to use that instead of old-fashioned pen and paper ... *just make sure you are competent with it, so it doesn't slow your progress or distract you from your study!*

5) It is very helpful to have a way to search your Bible. The optimal method of searching would be with electronic Bible software, either on your computing device or via the Internet. If that is not available, then a hardcopy concordance should suffice; many Bibles contain a small concordance in back.

6) You will need to be able to investigate words in the original languages of the Bible. Some excellent resources are available for this purpose, which we will discuss in Chapter 17 – Clarifying the Terms.

These items should be all you'll need to begin your study. Obviously, you can benefit from other study resources, but these items will take you a long way.

8
The Concept of Context

Introduction

The importance of knowing the context of your passage cannot be understated. Studying a passage as part of its context can unlock truths that would otherwise be lost, while studying a passage without considering its context can easily lead to erroneous interpretations. You should be aware, however, that a study that may have begun as a few verses can easily expand into a much larger study when the context is included.

Selecting your passage of study

There are many different ways to study the Bible, such as topical studies, character studies, verse studies, word studies, and more. Our focus, however, will be on studying *textual* portions of Scripture, such as verses, chapters, or entire books of the Bible. The principles for textual studies form the basis for other types of study, and once you are comfortable with the principles of textual studies, you can safely venture into the other types.

As you follow this approach, you will become very familiar with your *selected* passage of study. You may also become familiar with Scripture passages that you did not plan to study. We will spend a fair amount of time working through passages, seeking to understand their meaning and how they relate to each other as they were woven into the tapestry of their context.

So, what would you like to study?

If you are beginning a new study, it's time to select your passage. If you're new to the Scriptures, we recommend that you begin with a simpler genre of Scripture, such as a narrative or perhaps a passage from one of the shorter epistles.

In order to illustrate this approach to studying the Scriptures, we will use Jesus' parable of the Lost Sheep as our example. What was that? Did you say that Jesus' parable of the Lost Sheep is recorded in both Matthew and Luke? That's an excellent point. When you begin a study, it's of great importance that you are specific about what you want to study, so you can have a clear focus on your passage.

✦ **Our *example* passage will be Jesus' parable of the Lost Sheep in Matthew 18:12–14.**

I have recorded the specific passage at the top of my study notes as shown in Figure 4 (i.e. Matthew 18:12–14). I also wrote some additional comments that I felt would be helpful in this study. Take time to do the same in your notes to make them as personal and useful as possible. You may, of course, type your notes, if you prefer.

> *Nov 23   Study Notes: The Parable of the Lost Sheep - Matthew 18:12-14*
> *Note: I have heard this passage is about evangelism and Jesus' concern for unbelievers who have not yet, come to faith, but I am starting to think this passage is not about unbelievers, but about wayward believers. I hope to learn the correct interpretation.*

Figure 4—Study Notes Heading

✦ **Take this opportunity to initialize your notes for this study as I did in Figure 4 above.**

Contextual Boundaries

Recall that Hermeneutic Principle #6 teaches, "A Scripture passage should be evaluated within the flow of its textual context." It may be helpful for you to reread the guidance of this principle in Chapter 4, before proceeding with this section. In order to follow this guidance, we must identify the beginning of the context and its ending. We will the refer to these as **contextual boundaries** and for simplicity we will refer to the text that lies in within the boundaries as the **contextual section**. Refer to Figure 5 as an illustration of a contextual section from Matthew 8. The entire contextual section is now our new passage of study.

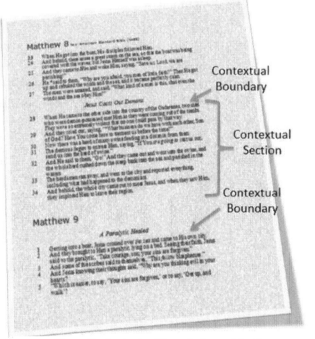

Figure 5—Contextual Boundaries and Section

How can you find contextual boundaries of a passage? Are they simply the beginning and ending of a verse, sentence, paragraph, story, or chapter? One way to describe beginning and ending boundaries is with the analogy of a scene change in a theatrical play. When the curtain opens and a new scene is presented, we *may* have the beginning of a *section* that is the beginning boundary of a contextual section. When the curtain closes and the scene ends, we *may* have an ending or closing boundary and, thus, the end of the contextual section. The opening and closing contextual boundaries are relatively easy to identify in narrative literature, but they can be more difficult to identify in other literary genres of the Bible, such as wisdom literature and epistles.

Let's look at several examples that will help clarify the concept of contextual boundaries. Open your Bible and try to identify the contextual boundaries for the Scripture passages in the left column of the following table. **Be sure to try to find the boundaries in your Bible before you look at the answers in the right columns.** Some of the boundaries will be relatively easy to identify, while others may be more challenging.

Scripture Passage	Opening Contextual Boundary	Closing Contextual Boundary
The Parable of the Lost Sheep in Matthew 18:12–14	Matthew 17:24—A new scene opens with "When they came to Capernaum …"	Matthew 18:35—the scene apparently closed here, since 19:1 opens a new scene with "When Jesus had finished these words …"

The Parable of the Lost Coin in Luke 15:8–10	Luke 15:1—The scene opens with the Pharisees and scribes grumbling.	Luke 17:10—The scene apparently closed in 17:10, since 17:11 opens a new scene with Jesus traveling to Jerusalem.
The account of the Tower of Babel in Genesis 11:1–9	Genesis 11:1—The previous scene (i.e. the genealogy of Noah's families) clearly ended in the previous verse 10:32) and the story of Babel began in 11:1	Genesis 11:9—The scene clearly changed with the genealogy of Shem's families.
Job's statement, "… I know that my Redeemer lives …" in Job 19:25	Job 19:1—Job's discourse begins after the phrase, "Then Job responded …"	Job 19:29—The scene clearly changed in the following verse (20:1), with "Then Zophar … answered …" *But we must be mindful that Zophar's words may be a response to Job's words in the previous contextual section!*

Psalm 107:23–24, "Those who go down to the sea in ships, Who do business on great waters; They have seen the works of the LORD, And His wonders in the deep."	Psalm 107:1—The opening of this Psalm is the opening contextual boundary	Psalm 107:43—The end of this Psalm is the closing contextual boundary.
Isaiah's vision of the Lord in Isaiah 6:1–5	Isaiah 6:1—The opening is clearly seen in the specific date of the event, "In the year of King Uzziah's death ..."	Isaiah 6:13—The scene clearly changed in 7:1, with the pronouncement of a new date and different kings.
Romans 10:9–10, "... if you confess with your mouth Jesus as Lord ..."	Romans 9:1—The opening boundary must be traced all the way back to this definite change of thought in 9:1, "I am telling the truth in Christ, I am not lying ..."	Romans 11:36—The closing boundary can be found as 12:1 introduces an entirely new train of thought regarding the believers' response, as compared to the case that led up to the thought.

Table 3—Examples of Contextual Boundaries

As you review these examples of contextual boundaries, you may be surprised to find that, in most cases, the amount of material in your passage of study grew dramatically, but this is normal and should be expected. It is by studying the full context that uncertainty will be removed and the truth will be revealed. Although these verses may seem to only supplement your desired passage, you will find that they often hold clues that unlock the truth and meaning of your original passage.

In our example of the Lost Sheep in Matthew 18:12–14, identifying the contextual boundaries extended our original study from three verses (18:12–14) to 39 verses (17:24–18:35). But a careful study of these additional verses sheds an enormous amount of light on the parable and reveals many additional truths that would otherwise be unnoticed.

Some of the truths we find in this passage include:
   a) who the lost sheep represents
   b) the little ones that Jesus mentions in the parable includes *anyone* who believes in Him (i.e. both children and adult followers of Christ)
   c) that we have angels who continually stand before our Father in heaven (not just children, but adults also have angels)
   d) the gravity of the offense of causing a little one to stumble, whether adult or child
   e) that Jesus' desire for lost sheep (i.e. straying believers) is restoration—discipline is the last resort
   f) we see the tender love of our Lord Jesus
   g) that something mystical happens in heaven when the church on earth agrees on a course of action
   h) that heaven hears and abides by the decisions of the church on earth … where two or more are gathered
   i) Jesus is still with us, even if we are completely alone

You may be asking if all of these points came from studying the contextual section within the Matthew 17:24–18:35 contextual boundaries and the answer is, "Yes!" It's tempting to want to distill a passage down to a main theme so we can summarize an overarching point of the teaching or for the sake of recall. But our goal is not to reduce God's Word to something that we can simply recall for a final exam or reduce to summary form. It is to become intimately familiar with it so we can know the heart of God. Our desire is to dive into passages and dwell on them and taste and savor the banquet of God's Word. This is the type of studying that will produce a heart of understanding and joy in the journey.

Lessons within a Lesson

As you would expect, when you expand a small area of study into a much larger section, you will certainly encounter much more teaching from the Word. This additional teaching comes in the form of the writer or speaker's points and sub-points, lessons that the Lord wants us to understand. We will also come face to face with the points and sub-points of the opposition—that is, those who oppose the ways of God, and we want to understand their perspective and arguments as well, since the Spirit placed them there for our instruction. There may be multiple lessons within the section—lessons that are explicitly taught and lessons that are inferred or implied. These small treasures can be easily overlooked if we don't give them the careful study and meditation they deserve.

In all cases, we must apply careful thought and meditation to every word and concept within the contextual section. Some refer to this as observation and suggest that it is the most important ingredient of studying the Word. I do not disagree with that, but I would add that the most fruitful observation is realized through careful familiarization with the Word by meditating on its details. Is this just quibbling over words? I don't think so, because familiarization through meditation will add context and meaning to the things we observe. It is analogous to the difference between knowledge and understanding. We strongly encourage you to be keenly observant as you read and study, and consider the significance of even the smallest details of the Word. The old adage is certainly true that "the difference between the master and the novice is detail!"

Even though your desire may be to understand a small passage of Scripture (the Lost Sheep in our example), our approach will be to study it as part of the larger section that lies between the contextual boundaries. We cannot isolate a section of Scripture from the rest of its context, book, or the rest of the Bible. The meanings of a contextual section are usually colored by the bigger picture, events or conversations of previous contextual sections. For our purposes, however, we will begin our study by understanding the immediate message within its contextual section and then weave that understanding into the entirety of the Scriptures.

Where Are the Boundaries?

How do we determine where the contextual boundaries of a passage lie? Would it suffice to simply start at the beginning of a paragraph and stop where it ends? Would it be safe to assume the boundaries begin and end where a chapter begins and ends? Unfortunately, neither of these methods are reliable, since all of the divisions in the text—sentences, paragraphs, verses and chapters—were determined by the translators. The oldest manuscripts do not have such divisions. What about the subject headings printed within the text of our English Bibles? Could they give us reliable insights about the content and context? Once again, the answer is "No." Subject headings were added by well-meaning translators many centuries later, but they are not inspired and are sometimes misleading about the content of a passage.

The fact is that there is no magic formula that can tell us where a contextual boundary lies within a passage. The principle, however, is that we are looking for a contextual section that is generally complete within itself and does not rely on other passages to clarify its message. On the other hand, as mentioned earlier, it would be misleading to suggest that any section of Scripture is truly a standalone message—the message of each passage must be considered in light of the message of the book in which it resides and in light of the overall message of the Bible. Thus, we cannot completely isolate any section of Scripture from the whole, but we can study smaller portions to determine their intended meaning.

In our example of the parable of the Lost Sheep in Matthew 18:12–14, the process of finding the opening boundary was quite easy... I simply scanned the preceding text in my Bible, until I found a statement that indicated the opening of a new scene or thought. It's not a matter of reading backward—that *would* be difficult! I quickly read the beginning and ending sentences of each of the preceding paragraphs until I found a scene change.

But didn't we just establish that we cannot rely on a paragraph beginning or ending as a contextual boundary? Yes, we did—we cannot safely assume that we've encountered a boundary simply because we've encountered the beginning or ending of a paragraph. On the other hand, it is unusual for a contextual boundary to begin in any place other than at the beginning or ending of a paragraph. This is because a contextual boundary is actually a change in thought or idea, which is the same purpose of a paragraph. Thus, the translators simply rendered it as a new paragraph. It is very natural for a contextual boundary to be found at the beginning or ending of a paragraph, although not every paragraph contains a contextual boundary—a contextual *section* frequently contains many paragraphs.

Finding the Contextual Boundaries for the Lost Sheep
Let's illustrate *boundary hunting* with our example passage of the parable of the Lost Sheep in Matthew 18:12–14. We will begin by searching backward to find the **beginning** contextual boundary. The first step is to see if our passage is actually the beginning of the context.

Our passage, Matthew 18:12 begins with, "What do you think? If any man has a hundred sheep ..." Does that sound like the beginning of a new context? When we read those words, it actually sounds like we tuned in to a conversation that was already in progress, which we did, so that cannot be our beginning boundary. We will continue to move backward until we find a statement that might indicate the beginning of a new contextual section.

When we scan the previous paragraphs, we find a possible indication of a context change in Matthew 18:1–2, which begins with "<u>At that time</u> the disciples came to Jesus and said, 'Who then is greatest in the kingdom of heaven?' And He called a child to Himself and set him before them..." In these two verses, we see an indication of *time* and a change of subject that was prompted by the disciples' question, so it is tempting to accept this as the beginning of a new contextual section ... but be careful! Do not quickly jump to a conclusion. The indicators that we described simply signal that we need to review the context to see if it has actually changed; we cannot rely on them solely to indicate that it is truly a contextual boundary. We must study the surrounding text to see if we are correct.

As it turns out, the previous paragraph in Matthew 17:24–27 contains a brief dialog between Peter and some tax collectors. Close examination of the passage suggests that the disciples' question in Matthew 18:1–2, regarding "who is the greatest in the kingdom of heaven?" was prompted by Jesus' words about the **kings of the earth** (i.e. kingdoms) collecting taxes from sons or strangers (Matthew 17:25). Furthermore, Jesus implied the subject of the Kingdom of Heaven in 17:25–27. Because of this, we will consider the paragraph in Matthew 17:24–27 to be part of the **same** contextual section that contains the parable of the Lost Sheep.

We continue our boundary hunt by scanning backward. The beginning of the previous paragraph also contains some possible indicators of a contextual boundary. The first sentence of the paragraph, Matthew 17:24, says:

> "When <u>they came to Capernaum</u>, those who collected the two-drachma tax <u>came to Peter and said</u>, 'Does your teacher not pay the two-drachma tax?'"   [Emphasis added]

In this verse, the indicators are a <u>change of location</u> and a new conversation or <u>change of subject</u>. Does this establish that we have a new context? No, it does not, but it indicates that this is a good place to examine the preceding text to see if the context might be different. As we read the preceding text, we find the subject matter and the characters to be very different than those in Matthew 17:24–27. It is a completely different context. We will, therefore, use Matthew 17:24 as our **beginning contextual boundary**.

Now that we have established our *beginning* contextual boundary, let's begin searching for our *ending* contextual boundary. We will begin with our selected passage, Matthew 18:12–14 and scan forward. As always, we must ask if the contextual section might end with our selected passage in verse 14. In other words, does the end of the parable signal the end of the discussion? It is tempting to accept the parable of the Lost Sheep as a stand-alone message, but when we examine the text that follows it, there is no reason to believe the context has changed. We must, therefore, read onward to find indicators that this contextual section has ended and a new one has begun.

As we continue reading, we will come to Matthew 19:1, which is a clear example of a contextual boundary being found at the beginning of a paragraph:

> "When Jesus had <u>finished these words</u>, He <u>departed from Galilee and came into the region of Judea beyond the Jordan</u>;"
>   Matthew 19:1

Notice this verse has two indications of a change of context. The first
is a clear statement that Jesus had finished His words, which suggests
the subject is moving on to something else. The second indication of a
context change is that He moved to a different location, similar to a
change of scenes in a theatrical play. As we encounter indicators such
as these, we must read the text that follows to determine if the
context has truly changed. If so, we can safely assume this is the
ending contextual boundary for our Matthew 18:12–14 passage.
(*Note: Matthew 19:1 would also be the beginning contextual
boundary for the contextual section that follows it.*)

The parable of the Lost Sheep—Matthew 18:12–14	
Beginning Contextual Boundary:	Matthew 17:24
Ending Contextual Boundary:	Matthew 19:1
The Contextual Section:	Matthew 17:24–18:35

What seemed like a tedious process was only tedious because we
included explanations about finding the boundaries. In reality, when
you seek the boundaries of the context of your passage, it will
probably require less time than it took to read my explanation above.
It's something relatively easy, and you will find it becomes easier with
practice.

Characteristics of a Contextual Section
Now that we've identified both the beginning and ending contextual
boundaries for Jesus' parable of the Lost Sheep in Matthew 18:12–14,
I would like to point out some characteristics of a contextual section.
As you read through Matthew 18, looking for indicators of context
changes, you probably observed several *possible* changes in the
subject matter in chapter 18 that might lead us to believe that the
context has changed.

For example, in 18:15, we should ask how Jesus' statement, "If your brother sins, go and show him his fault in private…" is related to the parable of the Lost Sheep. At first glance, it does not seem to be, but there are no indications that the participants in the conversation have changed or that the time or location have changed. It seems to be a continuation of the same discourse of the parable of the Lost Sheep, so we must include these verses in our contextual section.

Similarly, at an initial glance it is difficult to see the relationship between the parable of the Lost Sheep and church discipline Jesus described in 18:17; the things we bind on earth being bound in heaven (18:18); where two or three are gathered in My name, I am there in their midst (18:20); Peter asking if he should forgive an offender seven times (18:21); or Jesus' response via the parable of the unforgiving slave in 18:23-34. But the passage progresses logically and in order, and a close examination reveals that all of these teachings are related to each other in some way—they are woven together by a common theme.

All of these passages are in the same context as the parable of the Lost Sheep and our task is to understand how they were woven together to form the tapestry of the message. You may find that some stories are closely intertwined, while others are not as closely connected. Still others may be parenthetical stories with a distant relationship to your passage. You may be wondering how they relate to each other and what they mean. We will explore the process of seeking understanding in a later chapter, but for now, let's continue learning the steps that will lead to that point.

Record the Boundaries for Your Passage
At this point, we have explained the concepts of *context* and *contextual boundaries*, so you should have a solid understanding of these concepts and be able to identify them for your passage of study. Now you can update your study notes with the contextual

boundaries for your passage and explain your reasoning for selecting them. Refer to Figure 6 for an example of how I updated my notes for my Lost Sheep study in Matthew 18:12–14.

Nov 23 Study Notes: (Cont'd) - The Parable of the Lost Sheep - Matthew 18:12-14
Contextual Boundaries:
Beginning CB: Matt 17:24 – Reason: Change of location and dialog.
*   (i.e. "When they came to Capernaum...")*
Closing CB: Matt 18:35 – Reason: Clear end of dialog and change of location
*   (i.e. "When Jesus had finished these words, He departed from Galilee...")*
Contextual Section: Matt 17:24 – 18:35

Figure 6—Example of Recording Contextual Boundaries in Study Notes

Print It

Once you have identified the contextual boundaries for your passage of study, we suggest that you print your entire contextual section. If possible, print it with a large border for your notes. Be sure to use a font that is comfortable for you. Refer to Figure 7 as an example.

✦   ***Print It****—this is a required step! You will need to have a*
      printed copy of your Contextual Section for the remainder of
      your study!

Figure 7
Printout of Contextual Section

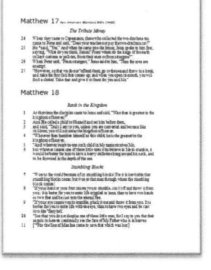

Why is it important to print the contextual section for your passage? In this approach to Bible study, you will use pens and highlighters to mark up the printout of your contextual section—to highlight important points of the text; to draw lines between related points; to circle, scribble, make notes, and anything else that might help you connect the dots of the text to better understand its meaning. It would be possible to make notes in your Bible, but it's probably better if you transfer only your final, more meaningful notes to your Bible, using your printout for your study notes. You can save your printout with your study notes and refer to them in the future if you revisit a passage. There's nothing magic about printing your contextual section, but it will certainly help you learn!

Summary

You may be wondering why we place such a great emphasis on understanding the context. The importance of context will become clear as you study the examples in the remaining chapters of this book. We encourage you to take some time and read the advice that is provided in Appendix C—Guidance for Identifying Contextual Boundaries. The examples will increase your understanding of the concept of context and help you determine the contextual boundaries for your passages of study. It provides both general guidance for identifying contextual boundaries and specific guidance for identifying boundaries in various literary genres of the Bible. It may be wise to bookmark Appendix C for your future reference.

9
Behind the Scenes

Have you ever started watching a movie after it was already underway and found that you were still able to understand the situations, tensions, humor, and excitement, even though you missed its beginning? If you were able to watch the same movie from the beginning, when the setting, characters, and context were introduced, you would, no doubt, have detected many more of the subtle character and situational developments that could have made the entire story unfold with greater meaning.

In a similar way, when we read the Bible, it's like joining a movie that is already underway. We are able to comprehend words, meanings, and implications, even though we have limited information about the background and the characters. The limitation is even more pronounced when trying to understand the message of the Scriptures, due to the vast separation between our world and the ancient world of the Bible. Differences in language, culture, technology, religion, government, agriculture, industry, geography, and, thousands of years of social change all create interpretation uncertainties with each layer of separation.

It is possible for us to narrow the divide between our world and the Scriptures by researching the background of a passage and the book that contains it. Think of it as setting the stage for a play. Once the stage is set, the story can be played out in a way that increases the comprehension of the viewer. Let's take a look at the steps involved in recreating the background.

>   *Step 1: Research the background of the author and the book*
>   *that contains your passage*
>   *Step 2: Research the Big-6 contexts of your passage*

Step 1: Research the author and the book
Researching the background is an effort to understand the author and the situation in which he wrote the book or letter. Was he a king, farmer, or priest? What were his concerns, goals, desires, political or religious situation, and fears? Was he a prophet of God who had no fear of his security, like Nathan or Samuel, or was he a prophet of God who was being pursued and tormented by the wicked, like Elisha or Jeremiah? How much revelation did this prophet have when he wrote his message? How much revelation did Solomon have when he wrote Ecclesiastes, or how much did John have when he wrote his gospel many years after Christ ascended to heaven?

Reconstructing the background also requires an understanding of the audience. Were they familiar with Jewish customs, or were they Gentiles who had converted to Judaism? Did the writer or speaker assume the audience had a certain level of understanding about his subject? Based on the audience's understanding, how much could the writer assume before he wrote the letter? Even though the message of the Bible is for the entire world, we must understand that it was written from a predominantly Jewish perspective, which must factor into our interpretation.

The items of interest for this research include:
- The name of the author and biographical information about him
- The date or range of dates when the book was written
- The dates when the events of the book took place
- The intended audience

The Human Author of the Book
Many books of the Bible do not explicitly name the author, even though they may provide some insightful biographical information about him. It is usually necessary to consult the work of Bible scholars to gather this information, but it's surprising how much information

we can find within the writings. When seeking the author's identity, do not be too quick to believe it is the name or title of the book, since the titles of some books refer to the recipients rather than the authors, such as Philemon, 1 & 2 Timothy, and Titus.

As you research the author and book, you should look for the following information:

Author—Try to learn the name of the *human* author of the book of the Bible—who wrote it? The authorship is sometimes difficult to determine, which means you may have to rely on the insights of Bible scholars. If you are unable to identify the author, simply write "author unknown." You can update this note if the answer become clear later.

Place of writing—Try to determine the most likely place or places where the book was written. Once again, this information may be difficult to find, but it can yield valuable insights about the meaning of passages in the book. For example, did you know that both Daniel and Ezekiel were probably written in Babylon during the exile? Where was Moses when he wrote Genesis? It is very likely that he wrote it while he was still a prince in Egypt with access to the Egyptian libraries and record archives. His other books, Exodus, Leviticus, Numbers, and Deuteronomy, were written during Israel's wanderings in the wilderness. It is likely that some of Paul's letters (epistles) were written while he was confined by the Romans awaiting trial, a fact that could explain the some of his statements. These simple facts give much color and richness to your understanding of the books of the Bible!

Date of writing—The date of authorship of a book can be very enlightening. Becoming familiar with some of the key dates of the Bible act as a structure for organizing its history in your mind. Some books of the Bible were written over a very short period of time, while others are records of history and were probably updated throughout the years as events occurred. Philemon and 3 John, for example, were most certainly written within a short time, while the books of Israel's history were probably on-going annals that were updated during or after significant events.

For example, 2 Chronicles 16:11 tells us, "Now, the acts of Asa from first to last, behold, they are written in the Book of the Kings of Judah and Israel." This is one of many statements that indicate that some of the books of the Bible were written over a long period of time, such as 1 & 2 Samuel, I & 2 Kings and I & 2 Chronicles. We have created a very helpful chart of the dates of the Kings and Prophets, which is available through the web site, at www.AncientWords.us.

Date(s) and era of the book's events—We sometimes assume the date of a book's writing coincides with the events of the book, but that is not always the case. For example, it would seem logical that the four gospels were penned soon after Jesus ascended or shortly after Pentecost (possibly 30–33 A.D.). But in reality, they were written years later. As students of the Word, it is helpful to have an idea about the timing in which a book was written since it can sometimes give us insight for understanding the message.

Intended audience—Knowing the intended audience of a book gives insight into how it was to be received by others and may give us insight into how we should receive it. Some books of the Bible clearly and concisely list the intended audience, including Titus (see Titus 1:4) and Luke (see Luke 1:3–4), although there was most certainly an expectation that they would have been shared and read by many. Other books seem to have been written for the benefit of many people, such as Galatians (see Galatians 1:2), the historical books, and the epistles. Epistles that do not list a specific audience are referred to as *general* epistles.

You may be wondering where you can find this type of background information, since it is not always found in the Bible. One of the best options is to consult books that *survey* the Old or New Testaments or books that specifically address the book of the Bible that interests you. These types of books often provide information about the author, date and place of writing, and the intended audience.

We have compiled a simple *Fact Book* that provides this type of information about each of the sixty-six books of the Bible. The *Fact Book* was designed simply to provide the facts about the books of the Bible, including biographies of authors and some of the leading characters, the Big-6 information, maps, charts, and other information that can be very helpful as you prepare to study the Bible. Information about obtaining a copy of the Fact Book can be found on our web site at www.AncientWords.us.

As you research this information, remember that you are only looking for the facts rather than seeking a person's commentary or theological perspective of the facts. Once again, the reason is because we do not want to bias our interpretation of the Scriptures before we begin our study. If your only access to this type of background information is in a commentary, proceed cautiously and just focus on the facts about the author, dates, audience, and book. After our study is complete, we will compare our learning to that of other believers who have also studied the Word in a careful, prayerful manner.

Since our example study of the parable of the Lost Sheep is in the gospel of Matthew, I've updated my study notes to record the background and authorship of the book of Matthew and placed a copy in Figure 8 as an example for you. Feel free to include as much information in your study notes as you desire—their purpose is to help you learn and recall.

Background Research:
Author: Matthew (aka. Levi) - Disciple/Apostle – Tax collector, called by Jesus (Matthew 9:9-13, 10:3, Acts 1:13)
Place of writing: Jerusalem? Antioch?
Date of writing: Probably between A.D. 58 - 70
Dates & era of the book's events: 5 BC – 30 AD (estimated) – During Jesus' earthly ministry.
Intended audience: Possibly intended for a Jewish audience because of its Messianic tone, but it also speaks of gentiles becoming part of the Kingdom of Heaven, which implies that non-Jews clearly have a vested interest in Matthew's message.

Figure 8—Background Research Notes

Give it some thought …

Based on the background information recorded in our example in Figure 8, what questions could you ask to help you gain a deeper sense of its influence on the message of the book? We've provided some examples below:

- What might Matthew's past as a tax collector say about his pre-Christ lifestyle or character?
- How were tax collectors viewed by the Jews? What might it say about his friends?
- What does his past as a tax collector suggest about his conversion to Christ?
- How might Matthew's past affect his outlook as an apostle?
- Is it possible that his life as a despised tax collector might influence his emphasis on righteousness?
- Does the place of writing seem to have any impact on the message of his gospel?
- Matthew was an apostle—what is an apostle?

- Matthew was a disciple—what is a disciple? Am I a disciple? Am I an apostle?
- What is the significance of his gospel being written before A.D. 70?
- Why do you think he waited so long to record his gospel after Jesus ascended?
- Why would Matthew write his gospel with a typically Jewish flavor (i.e. with Jewish terms & idioms)?
- What is meant by "Messianic" tone? What does "Messiah" mean and how is it significant?

These questions are just a sampling of many possible questions that could lead to more questions, answers, and deeper insights about the message of the book. Make a point of musing on the facts you learn during your research and seek to understand how they might affect the message.

Step 2: Research the Big-6 environmental contexts of your passage

Now that we've learned about the background of the *book* that contains our passage, let's consider the Big-6 environmental contexts that may also color its message. Recall from Chapter 4 that the Big-6 contexts refer to the six arenas that could influence the meaning of a passage. The Big-6 environmental contexts are listed below and illustrated in Figure 9. The illustration depicts how the Big-6 contexts underlie the original message of the Biblical message, and also shows how the various contexts can overlap each other.[58]

✦ **Historical**

✦ **Cultural & Social**

✦ **Geographical**

✦ **Political & Governmental**

✦ **Religious**

✦ **Military**

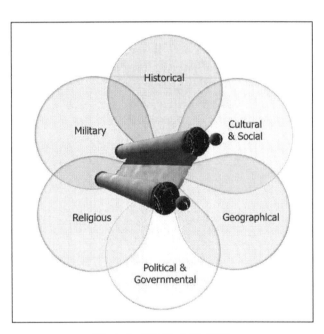

Figure 9—The Big-6 Contexts

---

[58] Figure 9 is not intended to show all of the possible overlapping of the contexts. In reality, there is probably overlap between every context.

Having knowledge of this information will help us avoid some of the classic interpretation errors, especially the very common error that assumes the Scriptures were written from the same perspectives of life in our 21st century world. The world of the Bible was very different from ours, and we must make every effort to interpret it through the eyes of the Bible's writers and their audiences.

The Big-6 Environmental Contexts:
1. Historical Context

The Historical Context refers to the events that led up to your passage of study, including both the distant past and recent events that set the stage. These may include, among other things: economic well-being, prosperity, famine, and oppression by other nations or people. This context may overlap the military, geographical, and political/governmental contexts.

The historical context can have a very subtle influence on the writer's perspective that is not always explained in the text. For example, we find historical context of the latter part of the book of Daniel and the entire books of Ezra, Nehemiah, and Malachi under the world rule of the Persian Empire. But when the history of the Bible reopens 400 years later, we find a very different world, with Greek as the universal language and Rome as the dominant world empire. An understanding of the historical context of each of these books sheds much light on the correct interpretation.

An example of the importance of understanding the historical context may be found in the era of the Divided Monarchy. The nation of Israel was once united under the reigns of Kings Saul, David, and Solomon. But after Solomon's death, the kingdom split into two separate kingdoms, each with its own king and capital city. The cause of the deep rift between the tribes of Israel is described in 1 Kings 12:1–24, which provides the historical context and is the key to understanding some significant events of the historical books and prophets in the Bible.

Every student of the Word should endeavor to become a student of the history of the Bible. We're not suggesting that every believer return to college and become a history major, but the more you learn about the history of the ancient kingdoms, the more you'll understand and enjoy God's Word.

2. Cultural and Social Context

The cultural and social context refers to the customs, behaviors, and attitudes of a people group that characterize their way of life. In many cases, the Scriptures reflect the cultural and social values of the writer. Because of this, it is of great importance that students of the Word have an understanding of the influences that were prevalent during the writing of each book of the Bible. The cultural and social context may overlap the religious and political/governmental contexts, among others.

A common interpretation error occurs when students attempt to interpret a passage through the lens of their own culture, rather than through that of the Scripture writer. When we compare our modern world with that of the Biblical writers, we are separated by thousands of years, vast distances, an enormous technical divide, and varied cultural and social differences. Examples of cultural and social norms of the Bible include: reclining at the table while eating, greeting with a kiss, slavery as a common practice, bartering, an agricultural society, polygamy, and living under the occupation of a foreign army.

3. **Geographical Context**

   The geographical locations and terrain of the Bible greatly color its stories and events. The geographic arenas include the land of the Chaldeans, which is Abram's place of origin, Egypt, North Africa, the Sinai Peninsula, Palestine, Babylon, Persia, Asia Minor, and the nations surrounding the Mediterranean Sea, including Rome and Spain. The terrain includes snow-capped mountains, barren wildernesses, vast, craggy deserts, the Great Sea, the Dead Sea, hill country, and fertile plains, just to name a few. An awareness of the geography helps a student of the Word visualize the stories and, perhaps, unlock some of their mystery.

   Mental images of the Egyptian city of Rameses as Moses led the nation of Israel out of captivity, the tomb of the patriarchs in the cave of Machpeleh, the well outside the city where Rebekah drew water for Abraham's servant, Jesus preaching on the mountain, fishermen in boats on the Sea of Galilee, the tribes of Israel calling to each other on Mounts Ebal and Gerizim, Elijah and the prophets of Baal at Mount Carmel, and Jesus and Cleopas walking on the pathway between Jerusalem and Emmaus, can make the stories come alive in the mind of the reader, and can lead to a more informed understanding as we seek to interpret God's Word.

The geographical context will often overlap the military context, since the terrain can dictate the strategies for battles and plays a part in the outcome.

4. Political and Governmental Context

The political context refers to the influence of existing rulers—including emperors, kings, queens, princes, viceroys, governors, satraps, prefects, councils, senates, tax collectors, civic leaders, and various factions—as they governed and influenced the lives of the people at the time of the writing. For example, during New Testament times, the political environment of Israel was ruled by the Romans, who placed their procurators, governors, and kings, over the people. It is important to understand how Caesar, King Herod, Governor Pilate, the Sanhedrin, and the high priests influenced the thoughts and actions of the people through political and religious-political affluence.

The political and governmental context also overlaps the religious context, since the Sanhedrin, which was the governing religious body of Israel, also exerted a governing influence over the lives of the people. Furthermore, the high priests, scribes, lawyers, and temple guards also factored into the governmental influences over the nation of Israel.

5. Religious Context

The religious context refers to the influence of religious leaders, observances, rules and rites, and the mixture of various religions during the time that a portion of Scripture was written or occurred. It is fascinating to observe how the religious climate played such key roles in the history of Israel and Judah as the ages unfolded.

Although the Law of Moses defined the nation of Israel down to its core, it was the people's adherence to the Law—or lack of adherence—that determined the general well-being of the nation before God. An understanding of the Law of Moses is essential for fully understand the culture, social customs, prophecies, and the expectation of the Messiah and His kingdom. Without such an understanding, it is very difficult to understand the reasons behind the judgments of God on Israel and the nations of the world.

The Religious Context was often comprised of a dominant religion along with a mixture of other religions. For example, when King David fully followed the Lord, the nation of Israel prospered. His son, King Solomon, initially followed the Lord, but his heart turned away as he permitted and participated in the religions of his wives and concubines (1 Kings 11:1–8). As a result, the kingdom of Israel was divided because of Solomon's sin, and the religious climate seemed to progressively descend into greater corruption. During the rule of Ahab, for example, the worship of the Lord had actually become a punishable crime and the worshippers of Baal greatly outnumbered God's faithful worshippers.

Throughout the Old Testament, the words of the prophets were issued as warnings and indictments against Israel and Judah because of their disregard for the Law of Moses. Developing an understanding of the first five books of the Bible (also called the Pentateuch, the Law of Moses, and the

Law) can greatly increase a student's insights into the Religious Context and produce a greater understanding of the entire Bible.

6. Military Context

The Military Context refers to the influences, pressures, and invasions of warring nations, neighbors, kings, and allies. Grant Osborne noted in his book that "Palestine's position as the sole land bridge between Africa and Eurasia meant that for reasons of trade routes and strategic military position, it was essential for powerful nations to control it. No other portion of real estate in the world has been so embattled."[59]

Because of its strategic location, the nation of Israel has been the battleground for wars that were not just its own, but also those of surrounding nations, frequently resulting in collateral damage for the small nation. An example of this is found in 2 Chronicles 36:20-24 and 2 Kings 23:28-30, when Pharaoh Neco, King of Egypt, went up to meet the king of Assyria in battle at the Euphrates River, moving through Israel on his way. King Josiah of Judah was killed in battle trying to defend his kingdom from the perceived threat of Pharaoh Neco and the Egyptian army.

A great portion of Israel's history centered around its own military actions and those of its neighbors. The Lord frequently used the military might of others as a means of punishing and purifying the nation of Israel. The Bible contains records of the powerful militaries of other nations, including: Egyptians, Assyrians, Syrians, Persians, Romans,

---

[59] (Osborne 2006)

Greeks, and Ethiopians. Much of the historical context is defined by military campaigns that affected Israel and the surrounding areas.

Israel's oppression and chastening began with Egypt and continued with nations that occupied the Promised Land, and were not driven out. The Lord inflicted the ultimate punishment on the kingdom of Israel through the might of the King of Assyria, who invaded the land and completely removed the people from the land and repopulated it "with men from Babylon and from Cuthah and from Avva and from Hamath and Sephar-vaim, and settled them in the cities of Samaria in place of the sons of Israel."[60]

The Lord also used the military might of the Babylonians to bring a ruthless judgment on Judah and the city of Jerusalem, as they tore down its walls and burned the holy temple of God. Unlike the northern kingdom, however, God, in His mercy, spared a remnant of the nation and allowed to return to Jerusalem to rebuild the wall and the city, and repopulate the land.

Some very significant military events took place during the interlude between the Old Testament and the New Testament. The time period from the closing of the book of Malachi until the opening of the gospel of Matthew is referred to as the *Intertestamental Period*. Within this timeframe, Alexander the Great conquered most of the known world and made Greek the universal language, which played a key role in the language of the New Testament and

---

[60] 2 Kings 17:24

the Septuagint (the Greek translation of the Old Testament). The Intertestamental Period also saw the emergence of Rome as the dominant world power that occupied the nation of Israel during the time of Christ and the apostles.

The Military Context can overlap all of the other environmental contexts and have a profound influence on the meaning of the Scriptures. As you study God's Word, you should seek to understand the influence of the *Big-6* on each passage of the Bible in order to arrive at a well-rounded interpretation.

As you gather information about each environmental context, you should record a summarized version of it in your study notes. The task of researching a book of the Bible may sound intimidating, but it can be quite enjoyable, as the Bible, itself, is an excellent source of information. For example, Luke 3:1-2 sheds some very interesting light on the Political/Governmental context that played a significant part in all four gospel accounts. Once you find this information, it is up to you to consider it further so you can understand the implications. Such information can generally be found in historical reference books, as well as in our *Fact Book*, available at www.AncientWords.us.

If you find a particularly valuable study resource, record it in your study notes, along with the page(s) that apply, so you can refer to it in future studies. We recommend the following:
- *The Annals of the World*[61] by James Ussher, which was first published in 1658
- *Antiquities of the Jews*[62] by Titus Flavius Josephus (translated by William Whiston)

---

[61] (Ussher, 1658)

Take time to review the information in Figure 10, where we have recorded a summary-version of our Big-6 research in our notes. It would, of course, be great if you want to provide in-depth detail, but for the purposes of your study notes, it is sufficient to provide summary-level information. Our purpose is to cull through the information, seeking details that might influence the message of the book. You may want to record more detailed information on additional sheets of paper and reference it in your study journal.

The Big-6 Influences

Cultural/Social: The culture of Israel was primarily Jewish, dominated by the laws and customs of Judaism, but the influences of the Romans, Greeks, Samaritans, Herodians, and others were significant.

Geographical: The narrative of the book spans the land of Israel: Galilee, Judea, Jerusalem, Samaria, the wilderness, the mountains, the Sea of Galilee, the Jordan River, etc.

Political/Governmental: The nation of Israel was occupied and ruled by Rome. In Luke 3:1-2, we learn about the Political environment when John the Baptist began his ministry:

- In the fifteenth year of the reign of Tiberius Caesar,
- Pontius Pilate was governor of Judea (see Luke 13:1),
- Herod was tetrarch of Galilee (see Matthew 2:16), his brother Philip was tetrarch of the region of Ituraea and Trachonitis, and Lysanias was tetrarch of Abilene
- in the high priesthood of Annas and Caiaphas...".- Israel was governed by the Sanhedrin – The Jewish people were allowed to govern themselves in smaller matters, but significant cases, including those which called for capital punishment were to be decided by their Roman captors.

Figure 10—Big-6 Influences Notes

---

[62] (Josephus)

✦ **Give it some thought ...**

Researching the environmental contexts is very important, but the research is only part of the task. We must step beyond the task of gathering and consider how the information could affect our passage. We can accomplish this through the use of exploratory questioning, which we will discuss further in Chapter 16.

Based on the Big-6 information recorded Figure 10, what questions could you ask to help you gain a deeper understanding of the Big-6 influences on the book? We've provided some example questions below – take some time to review and answer the questions, and then compose some additional questions of your own that might help you gain insight into the situation of the book.

A few questions about how the Big-6 environmental contexts of the book might influence the message:

- What does the Bible tell us about the character of Pilate? (Hint: do a Bible search on "Pilate" and read all of the resulting verses). Was he a benevolent procurator?
- What is a procurator? What is a Caesar?
- What year did Tiberius Caesar rule over the Roman Empire?
- How might the political climate have influenced the accounts in the gospel of Matthew?
- Did the people live in fear of their government or enjoy relative freedom?
- Was their government kind, cruel, or something in between?
- Were they occupied by a foreign army and government, were they self-governing, or something in between?
- Was freedom a reality or did the people live in fear of the government or religious leaders?

- To what extent were the Jewish people able to govern themselves?
- What is the Sanhedrin? What is its purpose?
- How was the leadership of Israel structured (i.e. the Sanhedrin, High Priest, etc.)?
- Who were the Pharisees? What did they believe? How dominant were they in the Jewish religion?
- Who were the Sadducees? What did they believe? How dominant were they in the Jewish religion?
- What is the relationship between the Pharisees and the Sadducees?
- Was the Sanhedrin comprised of both Pharisees and Sadducees? Others?
- Was the temple in operation during the events of the book of Matthew?

We cannot be certain which information will have an influence on a specific passage. Although it is unlikely that Israel's occupation by Rome would have a significant impact on the parable of the Lost Sheep in Matthew 18, we cannot be certain until we explore the various aspects of the context.

This would be a good point for you to take some time to reread the entire book of the Bible that contains your passage, so you can see it in the light of its background information and the Big-6 contexts. Chapter 14 – Reading Basics, explains that you should simply *skim* the chapter via *inspectional* reading, rather than engaging in a deep study via analytical reading. The purpose is to gain an overview, rather than seeking to fully understand the book at this time.

As you read the book, look for statements and hints that may indicate the reason the book was written. For example, the gospel of John clearly tells us "... these have been written so that you may believe that Jesus is the Christ, the Son of God; and that believing you may have life in His name."[63] Not all books of the Bible are as clear about their background or purpose as is the Gospel of John.

Lightening the Load

Although some of the tasks may, at first, appear to be tedious and time consuming, you should know that many of them need not be repeated for your future studies. For example, if you were to study the book of Colossians and spend time researching Paul, the author, you would not need to repeat the same research about him when you study his other epistles. In a similar same way, if you were to study a passage from the gospel of Matthew, your research about the Big-6 would probably not have to be repeated as you study the other three gospels. Our point is that Bible study need not be a difficult or tedious effort, although it certainly requires effort. Jesus told us to *learn* from Him and we will find rest for our souls.[64] God's Word brings the hope of abundant life and rest for our souls, which energizes us far beyond the effort we give.

We are students of God's Word engaged in a life-long endeavor to understand and honor Him. During this journey, we will become increasingly familiar with His Word and with the contexts that color it. Unexpected insights will come to light as you continually learn and gain new information about the various Big-6 contexts of the Bible. You will observe that the more we learn, the more we are able to learn. As we increase our awareness of the contextual settings of the Bible and the events that God used to shape it, we will have a greater chance of arriving at an accurate understanding of His Word.

---

[63] John 20:31
[64] Matt 11:29

10
Figures of Speech in the Bible

"All language is governed by law; but, in order to increase the power of a word, or the force of an expression, these laws are designedly departed from, and words and sentences are thrown into, and used in, new forms, or *figures*."

E.W. Bullinger—*Figures of Speech Used in the Bible*

*I'd like to introduce you to someone whom I've come to greatly appreciate. His name is ETHELBERT W. BULLINGER—we'll call him EWB for short. EWB has created an amazing, scholarly work that categorizes and describes all of the figures of speech in the Bible. He is truly a master of his trade—probably the foremost expert on the subject of figures of speech in the Bible of his time. He was fluent in Hebrew, Classical Greek, Biblical Greek, Latin, French, and of course, English. God has lavishly equipped him to help us gain an understanding of this very important subject. I highly recommend that you obtain a copy of his book, *Figures of Speech in the Bible*, but make sure there's room on your bookshelf, since it contains more than 1,100 pages!*

E.W. Bullinger – 1837 – 1913
This image is in the Public Domain in the USA – PD-1923

> *I'm not suggesting that you agree with all of EWB's positions, because you will probably recognize that he approaches the Scriptures with a set of assumptions and presuppositions that influenced his perspective. But that's okay—he seems to be a man who dearly loved the Lord and approached the Word with the greatest humility and respect and there is so much we can learn from him. I will be referring to his work quite often within this chapter, so please allow me to stand on the shoulders of a giant as we explore figures of speech together.*
>
> **DEM**

Introduction

As we continue to set the stage for our study, we will explore figures of speech, which is a realm of literature that seems to bend the rules of grammar, linguistics, and sometimes even common sense. The Scriptures are abundant with figures, but they can easily become a source of confusion to an interpreter. Because of this, we have devoted two entire chapters to introducing some of the more common *types* of figures in the Bible and have provided guidelines for determining when a word or phrase should be understood figuratively or literally. Armed with an understanding of how the Bible characters wrote and spoke, we can remove much of the mystery and sense of alienation that we feel as we study the text.

When words or phrases are used in their direct or primitive sense (i.e. by their simple dictionary definition), they are said to be used *literally*. On the other hand, when they are used in a manner that is *different* from the literal sense, they are said to be used *figuratively*. For example, when Jesus wrote on the ground with His finger (John 8:6), it is clear that *finger* is being used in its literal sense. But when He said, "If I cast out demons by the finger of God..." (Luke 11:20) then we might assume this use of *finger* is probably in a figurative sense.

Why would a writer or speaker use terminology in a way that it was not intended? Wouldn't a point be more clearly conveyed by through the literal use of a word or phrase? E.W. Bullinger, author of the classic work *Figures of Speech Used in the Bible*, emphasized that figures of speech are **always** used "for the purpose of giving additional force, more life, intensified feeling, and greater emphasis... an unusual form (figura) is never used except to add force to the truth conveyed, emphasis to the statement of it, and depth to the meaning of it."[65]

Even in cases when a figure understates a point, its ultimate purpose is to strengthen it beyond the capabilities of the literal usage of a word or phrase. For example, if a person were to open the door and come in from a fierce blizzard, they might say, "It's a bit chilly out there!" and their point would be clearly understood. If you were told that something "is not a pretty sight," you would immediately understand the magnitude of this understatement. It is this added power that makes figures of speech powerful tools for writers and speakers as they endeavor to move their audiences.

Figures of speech are abundant in every language of the world, including the original languages of the Bible. In the same way that a picture paints a thousand words, a figure of speech is able to convey the writer's point, while stirring the senses and emotions of the reader. Concepts that are complex, hidden, or abstract can be brought to life through a simple metaphor or simile.

Through an aptly phrased figure of speech, color, strength, and emphasis can adorn our words, and conjure mental images, feelings, and passion in the minds and hearts of the listener. Through an aptly phrased figure of speech, mundane formulae, lifeless rules, and everyday routine can be vividly envisioned in the mind of the reader

---

[65] (Bullinger, 2012—First Published in 1898) (v-vi)

with captivating form, color, and life. Through an aptly phrased figure of speech, the words of the speaker can sow understanding in the heart of the listener. Through the use of figures of speech, our words become easily visualized and alive to the listener. They can be consoling or terrifying, tender or harsh, or tranquilizing or inspiring.

But what is the real essence of a figure of speech? We should not think of them as mere beautifications of truth. Although they add heart and beauty to common words, they excel far beyond, since they are the vehicles that God's Spirit chose to relay His truth. The figures of the Bible were inspired by the Spirit for the purpose of conveying truths that transcend the literal bounds of language. It is for this reason that speed reading will not produce understanding and an appreciation of God's Word. All aspects of His Word, including its figures of speech, must be considered carefully so we can grasp all of the intimations of truth and emotion that are hidden within. Figures of speech require prayerful meditation, so we can discern the multi-facetted aspects of truths they teach.

It is not necessary to become a grammarian to interpret the figures of speech in the Bible. In many cases, it is enough to be aware of their existence and abundant usage by the prophets and apostles and devote the time to prayerfully muse on them, as we consider how they unveil the message that is being conveyed.

Our Lord frequently used figures of speech to convey the gravity of His words. For example, "... but whoever causes one of these little ones who believe in Me to stumble, it would be better for him to have a heavy millstone hung around his neck, and to be drowned in the depth of the sea."[66] Would His points have been made as vividly if He spoke them literally? Perhaps, "You will endure severe punishment if you cause someone to sin."? I don't think so! Figures of speech are given to provoke thought; if ordinary speech were used, the point might slip past unnoticed.

These words of Jesus also illustrate the great care that must be exercised as they are interpreted. How different will be the listener's response if the words are interpreted literally versus figuratively! It is, perhaps, figures of speech that create the most confusion and controversy among sincere, God-fearing believers who truly desire to interpret the Scriptures accurately. In this chapter, we will provide some guidelines that will assist in determining if a word or phrase is to be understood literally or figuratively. Although we deeply desire to interpret the Word accurately, we frequently walk a fine line in interpretation decisions that deal with figures of speech.

Figures in the Bible

When the figures of speech of the Bible are mentioned, many people immediately think of Jesus' parables. But His parables are just one example of the Bible's many figures. In reality, the Scriptures are peppered with figures of speech and they are found in every one of its literary genres, including narratives, epistles, poetry, wisdom, prophecy, and yes, even in the Law of Moses. Refer to Table 4 for examples of their widespread usage in each literary genre of the Scriptures:

---

[66] Matthew 18:6

Literary Genre	Reference	Figure of Speech
Narrative	Luke 10:3	"… behold, I send you out as lambs in the midst of wolves."
	John 10:9	"I am the door; if anyone enters through Me, he will be saved, and will go in and out and find pasture."
Epistle	2 Timothy 2:17	"… and their empty talk will spread like gangrene …"
	James 3:6	"And the tongue is a fire, the very world of iniquity;"
	Romans 9:21	"Does not the potter have a right over the clay, to make from the same lump one vessel for honorable use and another for common use?"
Poetry	Song of Solomon 6:10	"Who is this that grows like the dawn, As beautiful as the full moon, As pure as the sun, As awesome as an army with banners?"
Wisdom	Proverbs 9:1	"Wisdom has built her house, She has hewn out her seven pillars …"
Prophecy	Jeremiah 15:16	"Your words were found and I ate them, and Your words became for me a joy and the delight of my heart; for I have been called by Your name."
	Ezekiel 21:5	"Thus all flesh will know that I, the Lord, have drawn My sword out of its sheath …"
	Zechariah 2:8	"… for he who touches you, touches the apple of His eye."
Law of Moses	Leviticus 26:19	"… I will also make your sky like iron and your earth like bronze."

Table 4—Figures in Each Literary Genre of Scripture

Figures of speech were so common among the ancient Greeks that they had identified and categorized over two-hundred of them.[67] Due to the influence of Alexander the Great, the Greek language had become the universal language of much of the known world long before the birth of Jesus. As the Holy Spirit breathed His word through the evangelists and the apostles, they used the richness of this language with its abundant figures of speech to relay the words of Jesus to mankind.

Today, figures are found in every language and culture. They grow from the need to express ideas in a simple manner that is easily understood among their own people. If, for example, a western businessman were teaching in rural Nepal, it would probably be unwise to attempt to explain a concept figuratively by saying "we need to reboot." On the other hand, it may be more appropriate to suggest that they "get the oxen back on the path," since much of their culture is agriculturally based and unacquainted with modern technology.

In a similar manner, a modern-day North American may need to investigate Jesus' figurative use of a *yoke* in order to properly understand His words "Take My yoke upon you and learn from Me, for I am gentle and humble in heart ... For My yoke is easy and My burden is light."[68] The verses in Table 5, below provide examples that illustrate that the Bible was inspired through personalities who were familiar with an agricultural society:

---

[67] (Bullinger, 2012—First Published in 1898) (v)
[68] Matthew 11:29–30

"My yoke is easy and my load is light."
(Matthew 11:30)

"... unless a grain of wheat falls into the earth and dies,
it remains alone; but if it dies, it bears much fruit."
(John 12:24)

"For the Scripture says,
'YOU SHALL NOT MUZZLE THE OX WHILE HE IS THRESHING,'
and 'The laborer is worthy of his wages.'"
(1 Timothy 5:18)

"Where no oxen are, the manger is clean,
but much revenue comes by the strength of the ox."
(Proverbs 14:4)

"Then they will hammer their swords into plowshares
And their spears into pruning hooks;
Nation will not lift up sword against nation,
And never again will they train for war."
(Micah 4:3)

Table 5—Agricultural Orientation of the Bible

Literal or Figurative?

How can we know when a word or phrase is being used literally or figuratively? Whichever way we choose will take us down a different interpretation path, so we must exercise caution. It's easy to get off the path and stray into the woods where many interpretation perils lay. There are some simple checks and balances that will help clarify whether a statement should be taken figuratively or literally.

1) Whenever possible, the Scriptures should be understood in a plain, ordinary sense. Our **Hermeneutic Principle #14** guides us to "Interpret each passage in the natural, intended sense of the writer or speaker." The best way to begin is with an attempt to understand the words in a literal sense unless it becomes nonsense.

2) When a statement seems to be contrary to
    a. our experience (i.e. our experience as it aligns with the Scriptures),
    b. known fact,
    c. revealed truth, or
    d. the general teaching of the Scriptures,
   then we should assume that a figure of speech is being used and we must investigate how it was used from the perspective of the original speaker or writer.

With these guidelines established, let's take a look at some passages and try to determine if they should be interpreted figuratively or literally (*Note: focus on the italicized words*):

Passage	Literal	Figurative
"Why do You *hide Your face* and forget our affliction and our oppression?" <div align="right">Psalm 44:24</div>	☐	☐
"Then the LORD *opened the eyes of Balaam*, and he saw the angel of the LORD standing in the way with his drawn sword in his hand;" <div align="right">Numbers 22:31</div>	☐	☐
"and *you shall strike the rock, and water will come out of it*, that the people may drink." <div align="right">Exodus 17:6</div>	☐	☐
"*I am the vine, you are the branches*; he who abides in Me and I in him, he *bears much fruit*" <div align="right">John 15:5</div>	☐	☐
"And the priests who carried the ark of the covenant of the LORD *stood firm on dry ground in the middle of the Jordan while all Israel crossed on dry ground*, until all the nation had finished crossing the Jordan." <div align="right">Joshua 3:17</div>	☐	☐
"...behold, *the Lion that is from the tribe of Judah*, the Root of David," <div align="right">Revelation 5:5</div>	☐	☐
"But if I cast out demons by *the finger of God*, then the kingdom of God has come upon you."	☐	☐

Common Figures of Speech in the Bible

I've come to the belief that the names of the common categories of figures of speech should be part of the normal vocabulary of every student of the Word. They are really quite simple, yet an awareness of these figures can yield a profound increase in understanding. Figures of speech are not rocket science, nor are they overly academic—we are all familiar with them and use them in our everyday lives, so this is just a matter of giving a name to something that you already know.

It is important that students of the Word be aware of common categories of figures of speech so they will know when they have encountered a figure in their study. Our purpose is not to explore all of the literary details of figures of speech, but we'll look at some of the more common types, with a focus on the interpretation aspect. In most cases, you will be able to recognize a figure of speech, even if you are not able to name its category. The image in Figure 11 lists the figures that we will explore in this chapter to better equip you for your studies.

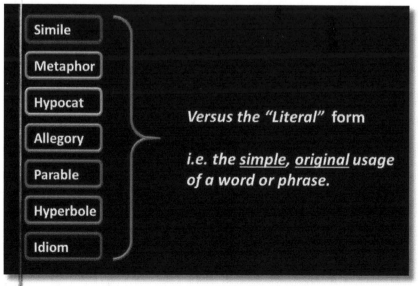

Figure 11—Common Figures of Speech in the Bible

Why is it important to understand when a figure of speech is being used in the Scriptures? The opposite of a *figurative* interpretation is a *literal* interpretation. A *literal* interpretation means that the words are understood in their "simple, original form (i.e. *literally*)"[69]. If a reader were to interpret a word or phrase as a figure of speech in a case where it was intended literally, then the resulting meaning could land him or her far from the truth. The opposite is also true: if the writer intended a literal meaning and the reader interpreted it figuratively, it would most likely result in a significant interpretation error.

Let's use Luke 14:26 as an example: "If anyone comes to Me, and does not hate his own father and mother and wife and children and brothers and sisters, yes, and even his own life, he cannot be My disciple." If the reader were to understand Jesus' usage of the word *hate* literally, the result for the reader and for his or her family relationships would be catastrophic and God's law and desires for His children would be undercut. If *hate* were understood figuratively, then the reader would have to be convinced that this is, indeed, being used as a figure of speech and then determine how it should be understood and obeyed.

As we study the Scriptures, we must be mindful that God's Spirit inspired each figure of speech as His chosen vehicle for conveying truth just as carefully as He inspired each "letter or stroke of the law."[70] The figures of speech are inseparable from the truths that they convey, as their imagery reveals aspects that would otherwise remain unknown. They are more than flowery adornments of the language—truth is to be found within the artistic beauty of their

---

[69] (Bullinger, 2012—First Published in 1898) (xv)
[70] Matthew 5:18

words. In many cases, a casual reading or hasty glance will miss the richness that only thoughtful meditation can reveal.

Michael Travers correctly observed that "Figures of speech find similarities in objects or ideas we would not normally find similar. They use concrete objects that appeal to our senses and thereby show rather than tell. They appear in even the strongest theology in the Bible (consider the image of slavery either to sin or to God in Romans 6:15–23, for example). Furthermore, they provide the form in which their theology is set; they are indispensable to meaning."[71] It is the responsibility of each student of the Word to prayerfully consider each figure, to determine which aspects apply to the context and the truth that is being taught by the Spirit.

Figures of Comparison
Let's take a closer look at some of the more common types of figures that are found in the Scriptures.

The first three figures that we'll explore are simile, metaphor, and allegory, which are figures that draw *comparisons* in different ways:
- o   Similes compare through **resemblance**
- o   Metaphors compare through **representation**, and
- o   Allegories compare in two ways:
  - ▪   as a **continued metaphor** or
  - ▪   through **continued implication**

The purpose of comparison figures is to associate the feelings, thoughts, and images of a commonly understood object (noun or verb) with an object that is not as easily known or visible. Psalm

---

[71] (Travers, 2003)

42:1[72], for example, compares the commonly understood imagery of a deer panting for water with the less evident feelings of the psalmist's soul, thus revealing his heart to the reader.

Simile

A simile is the simplest of the "comparison" figures of speech. Similes are easily identified by words that we often use when comparing things. For example, "gentle **as** a dove," or "time flies **like** an arrow." The first example uses "as" as the comparing word and the second uses "like," both of which indicate that we've encountered a simile.

Common indicators of a simile are *like, as, like as,* and *even as.* There are many more words that can signal the presence of a simile, but the words that we've listed are the most common.

The Scriptures contain such a large number of similes that it's difficult to select just a few for demonstration purposes. None the less, consider the similes in Table 6, below:

Similes in the Scriptures	
Psalm 42:1	"**As** the deer pants for the water brooks, so my soul pants for You, O God."
Isaiah 5:28	"Its arrows are sharp and all its bows are bent; the hoofs of its horses **seem like** flint and its *chariot* wheels **like** a whirlwind."
Isaiah 41:25	"I have aroused one from the north, and he has come; from the rising of the sun he will call on My name; and he will come upon rulers **as** upon

---

[72] Psalm 42:1 "As the deer pants for the water brooks, so my soul pants for You, O God."

	mortar, **even as** the potter treads clay."
Isaiah 53:2	"For He grew up before Him **like** a tender shoot, and **like** a root out of parched ground;"
Matthew 9:36	"Seeing the people, He felt compassion for them, because they were distressed and dispirited **like** sheep without a shepherd."
Luke 7:32	"They are **like** children who sit in the market place and call to one another, and they say, 'We played the flute for you, and you did not dance; we sang a dirge, and you did not weep."
Luke 13:19	"It is **like** a mustard seed, which a man took and threw into his own garden; and it grew and became a tree, and THE BIRDS OF THE AIR NESTED IN ITS BRANCHES."
1 Corinthians 15:22	"For **as** in Adam all die, so also in Christ all will be made alive."
James 1:6	"But he must ask in faith without any doubting, for the one who doubts is **like** the surf of the sea, driven and tossed by the wind."
1 Peter 1:24	"For, 'ALL FLESH IS **LIKE** GRASS, AND ALL ITS GLORY **LIKE** THE FLOWER OF GRASS. THE GRASS WITHERS, AND THE FLOWER FALLS OFF'"

Table 6—Similes in the Scriptures

Similes are quite simple and require little explanation, but the Spirit placed them in His Word because there is something for us to learn through them. It is not uncommon for *human* writers and speakers to use similes that are not a true resemblance to their subject, thus leaving the listener somewhat perplexed about the message. In God's Word, however, every simile is accurate and worthy of our meditation and trustworthy for our understanding, giving greater insight into His message.

Metaphor

Now that you are armed with an understanding of simile, the concept of metaphor will be easier to grasp. Like simile, metaphor is a figure of speech that is used to compare things. According to Bullinger, simile compares via **resemblance**, while metaphor compares via **representation**. In other words, a metaphor is a statement that one thing **is** another, or it is **represented as** another.

A characteristic of this difference is that metaphors **do not** have indicator words, such as *like, as, like as,* or *as,* as do similes. Metaphors boldly declare something, **representing** it as if it were a literal fact. This is where much of the difficulty with metaphors resides—it can be very difficult to determine if the words were intended literally or figuratively, creating the possibility for profound interpretation differences.

What is the difference between metaphors and similes? Is it simply the absence of the indicator words (*like, as,* etc.)? Both metaphor and simile compare things, so how would you describe the difference between the two? The difference between metaphor and simile is in their strength; the amount of passion and feeling that is relayed in each. Metaphor boldly transfers the figurative notion and feeling to its subject, while simile "is clear, beautiful, gentle, true to fact, but cold and too deliberate for passion."[73]

---

[73] (Bullinger, 2012—First Published in 1898) (727)

The Mechanics of Metaphor

In order for a figure of speech to qualify as a metaphor, it must include two objects, each of which must be understood in their absolute literal sense. If the nouns cannot be understood literally, the entire meaning of the sentence is lost. This means that the figurative portion of a metaphor lives in the verb that joins the nouns, and the *comparison* of the metaphor lives in a characteristic that is shared by both nouns. In all metaphors, the verb could be replaced with "represents" or "signifies."[74]

Allow me to illustrate this by using a metaphor from Psalm 23: "The Lord is my Shepherd." The two objects are "Lord" and "Shepherd" and the figure is found in the verb "is." Notice that both Lord and Shepherd are used in their very real, absolute literal senses. The Lord is represented as "my Shepherd." Thus, from this brief statement, we learn many characteristics of the Lord because of our familiarity with the characteristics of an earthly shepherd. An earthly shepherd is a caring guardian who defends, feeds, leads, and even loves his or her sheep. We could probably muse on this passage to find many more common characteristics, but these are sufficient to explain the purpose of metaphor.

Just for fun, let's compare the strength and passion of a metaphor with that of a simile. Suppose Psalm 23 began with "The Lord is *like* my Shepherd." Does that convey the strength and passion of "The Lord *is* my Shepherd?" I think not! There's an enormous difference in the amount of feeling and conviction of the metaphor. Metaphor is skillfully used by the writers of the Scriptures to powerfully convey the passion and feelings of Jehovah throughout His Word.

---

[74] (Bullinger, 2012—First Published in 1898) (740)

Like similes, the Scriptures are also abundant with metaphors. As you review the list in **Table 7**, below, notice the differences between metaphors and similes, not just in the absence of the indicator words, but in the increased passion and thrust of the statements.

Metaphors in the Scriptures	
Genesis 49:22	"Joseph **is** a fruitful bough, a fruitful bough by a spring; its branches run over a wall."
Deuteronomy 33:27	"The eternal God **is** a dwelling place, and underneath are the everlasting arms;"
1 Chronicles 29:15	"For we **are** sojourners before You, and tenants, as all our fathers were;"
Psalm 91:4	"His faithfulness **is** a shield and bulwark."
Proverbs 14:27	"The fear of the LORD **is** a fountain of life, that one may avoid the snares of death."
Song of Solomon 2:4	"And his banner over me **is** love."
Matthew 5:14	"You **are** the light of the world. A city set on a hill cannot be hidden;"
Matthew 13:37	"And He said, "The one who sows the good seed **is** the Son of Man,"
John 15:5	"I **am** the vine ..."

Table 7—Metaphors in the Scriptures

What do you see in each of the above metaphors? Would readers think the writer or speaker is being misleading or even lying by making these figurative *replacements*? Of course not! Metaphor is a legitimate, universally accepted method of conveying truth and it is up to the reader or listener to understand the figure as intended.

Because of the abundance of figurative language in the Bible, we must always be on the watch for words and phrases that are used figuratively and interpret them accordingly. Metaphors cannot usually be interpreted as being true to fact, so great caution must be exercised as we consider them. But do not be led to believe that a metaphor has less truth just because it is a figure of speech— remember that figures are **always** used for the purpose of giving greater emphasis or intensity to a truth!

Hypocatastasis

You may never have heard of *hypocatastasis*, but don't feel too badly, since it's not even found in some modern dictionaries. We'll shorten the name to *hypocat* just to make this easier to read. Why are we looking at a concept that's so obscure? Primarily because it is a figure of speech that is frequently used in the Scriptures, which means we should know it for that reason alone.

Although *hypocat* is somewhat archaic, the concept that it describes is very much alive and well. A similar and more current concept is found in the figure of *metonymy*, which we will briefly explore later in this chapter. Since hypocat is somewhat more foundational, it is worthwhile to spend some time learning about the concept it describes. Fortunately, it's easier to understand the meaning of hypocat (hypocatastasis) than it is to pronounce, so let's take a look ...

Recall that we're focusing on figures of speech that *compare* things. Reviewing what we've learned:

- Simile is comparison by **resemblance**
- Metaphor is comparison by **replacement**, and
- Hypocat (Hypocatastasis) is comparison by **implication**

As we've explained, simile uses words such as "like," "as," etc., which make it clear that a comparison is being made. Hypocat, on the other hand, **implies** the resemblance, creating a much more subtle comparison. Hypocat also uses only one object for comparison, whereas metaphor uses two. Since only one object is named, the other is implied and its meaning must be carefully evaluated by the reader or hearer.

Why would a writer or speaker use hypocat? Recall that metaphor has a greater impact than simile as it is more direct and packs more passion. In the same way, hypocat has a greater impact than metaphor, since it creates even greater passion and force through its resemblance. Thus, hypocat offers the greatest degree of impact of these three figures of speech.

Psalm 22:16 is an example of hypocat: "For dogs have surrounded me;…" It sounds like a very literal statement, but should the reader really believe that David was concerned about being surrounded by four-legged dogs? It would certainly be possible, but without minimizing the protection of the Lord, I think he would be able to get out of that situation with the help of his mighty men and his own weapons. But there's more to it, as hypocat **implies** a resemblance or representation of something else.

Verse 16 continues and explains his meaning by:

> "A band of evildoers has encompassed me;
> They pierced my hands and my feet."

Thus, David's **implication** is that the evildoers or his enemies are like dogs in some way or ways. Why would he use hypocat in this situation? It is because he wants us to understand that the nature and character of his enemies are aggressive and have the killing instincts of a pack of dogs with voracious appetites and wild fervor. Did his point come through with strength and passion? Would we sense his fear and desperation as clearly if he said, "My enemies are **like** dogs that encompass me" (i.e. simile) or "My enemies **are** dogs that encompass me" (i.e. metaphor)? David clearly chose the figure of comparison that packs the greatest punch by directly **implying** via hypocat that his enemies are voracious dogs who have encompassed him.

As mentioned earlier, hypocat has only one noun, whereas metaphor has two. In this example, if David said, "They are dogs who have encompassed me", then he would have two nouns, *they* and *dogs*, and the figure would have been a metaphor. But he simply said, "dogs have surrounded me," and it is up to the reader to determine what the other object should be. But the clear implication in the following verses is that dogs represent his enemies.

Once again, we must ask if readers could be misled by the use of hypocat or implication. Clearly, the God of truth Who inspired the Scriptures would not mislead or lie in His Word. As we study His Word, we must embrace the fact that His Spirit freely used figures of speech as accepted tools of literature and rhetoric to convey His message. There is no intent to deceive or element of dishonesty in the message, but it is up to the maturity and learning of the reader to interpret and understand His meaning.

In Matthew 16:6, Jesus used a figure of speech about the teaching of the Pharisees, saying "Beware of the leaven of the Pharisees and

Sadducees,"[75] yet He had to chastise His disciples because they did not recognize that He was speaking figuratively.[76] Although Jesus' point was that the disciples lacked the faith to believe that He could care for their need for bread, He clearly expected them to understand His figurative speech!

Take a moment to review the passages in **Table 8**, below, for more examples of hypocat in the Scriptures.

Hypocat (Hypocatastasis) in the Scriptures	
Matthew 3:10	"The axe is already laid at the root of the trees;"
Matthew 7:3–5	"Why do you look at the speck that is in your brother's eye, but do not notice the log that is in your own eye? Or how can you say to your brother, 'Let me take the speck out of your eye,' and behold, the log is in your own eye?"
Matthew 15:13	"Every plant which My heavenly Father did not plant shall be uprooted."
Matthew 15:26	"It is not good to take the children's bread and throw it to the dogs."
Matthew 16:8	"I also say to you that you are Peter" (i.e. you are a stone—Gr. Πέτρος—petros)
Matthew 23:33	"You serpents, you brood of vipers, how will you escape the sentence of hell?"
Matthew 23:34	"You blind guides, who strain out a gnat and swallow a camel!"

---

[75] Jesus' figure of speech in Matthew 16:6 is technically **not** a metaphor—it is *hypocatastasis*, which is implication.
[76] Matthew 16:11

Mark 1:17	"Follow Me, and I will make you become fishers of men."
Luke 13:32	"And He said to them, 'Go and tell that fox, "Behold, I cast out demons and perform cures today and tomorrow, and the third day I reach My goal."'"
John 2:19	"Destroy this temple, and in three days I will raise it up."
Acts 26:14	"It is hard for you to kick against the goads."
1 Corinthians 11:25	"This cup is the new covenant in My blood;"
1 Corinthians 13:1	"I have become a noisy gong or a clanging cymbal."

Table 8—Examples of Hypocat (Hypocatastasis) in the Bible

Interpreting Figures of Comparison

Once again, figures of speech present a challenge to the interpreter. A literal interpretation of a hypocat will result in an interpretation error, and incorrectly identifying the unstated or implied object of a hypocat will also result in an interpretation error. Applying an unintended characteristic of the noun of the hypocat can also result in an incorrect interpretation. For example, if an interpreter inferred that David's enemies have four legs like the dogs of his hypocat, then an interpretation error would result.

How can we know *which* characteristics of the figure are meant to transfer to the actual subject? In the Psalm 22 example, how can we know which characteristics of dogs are intended to apply to David's enemies? The answer is generally found in the context of the hypocat. Since the surrounding verses speak of harm and fear and violence from his enemies, we would probably be correct to muse on characteristics of dogs that could inflict the same. In verse 16, David no doubt used the imagery of dogs to impassion the reader to relate to the horror that his enemies inflicted on him.

As you meditate on a figure of speech, the context will usually offer the greatest insight. But we must also seek to understand the objects that are being compared. Our understanding can be augmented by asking three simple questions: What does it look like? What does it feel like? And what does it mean? *Calculating* an answer by immediately consulting a dictionary or the meaning of a word in its original language will often yield a shallow and incorrect assessment. As a reader, you should imaginatively enter into the situations, considering the first two questions, and the question of meaning will follow.

Allegory
The modern meaning of allegory is "a fictitious narrative, drama, picture, etc., that has a deeper meaning than that which is actually stated." Well known examples of allegory include John Bunyan's classic work, *The Pilgrim's Progress*, published in 1678, which is allegorical of the life of a Christian in this temporal world as he journeys to heaven. C.S. Lewis's classic, *The Lion, the Witch and the Wardrobe* (1950), allegorically portrays Christ through the lion, Aslan, climaxing in his sacrifice of himself for another.

The allegories contained in the Scriptures are very brief when compared to these two works. Nevertheless, the idea is the same: the people and symbols within the allegory represent a deeper or hidden truth. Why do the Scriptures use allegory? As with other figures of speech, truth(s) can be conveyed with greater passion and color than through a simple, literal story.

One of the more well-known allegories of the Bible was spoken by Nathan the prophet to King David. Although his allegorical story was simple, it was so skillfully crafted and so believable that it filled the king with emotion and rage. His story was about a poor man who had a single lamb that he loved and cherished as a daughter. A wealthy neighbor of the man, who owned many sheep, chose to take the lamb of the poor man and prepare if for dinner for his guest, rather than taking a lamb from his own flock.

When Nathan finished telling his allegorical story, "David's anger burned against the man, and he said to Nathan, 'As the LORD lives, surely the man who has done this deserves to die. He must make restitution for the lamb fourfold, because he did this thing and had no compassion.'"[77] To which Nathan responded, "You are the man!"

The power of allegory is seen in this story, as it pierced King David directly through the heart. I imagine his mouth dropping open, speechless, as he dropped to his knees in shame, guilt, and humiliation while the simple story exposed his grievous sin like an open book before God and his people. Allegory is a tool, used by authors, speakers, and poets that allows them to simplify concepts through familiar words and concepts. In this case, the cold, compassionless sins of David were condensed into an impassioned, one-minute story.

A Word of Caution about Allegories
Before we continue with our discussion of allegories, it is important to give a word of caution. Although allegories are abundant in the Bible, we remind you that some theologians and religious groups have abused allegorical interpretation by suggesting that many

---

[77] 2 Samuel 12:5–6

stories, if not all stories of the Bible should be understood allegorically. Such interpretations frequently come at the expense of eclipsing or discarding the clear and obvious meaning of God's Word.

Once again, we refer you to Hermeneutic Principle #14 in Chapter 4, which guides us to "Interpret each passage in the natural, intended sense of the writer or speaker." Forcing an allegorical interpretation from a passage that does not warrant it will most likely result in a teaching that is other than the word of the Lord. On the other hand, we must recognize that allegories **do** exist in the Scriptures and we must interpret them as such. In order to be faithful to the truth, we cannot throw-out the allegorical baby with the bathwater.

Allegories in the Scriptures

Perhaps the most obvious allegory in the Scriptures is found in Galatians 4, where Paul uses the historical example of Sarah and Hagar, representing two covenants. How do we know this is allegory? Because in Galatians 4:24, Paul says, "This is allegorically speaking ..."

There are several important lessons to learn as we consider the allegorical implications this passage. First of all, Paul's use of this true historical event as allegory does not in any way suggest that the event was fictitious. It is perfectly valid for an allegory to be built on a true historical event or upon a fictitious event.

Secondly, Paul's use of a historical account from the Bible **does not** give us license to interpret other historical events in the Scriptures as allegorical. Although it may be possible to find parallels or similarities between a historical event of the Bible and a New Testament truth, we must be careful not to believe that **our** non-inspired allegorical interpretations are truly doctrines of God. Clearly, this form of interpretation would enable people to synthesize almost any doctrine they desire by creating their own allegories from the historical events of the Scriptures.

The reason Paul's allegorical usage of Sarah and Hagar is legitimate is because it was inspired by the Holy Spirit; the same cannot be said of our own allegories. It would be a very dangerous departure from sound interpretation principles if we were to use our own judgment in determining which historical events contain a hidden allegorical meaning and which do not.

We should also point out that every allegory, whether based on a true event or a fictional story, must have taken place in the past (i.e. must be in the past tense) and never stated as a future event. Any such figurative story that is stated in the future tense considered to be *prophecy*. The prophetic imagery in Revelation 17:3 is clearly in allegorical form, yet has a literal fulfillment, as explained in verses 7–13. It *cannot*, therefore, be classified as allegory.

"And he carried me away in the Spirit into a wilderness; and I saw a woman sitting on a scarlet beast, full of blasphemous names, having seven heads and ten horns. The woman was clothed in purple and scarlet, and adorned with gold and precious stones and pearls, having in her hand a gold cup full of abominations and of the unclean things of her immorality, and on her forehead a name was written, a mystery, 'BABYLON THE GREAT, THE MOTHER OF HARLOTS AND OF THE ABOMINATIONS OF THE EARTH.' And I saw the woman drunk with the blood of the saints, and with the blood of the witnesses of Jesus. When I saw her, I wondered greatly."[78]

---

[78] Revelation 17:3–6

Take a few minutes to read the allegories from the Scriptures in Table 9, below.

Allegories in the Scriptures	
Psalm 23	"The LORD is my shepherd, I shall not want. He makes me lie down in green pastures; He leads me beside quiet waters."
Isaiah 5:1-6	"Let me sing now for my well-beloved a song of my beloved concerning His vineyard. My well-beloved had a vineyard on a fertile hill. He dug it all around, removed its stones, and planted it with the choicest vine. And He built a tower … "
Matthew 9:15	"And Jesus said to them, 'The attendants of the bridegroom cannot mourn as long as the bridegroom is with them, can they? But the days will come when the bridegroom is taken away from them, and then they will fast.'"
Matthew 9:16	"But no one puts a patch of un-shrunk cloth on an old garment; for the patch pulls away from the garment, and a worse tear results."
John 4:35	"Do you not say, 'There are yet four months, and then comes the harvest'? Behold, I say to you, lift up your eyes and look on the fields, that they are white for harvest."
Romans 11:16–17	"If the first piece of dough is holy, the lump is also; and if the root is holy, the branches are too. But if some of the branches were broken off, and you, being a wild olive, were grafted in among them and became partaker with them of the rich root of the olive tree …"

1 Corinthians 3:6–7	"I planted, Apollos watered, but God was causing the growth. So then neither the one who plants nor the one who waters is anything, but God who causes the growth."
2 Corinthians 3:2–3	"You are our letter, written in our hearts, known and read by all men; being manifested that you are a letter of Christ, cared for by us, written not with ink but with the Spirit of the living God, not on tablets of stone but on tablets of human hearts."
Galatians 6:8	"For the one who sows to his own flesh will from the flesh reap corruption, but the one who sows to the Spirit will from the Spirit reap eternal life."
Ephesians 6:13–15	"Therefore, take up the full armor of God, so that you will be able to resist in the evil day, and having done everything, to stand firm. Stand firm therefore, HAVING GIRDED YOUR LOINS WITH TRUTH, and HAVING PUT ON THE BREASTPLATE OF RIGHTEOUSNESS, and having shod YOUR FEET WITH THE PREPARATION OF THE GOSPEL OF PEACE ..."

Table 9—Examples of Allegory in the Bible

We must exercise great caution when interpreting the allegories of the Scriptures. Clearly, the Holy Spirit has a specific message within His Word, including the messages within allegories; some are accompanied with an interpretation, while others are not, placing the responsibility on the reader to meditate on each passage and arrive at an accurate understanding. In most cases, however, the meaning of an allegory can be found within the context or else an explanation will be provided in the Scriptures.

Once again, we must emphasize that the interpretation of an allegory is **not** a matter of anyone's own interpretation—the correct interpretation is that which the Holy Spirit intended as He inspired the writer to pen the words. As Peter taught us, "no prophecy of Scripture is a matter of one's own interpretation,"[79] and in the same way, it follows that no other part of Scripture, including figures of speech, are a matter of one's own interpretation. If we endeavor to interpret each passage in the most natural, intended sense of the writer or speaker, we will be able to hone-in on the truth of the Scriptures and stay out of the woods of error.

Summary of Figures of Comparison

Figures of comparison adorn the Word of God with images and feelings that extend beyond the means of literal words. In order to for us to comprehend their meaning, we must take the time to consider which aspects of the figure relate to the message at hand. In the next chapter, we will explore other types of figures of speech that present truths through colorful expression. Like figures of comparison, these figures must also be understood as figures, rather than literal statements, and be carefully considered to discern their meaning. By understanding the role of all types of figures in the Bible, we can be freed from defending literal statements that were not intended to be literal. Tune into the next chapter and you will understand!

---

[79] 2 Peter 1:20

11
More Figures of Speech

Introduction

In this chapter, we will continue our exploration of Figures of Speech, turning our attention to figures that are designed to both illustrate and hide truth, which sounds like a paradox in itself. In other cases, figurative speech is sometimes misunderstood because it is assumed to be literal, creating serious difficulty for those who sincerely desire to honor the Word by interpreting it as stated.

As we investigate these unusual usages of words, we will highlight passages that make it clear that even the personalities of the Scriptures do not always hold to a strict literal usage. Thus, we will suggest four principles that can be used when evaluating some of the *universal* statements of the Bible. We hope this information will be insightful and liberating as you become increasingly comfortable interpreting God's Word.

Parable

Despite being highly misunderstood, some of the best-known stories of the Bible are relayed in parable form. For example, even many unbelievers could recount the story of the Good Samaritan or the Prodigal Son. A parable is simply an illustration that **likens** one set of circumstances to another by continuing the use of a figure of comparison. The parable of the Treasure Hidden in the Field, for example, is an extended simile, since it is introduced with **like** and continues to expand upon the figure in the rest of the story:

"The kingdom of heaven is **like** a treasure hidden in the field, which a man found and hid again; and from joy over it he goes and sells all that he has and buys that field."[80]

We also find some parables that begin with other types of figures. The parable of the Nobleman, for example, begins as hypocat (hypocatastasis) and then continues its story with a series of **resemblances**:

"So He said, 'A nobleman went to a distant country to receive a kingdom for himself, and then return ...'"[81]

Parables are easy to identify in the Scriptures when the writers introduce them as a parable. The synoptic gospels contain statements like: "Hear then the parable ..." or "Jesus presented another parable to them ..." or "Now learn the parable from ...", and so on. On the other hand, neither the parable of the Prodigal Son nor the parable of the Unrighteous Steward are introduced as parables—it is left to the reader to understand Jesus' usage of these stories.

We also face the challenge of knowing if some stories are parables or if they are accounts of actual events. The story of the Rich Man and Lazarus, which is recorded in Luke 16:19–31, is one such story. It is not introduced as being a parable and it has some differences from other parables, one of which is that the name of a person, Lazarus, is mentioned—none of Jesus' other parables mention an individual by name.

---

[80] Matthew 13:44
[81] Luke 19:12

202

Is the story of the Rich Man and Lazarus a parable? From a linguistic perspective, it certainly could be, since it is perfectly acceptable for a parable to be based on a true story. The real question about this particular parable is whether Jesus is relaying fact or imagery, since it colors the truths that He taught through it.

Does it really make a difference if the story is true or fictitious? If it is a parable then it may be possible to interpret the figures as symbolic representations of something else. For example, it has been said the flames may simply represent some form of punishment. On the other hand, if this story is not fictitious, but an actual eye-witness account, then Jesus might actually be relating an eye-witness account of actual visual images of torment in the afterlife, which give great insight into the reality of eternal punishment and reward!

The primary requirement for being a parable is that it must be based on a story that is believable by the audience, regardless of whether it's factual. If it is not believable, then it might be better categorized as a **fable**, which is a story of mythical happenings that is used to teach a lesson. For example, if someone told a story about trees talking to each other, as in Judges 9:8–15, it might be understood as a fable. The account in Judges, however, is not a fable, because it is followed by an explanation, which places it in the category of allegory.

What about talking animals? You may be thinking of Balaam's donkey. Is that story fact or fable? It is clearly a factual account, based on its context, which states that it was an act of God (i.e. a miracle of God) that enabled the donkey to speak ("And the LORD opened the mouth of the donkey …"). Thus, it is up to the reader to determine from the context if the story is believable or not—fact or fable.

Another important principle for interpreting parables is that we cannot press every detail of the symbolism in an attempt to extract further truths—the purpose of a parable is to teach one primary truth or lesson. Parables are simply truths that are illustrated through a literary device; they are not intended to convey extensive details through their symbolism. In the same way that we do not press a proverb beyond its limits or reasonable meaning, we should not press parables beyond their limits by expecting a message to be found in every possible detail.

For example, someone might suggest that different species of birds of the air could nest in the mustard tree of Jesus' parable of the mustard seed.[82] Although that would certainly be possible, it is not stated in the parable. Continuing on this assumption, the person might further suggest that the different species of birds represent different religions within the Kingdom of God, which is clearly outside of Jesus' other teaching.[83]

You can see from this example how Jesus' intended meaning in the parable could be pressed far beyond what He intended to teach about the kingdom. The principle that we must follow is that *parables cannot be pressed to teach more than the primary truth or lesson.* This does not suggest, however, that we should not seek to apply the parable to our lives! We must differentiate between the interpretation and application aspects of our study.

---

[82] Matthew 13:31–32
[83] John 14:6 "… no one comes to the Father but through Me."

As always, our goal in interpretation is to understand the intended meaning of the writer or speaker and we must be careful not exploit parables to provide illustrations or analogies for our own purposes. Fortunately, some parables are accompanied by explanations that keep us on track about their intended meaning, while for others, hints about their meaning are provided within the context. In other cases, the meaning must be determined by the broader context, along with an understanding the overall message of the writer or speaker. In all cases, we must avoid clouding God's intended meaning by forcing a parable to support our own agendas.

Hyperbole

Have you ever read a passage in the Scriptures and been startled by its extreme implications? In some cases, we immediately understand the meaning of such statements and continue reading without even pausing for a second look. With other passages, however, we pause, almost in shock at what we just read, even stumbling in our confusion. We sometimes shake our heads and ask how anyone could believe and follow something like that.

These types of statements often fall into the category of *hyperbole*. As the name implies, there is something *hyper* or extreme about it. The Greek prefix, *hyper* or *huper*, actually means over and above, or beyond. In other words, a *hyperbole* is a word or phrase that is an intentional exaggeration, going above and beyond the actual meaning in order to emphasize a point. Such statements are *usually* not intended to be taken literally.

Here's an example of a hyperbole that would probably not even cause you to stop and ponder, because its meaning is clear:

"Where can we go up? Our brethren have made our hearts melt, saying, 'The people are bigger and taller than we; the cities are large and fortified to heaven. And besides, we saw the sons of the Anakim there.'"[84]

When you read this verse, did you believe, even for a moment, that the people's hearts really melted? Did you actually wonder if their cities were fortified to heaven? Probably not—you most likely understood the words as a figure of speech that emphasized their extreme concern about the situation.

Have you ever seen someone walk into a warm room and heard him or her exclaim, "It's burning-up in here!"? Was it really burning-up? Did anyone call the fire department to take care of the problem? Did you consider the person to be deceitful or even a liar for making such a statement? By the way, I'm starving—I haven't eaten since breakfast! Whoops—did I just lose credibility in your eyes for making such a statement? Probably not, the chances are good that you have also made a similar statement at one time or another in your life. These statements are hyperbole—an intentional exaggeration for the purpose of emphasizing a point.

The hyperboles of the Scriptures have been the source of serious interpretation errors as well as causing grief and confusion among sincere followers of Christ throughout the centuries. How should we view these difficult statements in the Scriptures? "If your eye causes you to stumble, pluck it out and throw it from you. It is better for you to enter life with one eye, than to have two eyes and be cast into the fiery hell."[85] Should we consider literally plucking out our eye and casting it away? Did Jesus intend these words to be taken literally or figuratively?

---

[84] Deuteronomy 1:28
[85] Matthew 18:9

Perhaps you are more comfortable with some of Jesus' other words: "Whoever does not carry his own cross and come after Me cannot be My disciple."[86] There are people in various parts of the world who literally carry a wooden cross and have themselves crucified every year because of these words. Was that Jesus' intent when He made this statement? Or "So then, none of you can be My disciple who does not give up all his own possessions."[87] If a person owns a single possession, including a single article of clothing, is he or she disqualified from being Jesus' disciple? Is Jesus instructing us to become social liabilities in order to be His disciples?

There is no question that these are difficult words, but we must consider the possibility that Jesus spoke them as hyperbole. Does hyperbolic speech negate the truths that are being taught? No, they do not negate it, instead, they serve to emphasize the gravity of His teaching. So the question that we must ask is, "What point did He intend to convey?"

In His statement about plucking out your eye if it causes you to stumble,[88] He's clearly emphasizing the eternal importance of fleeing from lust and immorality, as there will be an extremely high price to pay. Is it possible that plucking out an eye could atone for the lust of the heart? No, He did not suggest that, even though some guilt-ridden people have literally plucked out an eye because of this passage. Would it be possible for a person who became blind later in

---

[86] Luke 14:27

[87] Luke 14:33

[88] Matthew 18:9 "If your eye causes you to stumble, pluck it out and throw it from you. It is better for you to enter life with one eye, than to have two eyes and be cast into the fiery hell."

life to lust in his heart? Of course it would, based on memories of past images. So it does not follow that Jesus was speaking of literally plucking out an eye.

So how should we understand this statement? Should we dismiss it in its entirety since it is, most likely, a hyperbole? May it never be! The purpose of the hyperbole was to dramatically emphasize the need to fervently pursue holiness—sexual purity and purity of heart in this case. **But we must always be very careful to separate the hyperbole from the related *direct* or *literal* teaching**. Jesus was speaking very literally when He followed the hyperbole with, "It is better for you to enter life with one eye, than to have two eyes and be cast into the fiery hell." That is not a figure of speech! He caught your attention with the hyperbole and immediately established the truth that fiery hell is a reality, and our behavior in this life has a bearing on our eternal well-being.

Extreme Truths—Non-Hyperbole

Before we leave the subject of hyperbole, we need to consider extreme statements that may actually be intended in a literal manner. For example, in John, chapter 6, Jesus told the Jews, "I am the living bread that came down out of heaven; if anyone eats of this bread, he will live forever; and the bread also which I will give for the life of the world is My flesh."[89] It sounds like a figure of speech— perhaps a hyperbole—and the people were certainly perplexed by it. But when they questioned Him about it, rather than explaining that He was speaking figuratively, He said,

"'Truly, truly, I say to you, **unless you eat the flesh of the Son of Man and drink His blood, you have no life in yourselves.** He who

---

[89] John 6:51

eats My flesh and drinks My blood has eternal life, and I will raise
him up on the last day. **For My flesh is true food, and My blood is
true drink**. He who eats My flesh and drinks My blood abides in
Me, and I in him. As the living Father sent Me, and I live because of
the Father, so he who eats Me, he also will live because of Me.
This is the bread which came down out of heaven; not as the
fathers ate and died; he who eats this bread will live forever.'"
(John 6:53–58; emphasis added)

How should we interpret these words of Jesus? Even His disciples
struggled with them! In some sense, His flesh is true food and His
blood is true drink. I will be the first to admit that I do not fully
understand His meaning, but I certainly believe His words. The Roman
Catholic Church explains this passage through their doctrine of
transubstantiation of the bread and the cup; the Lutheran Church
explains it as *consubstantiation*, while the modern Evangelical
churches explain it as *symbolic*, and others believe these words have
nothing to do with the Lord's Supper. I am content, however, to say
that I do not have an explanation that answers all of my questions—it
is and will be whatever God intended it to be, regardless of my theory
about it. I simply believe that somehow, Jesus' flesh is true food and
His blood is true drink, and whatever is occurring behind the spiritual
veil will be taken care of by God, regardless of my understanding.

We will, no doubt, understand these difficult passages someday. But
for now, let me caution you to be very careful about relegating all
extreme passages to the realm of hyperbole. You must exercise great
care to keep from dismissing a literal truth, simply because it is
difficult to understand. After all, the Scriptures teach truths that were
given by the infinite God and are supernatural by their very nature

are quite foreign to our natural inclinations. Our acceptance of such truths must be through childlike faith.

Cascading Figures

As we've mentioned, there are literally hundreds of different types of figures of speech, and as you would expect, it is very common to find figures *within* figures. We've already discussed simile, metaphor, hypocat, allegory, parable, and hyperbole, but other common figures include metonymy, personification, and synecdoche. For the purposes of interpreting the Scriptures, it is not of great importance to be able to name the figure's type, but you should be able to recognize them as figures of speech when you encounter them in your studies. This will help you as you face the decision of interpreting something as literal or figurative. Let's take a moment to look at three more important figures:

Figure
Metonymy (meh-ton-uh-mee)
A figure in which a name or noun is used in place of another. The figure is based on *relation,* rather than *resemblance.*   **Example**: "... you are teaching all the Jews who are among the Gentiles to forsake Moses, telling them not to circumcise their children nor to walk according to the customs." (Acts 21:21)—a metonymy that uses *Moses* in place of *the law of Moses.*   **Example**: "I will also redeem you with an outstretched arm and with great judgments." (Exodus 6:6)—a metonymy that renders *punishment* or *plagues* as *judgment.*   **Example**: "That they might take possession of *the fruit of* the peoples' labor ..." (Psalm 105:44)—the original language omits "*the fruit of,*" saying "... take possession of the people's labor ..." thus we find a metonymy that renders *labor* as *produce.*

Personification

A figure by which inanimate objects or abstract ideas are spoken of as persons or associated with characteristics or abilities of a person, including intelligence, words or actions.

Example: "the voice of your brother's blood is crying to Me from the ground." (Genesis 4:10)—We find a personification of *blood,* suggesting it is able to cry out.

Example: "Therefore my heart is glad and my glory rejoices;" (Psalm 16:9)—the *heart* is personified as being glad and *glory* is personified by rejoices.

Example: "The mountains and the hills will break forth into shouts of joy before you, and all the trees of the field will clap their hands." (Isaiah 55:12)—A personification of the *mountains* and *hills* shouting with joy and the *trees* clapping their hands.

Example: "the lust of the flesh and the lust of the eyes and the boastful pride of life ..." (1 John 2:16)—We find a personification of *flesh, eyes,* and *life,* as the characteristics of a person or individual are ascribed to them.

Example: "Because He has inclined His ear to me ..." (Psalm 116:2)—A personification of the Lord having ears and hearing our voice and supplications.

Synecdoche (si-nek-duh-kee)

A figure that conveys an idea through a word or phrase that contains an associated idea. Synecdoche frequently interchanges a *part* of an idea with the *whole. (Note: The difference between Metonymy and Synecdoche is thus: Metonymy is a figure that interchanges two related nouns, whereas Synecdoche interchanges two associated ideas.*

Example: "If there is injustice in my hands ..." (Psalm 7:3)—A synecdoche of the hands representing the whole person.

Example: "Elisha the son of Shaphat is here, who used to pour water on the hands of Elijah." (2 Kings 3:11)—A synecdoche that

conveys the idea of Elisha's *entire* service to Elijah, through the
associated *partial* idea of simply pouring water on his hands.
Example: "How blessed is the man who does not walk in the
counsel of the wicked …" (Psalm 1:1)—A synecdoche that uses *man*
to represent all *mankind*—both *men* and *women*. This usage is
abundant in the Scriptures.
Example: "But blessed are your eyes, because they see; and your
ears, because they hear." (Matthew 13:16)—A synecdoche of the
eyes and *ears* conveying the *idea* of the entire person.

With this information we can now demonstrate how it is very
common for Scripture passages to contain figures within figures. For
example, recall that Psalm 42:1 contains a **simile**, "As the deer pants
for the water brooks, so my soul pants for You, O God." The dominant
figure of this verse is the simile that is indicated by "as," but we also
find **synecdoche** in the *panting* of the soul, as it relates to the
associated idea of the entire person. Furthermore, we find the
personification of *soul* panting as a *physical body* would do.

But you tell me that I make it sound so technical and he's just
speaking figuratively. And I would reply, "Yes, that's the whole point!"
The Scriptures overflow with rich figurative speech that God's Spirit
used to convey concepts that would require volumes to convey
through literal speech! The meaning and truth of the Scriptures
cannot be caught by a casual reading; its truths cannot be correctly
understood apart from its figures. We often view the Scriptures from
a superficial perspective as we would view a reflection on the surface
of a pond, but it is only as we gaze on them through meditation and
contemplation that we become aware of their depths, as they
cascade dimension upon dimension.

It is not just by learning the meaning of a figure that we come to understand truth. But in figures, we find new dimensions of truth residing far beyond the bounds of a superficial reading; truths that can only be revealed as we study meditatively with the assistance of the Holy Spirit. This, perhaps, is what the psalmist realized when he declared, "I have more insight than all my teachers, for Your testimonies are my meditation. I understand more than the aged, because I have observed Your precepts."[90]

Idiom

Idiom is a very interesting phenomenon of speech, offering insightful glimpses into the cultures of the world. Idiom describes the usage of words and phrases that are peculiar to a group of people, and are often based on concepts or sayings that are reflections of their culture. Although idiom "is not generally classed among *Figures* in the technical sense of the word, we must still explore them as figures, since their words do not mean *literally* what they say."[91]

Allow me to illustrate the concept of *idiom* from my personal experience. Many years ago, I worked with a Chinese lady who had recently immigrated to the United States. Although she was conversant in English, we had many funny conversations, since she was not familiar with American idioms. On one occasion, she asked a question and I responded, "I can't remember off the top of my head." She looked very perplexed and then asked why I was talking about my head. The idiom "off the top of my head" is familiar to many English speakers in North America, but the non-literal usage of the words was not part of her Chinese culture. We had some good laughs about other idioms from both of our cultures. On another occasion, she was

---

[90] Psalm 119:99–100
[91] (Bullinger, 2012—First Published in 1898) *Page 821*

trying to be a matchmaker between a man and woman who also worked in our building and I casually mentioned that "I don't think they have the right chemistry." Wow—did that one evoke the questions!

Travelers will encounter differing idioms even when their destination country speaks the same language. Although Americans and British may both speak English, differences do exist. It's useful to know the common idioms when you visit another country. If an American were to ask for a cookie in England, they might be surprised to receive a biscuit on their plate. If a Brit were visiting the USA, and referred to the *bonnet* of their car, they would probably receive a blank look from most mechanics, until they realized it was a reference to the car's hood. It might even be more surprising to a mechanic when our British friend refers to the car's *wing*, which is just an idiomatic term for the *fender*.

Idiomatic differences are found even within the same country—it is only necessary for people to be in different locales or subcultures to have different idioms. Consider the world of soft drinks: people in the Midwestern sections of the United States refer to carbonated soft drinks as "pop", which is short for "soda pop". If a Midwesterner were to ask a New Jersey waiter, "What kinds of pop do you have?" he would probably receive a blank look, since much of the Northeastern United States refers to carbonated soft drinks as *soda.* If a native of New Jersey were to order a *soda* in Texas, they'd probably hear, "Yer not from around here, are ya?" The reason is that much of the southern United States refers to carbonated soft drinks as "coke"—*I'll have an orange-coke, please.* All of these designations for soft drinks—pop, soda, and coke—fall into the category of *Idiom.*

Idiomatic expressions can also be peculiar to industries, as well as to people groups. For example, a group of computer programmers will certainly use expressions that are specific to their work. In a similar manner, most fields and industries will have their own set of idiomatic expressions. Refer to Table 10 to see a few examples of common modern idioms.

Common Modern Idioms	Meaning
An elephant in the room	A reference to something very obvious, that no one would acknowledge or discuss.
Go figure	Try to understand *that* ... or It doesn't make sense
Kick the bucket	A euphemism for death
Blank look	The implication is that a person obviously does not understand a question or comment, thus they give a *blank look*
It's not rocket science	It's not difficult
At my wit's end	When a person has struggled with a problem or situation and finally have no solution or relief, they have come to their wit's end
Love is blind	When someone is in love, they cannot see the faults of the one they love
Collect your thoughts	Try to think calmly and rationally about something without stress or distraction
He/she is clueless	Referring to a person who is completely unaware of something— usually referring to a solution or situation
Crazy like a fox	Referring to someone who appears to

	be acting irrationally, but in reality, he knows exactly what he is doing; a reference to the *savvy nature* of a fox.

Table 10—Common Modern Idioms

Why have we spent so much time introducing Idioms? The reason is because they are abundant in the Scriptures and often hold the key to correctly understanding a passage. They can hide the intended meaning of a passage if not correctly understood or they can unlock its meaning when we understand them as intended. A correct understanding of an idiom can illumine our understanding from shades of gray to living color.

Idioms that originated from the ancient Hebrew culture are referred to as *Hebraisms.* Many Hebraisms have been preserved in God's timeless Word and have therefore, become woven into the fabric of modern cultures that esteem the Bible. Some of them are so common that people often believe they originated from their own culture. Take time to review Table 11, which contains some of these familiar idioms.

Idioms that Originated in the Bible	Meaning
"The skin of my teeth" (Job 19:30)	A very fine margin of escape (between life and death in Job's case)
"A drop from a bucket" (Isaiah 40:15) Also: "A drop in the bucket"	Referring to an immaterial part of the whole—an irrelevant amount
"A man after His own heart" (1 Samuel 13:14)	Referring to someone whose heart is in alignment with God's ... or whomever the speaker is referencing.

"Two-edged sword" (Hebrews 4:12)	This figure is now used to refer to something that is very sharp (effective) *or* something that can cut both ways— to our advantage and disadvantage
"Wolves in sheep's clothing" (Matthew 7:15)	Referring to someone who has an innocent appearance, but has malicious intent.
"My brother's keeper" (Genesis 4:9)	Referring to one's responsibility for another
"Become all things to all men" (1 Corinthians 9:22)	Referring to pleasing anyone with whom you associate
"Born again" (John 3:3)	Originally referring to the rebirth through Christ, but the idiom is used to refer to any form of new beginning
"Forbidden fruit" (Genesis 2:17)	A reference to something that is desirable but forbidden to have
"Pearls before swine" (Matthew 7:6)	Something that is of great value, but completely unappreciated by the receiver

Table 11—Idioms that Originated in the Bible

Let's get down to business (idiom intended ;-) and look at some more idioms of the Bible. Appendix B—Common Idioms in the Bible, contains a list of some common idioms, along with the most likely intended meaning of the speaker or writer. Refer to this table to familiarize yourself with some examples of this common, yet sometimes misleading form of communication. Since the very nature of idioms suggests that a literal interpretation would most likely result in error, you will find that becoming familiar with these Hebraisms can greatly improve your skill in correctly interpreting the Scriptures.

Colloquial Conversation

Let's step back from figures of speech for a moment and consider some fundamental concepts of understanding a writer or speaker. When we read the Bible or any text, we should ask ourselves if the words should be understood in a formal sense with full accuracy intended, or if they should be understood in a more casual sense, which we refer to as colloquial speech. If we determine that we are dealing with colloquial speech, then we must adjust our interpretation accordingly.

When people casually converse with each other, there is a tendency to generalize or round off the details without any indictment of misleading the listener. For example, "It's 300 miles from here to Chicago," when in reality it might be 295 miles or 310 miles. Or perhaps, "She went to the store at 7:00, last night," when in reality it was 6:50. Have you ever heard someone say, "Everyone was there!"? Certainly, they did not mean every human being was there! These are examples of colloquial speech. It's the way of casual conversation, as compared to more formal and precise conversation.

Much of the Bible is also written in colloquial style. It is not uncommon to encounter statements that are casual in nature and were not intended to convey exact accuracy. Does this lessen the perfect inerrancy of the Scriptures? Not at all! Recall that the Holy Spirit inspired the Scriptures through the personalities of men—He did not dictate the word to them. In doing so, He used their individual personalities and styles of speech as He inspired His word through them, including their figures of speech and colloquialisms. In this section, we will explore some colloquialisms in the Scriptures that have caused much difficulty for students of the Bible, as they've attempted to press the words into a literal, formal sense.

Universal Statements—Does All Always Mean All?

Many years ago, I was in a church service, listening to a guest preacher. As he brought his message to a climax, he emphatically stated, "And when the Bible says *all* it **means** *all*!" I thought, "Wow— there's a nugget of truth that I can take to the bank!" But I found that his axiom actually led to more difficulties in my studies of the Scriptures than it solved. Does *all* really mean *all* … always?

When we read through the story of the plagues on Egypt, for example, Exodus 9:6 tells us, "… and **all** the livestock of Egypt died." This was because of the plague of pestilence that God brought on the Egyptian's livestock, which included horses, donkeys, camels, herds, and flocks. I did not have any difficulty with that statement until I read verse 19 of chapter nine, which warns of the impending deadly hail that will kill the *livestock* and men who are in the fields. But wait a minute … weren't **all** of the livestock already dead from the pestilence? Did the Egyptians import these animals from another country? Or is it possible that *all* did not actually mean *all without exception*?

Let's examine another use of *all* in the Bible to see what we can learn. The sixth chapter of Genesis describes the corruption of man on the earth and how it grieved the Lord. Verse 12 tells us, "… for **all** flesh had corrupted their way upon the earth." But earlier, in verse 9, we read that "Noah was a righteous man, blameless in his time." How can we reconcile the statement that **all** flesh was corrupt, yet Noah was righteous and blameless? Furthermore, in verse 13 we read, "Then God said to Noah, 'The end of **all** flesh has come before Me;… I am about to destroy them with the earth.'" Once again, we see an instance where **all** apparently did not mean **all** in the **all without**

exception sense, since Noah and seven others did not come to their end.

If **all** does not necessarily mean **all without exception**, what else might it mean? Let's consider several types of statements in the Scriptures that are stated in a *universal* tone, but may actually not be as sweeping in their intended meaning. Consider the following four principles regarding statements in the Bible that are of a *universal nature*:

1) **All** is commonly used to describe the majority or the greater part of a whole... not necessarily the whole. Consider the following Scripture passages:
   o Exodus 9:25 "The hail struck all that was in the field through **all** the land of Egypt ...", yet verse 26 tells us that the land of Goshen, which is the place in Egypt where the Israelites had settled, received no hail. In this case, **all** did not mean **all Egypt without exception**.
   o 2 Samuel 17:24 "And Absalom crossed the Jordan, he and **all** the men of Israel with him." There were certainly other *men of Israel* who were not with Absalom, including David, Joab, and Joab's ten young armor bearers (2 Samuel 18:15). So, once again, we find an instance of **all** not referring to **all without exception**.
   o Jeremiah 26:9 "... And **all** the people gathered about Jeremiah in the house of the LORD." But we learn that it could not have been **all** of the people, since the next verse tells us that the officials of Judah were not there—they were at the king's house when they heard of it.

- Matthew 10:22 "You will be hated by **all** because of My name..." This **all** probably did not include other followers of Christ.
- Philippians 2:21 "For they **all** seek after their own interests, not those of Christ Jesus..." Certainly, other people existed who could have been concerned for the Philippian believers' well-being, including the other apostles, Peter, James, John, etc. Once again, **all** probably did not mean **all without exception**.

Why is this important? It is important because it removes the shackles from students of the Word that would otherwise demand literal interpretations of **all**. Consider the following verses for example... if you were to contend that **all** actually means **all without exception**, then you might miss the point of the passage:

- Matthew 3:5 "Then Jerusalem was going out to him, and **all** Judea and **all** the district around the Jordan;" Should we understand this to mean that every individual in these regions went out to see Jesus or perhaps a *greater* part?
- Matthew 8:34 "And behold, the **whole city** came out to meet Jesus;" This passage does not use the word **all**, but it carries the same idea. Once again, should we believe that every individual from the city came out to meet Jesus or perhaps the greater part of them?
- Perhaps this understanding of **all** could shed light on some more difficult statements of the Scriptures. For example, when Paul told us that "... **all** Israel will be saved" in Romans 11:26, should we believe that *every* Israelite, including Judas (i.e. the *son of perdition*), along with those who rejected salvation by faith in Christ, will be saved? Or could it mean

some portion of Israel—possibly those who will be alive when Christ returns. Could it mean something else about Israel? We will leave this for you to consider.

2) When **all** and **every** are used in a universal sense, we should consider interpreting it as **all <u>kinds</u>** (i.e. all kinds that are specified or implied), rather than to **all individuals**.[92] Consider the following examples:

   o Joel 2:28 and Acts 2:17 "I will pour out My Spirit on **all** mankind." Should we understand this to mean that even those who reject Christ will have God's Spirit poured-out on them? A better understanding might be <u>**"all kinds of people from all nations"**</u>.

   o John 12:32 "And I, if I am lifted up from the earth, will draw **all** men to Myself." The best understanding of this passage would be that Christ would draw *all without distinction*, rather than drawing *everyone* to Himself, which is contrary to fact and to the other teaching of the Scriptures.

   o Hebrews 2:9 "… so that by the grace of God He might taste death for **everyone**." The best interpretation of this passage is that Christ tasted death for *everyone without distinction*, rather than *everyone universally,* since that would imply that *everyone* would be saved, which is clearly contrary to the overall teaching of the Scriptures.

3) A universal negative does not necessarily negate *every* aspect of what is mentioned.[93] Consider the following examples:

   o Exodus 20:10 "… the seventh day is a sabbath of the LORD your God; in it you shall not do any work …" Although this

---

[92] (Bullinger, 2012—First Published in 1898) (Page 616)
[93] (Bullinger, 2012—First Published in 1898) (Page 618)

statement universally forbids (*i.e. negates*) work on the
Sabbath, it does not actually mean *all* work, but rather that
which is *specifically* forbidden. This commandment is clarified
in Leviticus 23:7–8[94], which stipulates that **laborious** work is
the type of work that is actually forbidden.

- o 1 Samuel 20:26 "Nevertheless Saul did not speak anything
  that day..." Although it is certainly possible that Saul did not
  speak **anything** that day, it is more likely that he did not
  speak anything about David's absence from the New Moon
  feast.

- o John 15:5 "I am the vine, you are the branches; he who
  abides in Me and I in him, he bears much fruit, for apart from
  Me **you can do nothing**." In these words, Jesus is probably
  not suggesting that the disciples cannot do anything apart
  from Him, because they were certainly capable of doing sinful
  and cowardly deeds. It is best to understand this passage in
  its context, which would lead us to "...apart from Me, you
  cannot bear fruit."

- o 1 Timothy 6:3–4 "If anyone advocates a different doctrine...
  he is conceited and **understands nothing** ..." In this passage,
  Paul is, most likely, not suggesting that these people
  understand **nothing at all**. A better way of understanding his
  words is that he understands nothing about the doctrine that
  he is professing to teach, which Paul identifies as *the mystery
  of godliness* in earlier in the epistle, in 3:16:

"By common confession, great is the mystery of godliness:

---

[94] "On the first day you shall have a holy convocation; you shall not do any
laborious work. But for seven days you shall present an offering by fire to
the LORD. On the seventh day is a holy convocation; you shall not do any
laborious work." (Emphasis added)

> He who was revealed in the flesh,
> Was vindicated in the Spirit,
> Seen by angels,
> Proclaimed among the nations,
> Believed on in the world,
> Taken up in glory."

4) Words that seem to be used in a universal sense may actually not include every possible aspect.
   o Mark 16:20 "And they went out and preached everywhere …" It would be beyond the bounds of reason to understand *everywhere* as an actual universal statement. It is unlikely that they preached in Antarctica or in South America or even on the moon. The better understanding is that they preached "everywhere they went, or in every kind of place, or everywhere they were able to go."[95]
   o Luke 2:54 "and were continually in the temple …" This verse is most likely telling us that they were in the temple whenever it was possible for them.
   o Acts 28:22 "for concerning this sect, it is known to us that it is spoken against everywhere." Clearly, the sect would not be spoken against in places where it is not known—the gospel had not been spread throughout the entire world at the time this was written. The most likely understanding of this statement is that it is spoken against everywhere it is known.

From a close examination of the Scriptures, it becomes clear that universal statements were not necessarily intended to be fully universal. Perhaps we are seeing colloquial usages by the speakers or writers. We have cited some exceptions to sweeping, universal

---

[95] (Bullinger, 2012—First Published in 1898) (Page 619)

statements, but we are by no means saying that there are no sweeping, universal statements in the Scriptures. As we learned in Chapter 8, the context plays an enormous part in correctly interpreting the Scriptures and will help you determine whether a sweeping, universal statement should be understood as such.

Figures of Speech and Bible Versions

It is important to understand that idioms and figures of speech are rendered differently, depending on the translation model of the Bible version. For example, a literal version might render a figure with the same wording and grammar of the original text, while a thought-for-thought version might render its **intended** meaning, rather than using the actual figure. A paraphrase version of the Bible may go as far as replacing the original figure with a modern figure for the purpose of helping the reader relate to the message.

Although the intent is to improve the clarity of the version, such practices tend to distance the reader from the original language and cultural expressions. It is also possible for a version to render the same figure differently in different places, which may make the reading more interesting, but the reader may lose familiarity with the normal speech and character of the writer or speaker, which is very important as we grow in our overall familiarity with the Scriptures.

How does this affect us? As we study, we must always ask whether the figure of speech, as translated, truly captured the original intent of the writer or speaker. If it was incorrect or even close, then we may miss the intended meaning of the Holy Spirit—we may miss the truth, a risk that cannot be downplayed. If, for example, a paraphrase version substituted a modern metaphor in place of the metaphor that was used in the original text, how can we be certain that the replacement conveyed the figurative meaning that was intended? It is certainly possible that the modern translator selected a metaphor that conveyed an aspect that was very different from that which was intended.

How do we deal with such a risk? The first step is to consult a version of the Bible that is known for being faithful to the original text and the figures of speech of the original text. We recommend that you use a version of the Bible that includes notes about the *literal* meanings of words and phrases in the original language and allows the reader to consider if there might be room for an alternate interpretation of a passage.

Many Bibles include marginal notes that reveal the *literal* meaning of certain words. In our example from 2 Samuel 12:5, where David is quoted, "... the man who has done this *deserves* to die.", the NASB provides a note next to *"deserves"*, indicating that the original language says *"is a son of death,"* which is an idiom. Versions with these types of study aids can be an enormous help in increasing our understanding of the Scriptures, since they provide the *most likely* rendering and allow the reader to see the original wording. For additional information about these notes, please refer to the "Low-Hanging Fruit" section on page 280.

Another option for determining if the figure is a reasonable translation is to compare the renderings in multiple versions of the Bible. In all cases, we should spend time meditating on a literal translation of the figure, to try to understand its meaning and application. In Chapter 17—Clarifying the Terms, we will explore ways to find the original meanings of words and phrases. It is really quite easy and it will add a new dimension to your studies!

Figures of Speech—Go Figure...

We have covered a fair amount of ground introducing figures of speech—on the other hand, we have just scratched the surface, as this has been a simple introduction to a vast subject. It is, however, of great importance that we are aware of the abundance of figures in the Bible and the apparent expectation of the Author that we understand them as such. So the responsibility is on the reader—the student of the Word—to determine if a figure is being used and, if so, to correctly assess its meaning. This is one of the basic tasks for accurately interpreting the Scriptures.

Part Three

The Simple Machines of Bible Study

Lever | Wheel and axle | Pulley

Inclined plane | Wedge | Screw

The Simple Machines of Bible Study

It's funny how large tasks can be simplified by breaking them into smaller tasks using simple tools. It's a very old principle that applies to many areas of life, including Bible study. In Part Three of this book we explain how to divide your contextual section into bite-size portions and study each portion using the simple machines or *tools* of Bible study.

The tools that we will explore are:

- Meditation and Reflection
- Reading Basics
- Taking Notes
- Exploring through Questioning
- Clarifying Terms
- Follow the Weaver
- Juxtaposing

You may be surprised that we're approaching Bible study with a set of tools, rather than as a series of steps or phases. We do this because the idea of phases can be somewhat misleading. Even though our studies tend to have phases, the reality is that we frequently must go back and revisit a phase one or more times as we explore a paragraph or contextual section.

When we approach a task with a set of tools, however, it is quite natural to use a tool for a moment, set it down while we use another, and then reuse the original tool – a process that may be repeated over and over. It is similar to the way that a craftsman, a seamstress, a gardener, or even a golfer uses the appropriate tools to accomplish a task.

What is the task that we're trying to conquer? It is, of course, to understand the meaning of the original writer or speaker – *I'm sure you answered that question correctly*! Our task is to use our set of Bible study tools to examine the text and arrive at an understanding of the message within. Each tool will be explained in greater detail in the remaining chapters of Part 3 of this book.

Before You Begin

It is important that you are familiar with the principles that were introduced in the prior chapters of this book. The principles include esteeming the Bible as the Word of God, being aware of your assumptions so you can make sure they do not inadvertently influence your interpretations, and approaching the Word in the same manner as the Bible characters. You should also be sure you understand the hermeneutic, application, and meditation principles. If you do not have a solid understanding of these concepts, you should review the earlier chapters since they hold some fundamental principles that will help you understand the Word.

I would like to re-emphasize the importance of studying in the Spirit, as explained in Chapter 5. Studying in the Spirit is the essence of the way we study – it is not a preliminary step or a phase or a tool. It determines our attitude and helps us truly rely on God's Spirit for our source of understanding. Interaction with His Spirit must permeate our entire study, prayerfully inviting Him to guide our thoughts and our findings, incorporating them into our learning and leading us to understanding. It is this aspect that distinguishes our study from a strictly academic effort.

12
Paragraph by Paragraph

PxP – A Common Sense Approach to Study

You may be wondering how you will study your contextual section, now that you've identified the contextual boundaries and researched its background. How will you study it? Recall how a study that may have begun as a small passage can easily blossom into a much larger study, as did our example of the parable of Lost Sheep in Matthew 18, which grew from three verses to 39.

It can be somewhat intimidating to try to understand a large section of Scripture. But allow me to simplify things for you: we will tackle our contextual section by dividing it into its natural divisions of paragraphs and we will scrutinize it on a paragraph-by-paragraph basis – **PxP** for short. Why is this a legitimate method of dividing our contextual section? Recall from Chapter 7 – Selecting a Bible, we explained that the translation teams grouped ideas and similar thoughts into paragraphs. Because of this, it makes sense to explore each paragraph as a unit. This does not mean that we study them in isolation from each other. On the contrary, we will use our *Follow the Weaver* tool to help us find the connections and linkages that the writer or speaker used to weave the message into the context.

This Is How We Will Proceed

We will begin by reading our entire contextual section to get an overview of the flow. We will not race through it, but we will not pause to research words or seek to understand the entire message. The purpose of this initial reading is to simply get a feel for the passage and its overall direction.

We will then study the **first paragraph** of our contextual section, using the tools in our toolset, beginning with careful reading of the entire paragraph, taking notes as we go. We will compose thoughtful questions that will lead us to deeper understanding of the message and expose are areas that require greater understanding. We will use the *Clarify the Terms* tool to explore meanings of words and, if the need arises, we will use our *Juxtapose* tool to compare the renderings of our passage in different Bible versions.

As we give our best effort toward understanding the first paragraph, we will use our *Taking Notes* tool to record our understanding to this point. It is very likely that some of our notes will mention things of which we cannot be certain. But don't worry, as you will see, we will be returning to this paragraph repeatedly as we continue our study of the contextual section. You will have the opportunity to update your notes and record additional insights for each paragraph throughout your study.

Next
We will study the **next** paragraph in a similar manner as the first, but we will also be using the *Follow the Weaver* tool to help us follow the reasoning and logic that the writer or speaker developed in the preceding paragraphs. As we will explain in Chapter 18 – Follow the Weaver, we will trace the threads of the context from the *preceding* paragraphs, rather than from the *following*, to assure that we follow the threads of the weave. We must be mindful, however, that as we follow the weaver, we cannot remove our focus from the paragraph at hand!

If we were to illustrate the flow of this approach, it would look something like that of Figure 12. As you can imagine, you will become very familiar with your entire contextual section, especially with the initial paragraphs. But you will also gain familiarity with the latter paragraphs, since you will be able to apply adequate time to them – after all, what's your deadline?

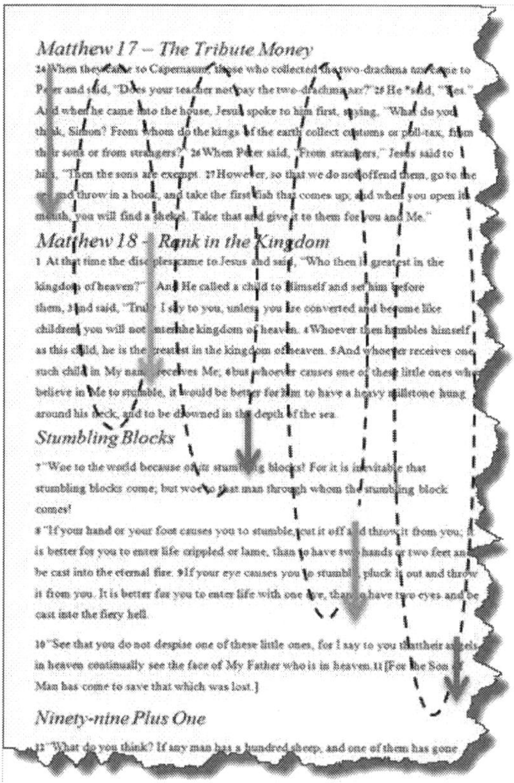

This procedure will be followed for every paragraph in the contextual section, from the first to the current. In other words, you will study each paragraph, looking to all of the *previous* paragraphs for clues about its meaning. After studying all of the paragraphs in the contextual section, you will then be able

Figure 12 - PxP Study Flow

to view the entire contextual section as a whole to weave the message together.

As you consider the image of Figure 12, you should not press it to imply more than it is saying. For example, it is not saying that you must always approach the previous paragraphs in a circular fashion. That would be the first step after studying your paragraph at hand, but after that, you certainly have the liberty to inspect any of the

preceding paragraphs in any order that you desire. Our primary goal
is to understand the context as a whole, rather than as proof texts.
Please refer to Figure 13 for a more concise description of PxP.

> **In more concise terms,**
>
> **With each paragraph:**
>
> + Carefully read the entire paragraph
> + Meditate on its points and message
> + Take time to reflect on the entire paragraph, making
>   notes of your observations
> + Trace the weaving, to determine how this paragraph
>   blends with the message of the previous paragraphs.

Figure 13 - PxP in Concise Terms

You may be wondering why we avoid jumping to *later* paragraphs to
gain insights. The reason is because we want to allow the writer or
speaker to develop the message in his or her own way. If we were
listening to a speaker, we would probably not interrupt to ask for
clarification about things that were unclear. Instead, we would follow
the logic, catch the figures of speech, and understand the points as
the message unfolds. The same is true when we study the Bible. We
can imagine that we are listening to a skillful speaker, who is
developing a message in his or her preferred way. Once we reach the
end of the contextual section, we can review all of the paragraphs to
assure that we understand the message in its entirety.

Long Paragraphs and Sentences
Have you ever read the first chapter of Ephesians? It contains some
fascinating insights into the mysteries of God, but they are condensed

into long sentences and paragraphs and difficult to grapple with. I'm sure the text was quite challenging to the translation teams! Even though most paragraphs will not be as long and complicated as this one, we still need to understand how to divide long paragraphs and sentences into bite-size portions so we can ingest, digest, and savor their full truth.

So how should we approach a paragraph like Ephesians 1:3–14? We don't want to miss a single concept within, so the best approach is to divide it into phrases and clauses at the punctuation marks: periods, commas, colons, semi-colons, question marks, etc. As you explore each phrase and clause, make sure that you fully understand each word and the connection to other parts of the sentence and paragraph. As you gain understanding of the smaller parts, you will be able to connect their thoughts to the overall meaning of the paragraph. We will explain this in greater detail in the coming chapters about Bible study tools, when we explain Clarifying the Terms, Follow the Weaver, and Exploratory Questioning.

The Entire Bible Is Within Reach
Approaching a contextual section on a paragraph-by-paragraph basis allows us to focus on the details, as the writer or speaker chose to present them. Now that you know the process, let's extend it to different types of Bible studies. How would you tackle the study of an entire book? Simply start at the beginning of the book and study it in order, contextual section by contextual section, until you finish it. Of course, each contextual section will be studied paragraph by paragraph, and you will follow the weaver through the contextual sections, making notes and articulating your learning as you go. Don't worry – we will explain the tools in the coming chapters.

How would you approach a character study or a topical study? The approach is very similar. You will simply find the passages that interest you and discipline yourself to understand them within their context so you will not be guilty of contextomy or proof-texting. This means that you will determine the contextual boundaries and study the passage to assure that you understand the character or topic in the spirit that the original writer or speaker intended. It sounds like common sense, doesn't it?

13
Meditation and Reflection

Meditation and reflection are two of the most powerful tools for gaining understanding of God's Word. What is the difference between the two? Meditation is simply the mental activity of considering a subject and applying effort to understand it (although we'll add a few more details to this definition in the following paragraphs). Reflection is meditation with a focus on your own life or to a particular situation. In other words, you are reflecting the Word back to yourself.

Meditation is the fountainhead of understanding. If a person's learning only consists of a diet of ingesting and memorizing facts that were fed through books or teachers, then his or her understanding will probably be somewhat deficient. On the other hand, if the learning came through a personal effort of researching facts, weighing the pertinent against the irrelevant, reasoning why one option has more validity than others, recognizing the error of various suppositions, and developing his or her own conclusions, then it is likely that this person either has gained understanding or has, at least, formed a foundation for understanding. Understanding is the product of the mental and spiritual exercise of meditation, which is truly the fountainhead of understanding.

In Chapter 5, we likened meditation to a man who wanted to build a piece of furniture; he went through the processes of envisioning, planning, and implementing until his goal was realized. When we apply this concept to studying the Bible, it includes the actions of reading, envisioning possible meanings, assessing the possibilities, developing conclusions, and following through with action. We have attempted to diagram the process of meditation in Figure 14– **please take a moment to study the diagram at this time**. Notice the components that flow into the meditative process. They include *knowledge, wisdom,* and *understanding,* which are distinctly separate entities, and all are key components of meditation. A brief explanation of these three will help you understand the concept of meditation and how it can help you reach your goal of understanding.

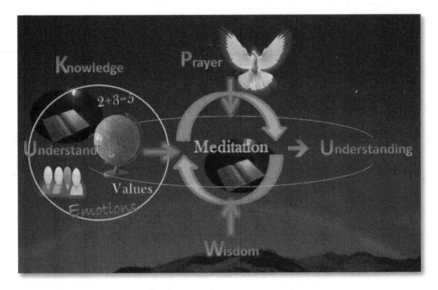

Figure 14—Meditation

Knowledge, Wisdom, and Understanding

Knowledge can be simply described as our cognizance or awareness of facts. These facts range from the very simple to the very abstract. For example, we know the alphabet, how to count, spelling, reading, arithmetic, and geography. We also know a certain portion of the Bible, as well as the information from other books and documents. We also know about people and relationships and we even know what other people know and think about us. Our knowledge also includes an awareness of our values, affections, emotions, vices, and experiences. All of the information that we've obtained is part of our knowledge, some of which is deeply engrained in our hearts (i.e. the heart of the mind ... not the pump!).

Wisdom, unlike knowledge, is a process. When we meditate on something, perhaps on a passage of the Bible, we use wisdom to apply our knowledge, values, and current understanding to our assessment of the passage. The image of the Bible in the Meditation process in Figure 14 represents our current knowledge of the Scriptures. It plays a key role in shaping the outcome of our meditation, keeping our understanding in alignment with the truth that we already know. Notice also that prayer is an essential part of our meditation effort. As we pray, we ask God's Spirit to guide our thoughts and meditations about our passage and lead us to an understanding of truth. Studying in the Spirit is of the greatest importance, since the truths of the Scriptures are spiritually discerned[96] and we must look to God's Spirit to guide us.

Understanding is the goal of our study—it is the fruit of sound meditation on God's Word. As we consider the Scriptures and prayerfully weigh the words before us in light of our knowledge and wisdom, we gain clarity and direction about the Word and its meaning, which result in understanding.

In a sense, understanding can be compared to motor skills. When people are learning to ride a bicycle, they need to make conscious decisions to apply pressure to the pedals with their feet, position their hands on the handlebars and brake, and shift their body weight for balance. But as they practice riding and become skilled, they no longer need to have these details in the forefront of their minds since

---

[96] "But a natural man does not accept the things of the Spirit of God, for they are foolishness to him; and he cannot understand them, because they are spiritually appraised. But he who is spiritual appraises all things ..."
1 Corinthians 2:14–15

their brains and nervous systems have hard-wired the motor skills—skills that are only attained by learning and doing.

In a similar way, the understanding that results from meditation causes our thoughts, actions, and responses to naturally gravitate toward the path of truth that we learn. As our motor skills enable us to competently ride a bicycle without requiring conscious thought, so our understanding hard-wires our minds in accordance with God's Word. Through meditation, our inner self is actually being transformed by renewing our mind by the truth of God's Word. We must, however, continue to fight with our old nature, which urges us to deviate from the way of truth, tempting us to disregard the thought structures and behaviors that we have been developing.

So, how does the meditative process actually accomplish its work? Believe it or not, it's actually quite simple, and because it is an intellectual skill, we are able to hone and fine-tune it for greatly improved results. We can improve our meditative skills through practice and augment them with the tools that are described in the following chapters.

The Power of Meditation

As we've explained, meditative Bible study yields the desirable fruit of understanding, but clearly, meditation also produces additional *knowledge* in our minds. The additional knowledge can come from multiple sources, including the Bible text, insights from the Holy Spirit, insights that we gain during our study, such as new comprehension and understanding about the message, new linkages within the context, and new facts that we learned from other sources during our study.

You may have noticed that understanding is shown in two places: in the outcome of meditation and as one of the components that feeds the meditative process, but in reality, they are referring to the same understanding. The purpose of the lines that connect the two understandings is to demonstrate how our understanding is actually enhanced, matured, and refined through the meditative process. This enhancement, regardless of how small, helps us view things a little bit differently—perhaps more accurately—each time we meditate on the Scriptures or on any subject. The result is an increasingly refined understanding with a more mature and Christ-like perspective.

It is also important to note that this enhanced understanding also refines and strengthens our values. This is significant since our desire is to become conformed to the image of Christ, to value and cherish the same things that He values and cherishes, which is the essence of sanctification or being set apart to Christ. This is the washing of the water of the Word, the refining and strengthening of our character, actually changing the way that we think and believe. It means the next time we apply our wisdom to a subject, we will have a somewhat improved system of knowledge, wisdom, and value, resulting in even greater understanding.

As we consider this diagram of meditation, it becomes apparent that knowledge and values are nourished as our understanding increases. Our spiritual growth—our sanctification—is accelerated by increased study of the Word. Conversely, a lack of study and meditation on God's Word will stagnate the process of sanctification and lead to malnourishment of the soul. Malnourishment and indirection are also caused by watered-down and elementary teaching of the Word, since they are unable to bring the student face to face with the details of God's truth. Thus, there is a clear case for the need of individuals and churches to faithfully study and teach God's Word for the growth and wellbeing of the body of Christ.

Meditation is the process of aligning the intellect with the soul and with the spirit and with the ways of God. The result is peace and harmony in our lives and with our God. Clearly, the interaction of the Holy Spirit with the Truth of God's Word are essential to have that kind of peace, but that is the whole point—we are seeking to know our Creator as He truly is. When we meet Him and come to an understanding of who we are—as He designed us—then we will truly be at peace with ourselves and with Him.

Putting Meditation Into Practice

Meditation is a very powerful tool in our pursuit of understanding. But it is far more than a standalone tool that is only used by itself—it is a tool that multiplies the effectiveness of our other tools. As you *Clarify the Terms,* you will use meditation to consider which term is the best fit for your passage. As you *Follow the Weaver*, you will use meditation to examine clues that might reveal a thread that connects one thought to another. As you use *Exploratory Questioning*, you will use meditation to craft questions that will help you zero-in on truth. And as you *Juxtapose* different translations of the Bible, you will use meditation to consider the implication of different renderings of the same passage. In a sense, meditation is the queen of learning, in the same way that mathematics is the queen of the sciences, since it has so many varied uses and applications.

Our meditation will be characterized by thoughtful, prayerful consideration of each detail throughout our study, compiling our insights into a comprehensive understanding of the whole paragraph. You will use the tools repeatedly, until you feel confident that you understand the paragraph to the greatest extent possible. Does this mean that you will fully understand each paragraph before moving on? Not necessarily, since it frequently happens that some questions are answered only by studying *subsequent* paragraphs. So, as you study, you should use all of the tools at your disposal as you prayerfully seek to understand the full message of each paragraph.

Final Thoughts about the Fountainhead

Meditation is the tool that we've been given to help us understand God. Through meditation, we immerse ourselves in the loving warmth of God's character and take refuge in the Shepherd who restores our souls. We learn the fear that keeps us from wrath, and we discern the path that leads to life. It is through meditation that knowledge is transformed into understanding and wisdom is honed; where we seek the presence of the Holy One and come to know Truth. It is the sanctuary where evils are purged, hearts are conformed, and worship and praise take flight, as we gain a glimpse of the beauty of our God. "One thing I have asked from the LORD, that I shall seek: That I may dwell in the house of the LORD all the days of my life, to behold the beauty of the LORD and to meditate in His temple."[97]

---

[97] Psalm 27:4

14
Reading Basics

Introduction

One of the most important tools of study is the ability to read – to read easily, clearly, and fluidly. In this chapter, we are going to cover some reading concepts that will become key tools in your study of the Word. Furthermore, it is my hope that we can reset and refresh your perspective of reading and comprehension.

I was very pleased when I read the words of Mortimer Adler in his book, *How to Read a Book*, as he was addressing the subject of how fast we should read. For many years, I felt pressured to read rapidly, even though my tendency was to read slowly and methodically to gain full understanding. But his words resonated when he said, "There is no single right speed at which you should read; the ability to read at various speeds and to know when each speed is appropriate is the ideal."[98] I felt somewhat liberated by his words and am able to enjoy reading at a speed that is appropriate for each occasion.

As we apply Dr. Adler's words[99] to studying the Bible, it also makes sense to vary our reading speed depending on the occasion. We do not want to read so fast that we overlook details that might be important, and we do not want to read so slowly that we miss the flow and continuity of what is being said. The best approach is to inter mix reading speeds or *types* of reading as follows:

---

[98] (Mortimer J. Adler, 1940) page 43

[99] Note: Dr. Adler identified three levels of reading: Elementary or Skimming, Inspectional, and Analytical. We will be using the same terms, but with slightly different meanings.

✦ Begin your study by skimming or *inspectional* reading of the **entire** contextual section. The purpose of inspectional reading is to get a general flavor and view of the overall structure. It is not necessary to fully understand every word, thought or concept in this type of reading. The purpose is to gain an overview of the section so you will know where it is heading.

✦ Since we are studying the contextual section with a paragraph-by-paragraph approach, the next step is to peruse your paragraph at hand with a more careful reading, observing the details and seeking to comprehend the thoughts, points, events, questions, and responses.

We must emphasize, however, that it is certainly possible to comprehend the meaning of thoughts and phrases and not understand the significance of what was said; comprehension and understanding are quite different. The Scriptures contain many profound statements that require meditation and reflection in order to truly understand. The truths of the Scriptures must be **spiritually discerned**, which, once again, requires prayerful meditation and reflection.

✦ We will refer to the third type of reading as *analytical* or *meditative* reading. After you have perused your paragraph and have comprehended its main points and direction, you must read it with the intent of understanding its meaning. This is accomplished through analytical, meditative reading of the text.

Meditative reading is most effective when used with other tools, such as clarifying the meanings of words, tracing the weave of the context, asking and answering thoughtful questions, making notes, and comparing other versions of the Word. These tools will be explained in the coming chapters.

As you work your way through each paragraph, you will employ the different types of reading at different times. Rather than using the types in their order, you will most likely use and reuse each reading type as seems best to you. You will use them along with the other tools of study until you have arrived at an understanding of the paragraph. In some cases, you may not fully understand a paragraph until you consider it in light of the following paragraph(s), since they may contain information that completes the picture.

How Should We Analyze?

What types of things should we look for as we read in a meditative way? What does it mean to read analytically? Studying meditatively means that we are seeking to understand the message of the text, exploring each detail in light of the context. Our investigation usually involves the following tasks:

✦ Meditation and reflection on the meaning of the words and message. Refer to Chapter 13 – Meditation and Reflection.

✦ Making simple notes about our new knowledge, insights, and questions that we encounter throughout our study. These notes will be reviewed and summarized at the end of our study when we *articulate* our learning. Refer to Chapter 20 – Articulating Your Learning.

✦ Composing questions that will help us explore the weave of the contextual section, the terminology, the meaning or substance, the possible meanings of words, the validity of our conclusions, how we might apply the passage, and questions about the validity of our own questions. Refer to Chapter 16 – Exploring Through Questioning.

✦ Clarifying the meaning of each word and phrase, using the powerful tools that have been given through godly scholars. Refer to Chapter 17 – Clarifying the Terms.

✦ Considering each figure of speech, how the writer or speaker used them to convey their meaning. Asking ourselves which aspect(s) of the figure should be applied to the point at hand. Refer to Chapters 10 and 11 – Figures of Speech.

✦ Tracing the threads of the context, seeking to understand how the writer or speaker interwove the message of our paragraph to other thoughts in the contextual section and the entirety of the Scriptures. Refer to Chapter 18 – Follow the Weaver.

✦ Reviewing or researching the Big-6 background of the text if we encounter something that requires more information than we found in our preliminary background check. This type of reading will take us through an investigation of the Big-6, turning over stones, looking under bushes, seeking clues from the environmental contexts that may affect its meaning. Refer to Chapter 9 – Behind the Scenes.

✦ Juxtaposing a passage in two or more different versions of the Bible, to see how experts dealt with translational questions that might indicate some latitude in interpretation. Refer to Chapter 19 – Dare to Juxtapose!

All of these tools are available to help us arrive at an accurate understanding of the message of our contextual section. It is helpful to view them as tools, rather than as phases, since each one will likely be used multiple times as you study each paragraph and your entire contextual section.

Literary Genres in Context

As you make your way through your contextual section, you should be on the watch for changes of literary genre. It is common to find different literature types within a single passage of Scripture and it would be incorrect to assume that a particular book contains only one literary genre. Matthew 13, for example, is a narrative that contains parables, teaching, and prophecy – each of which should be interpreted as its genre requires. Another example is the book of Leviticus, the majority of which contains laws and rules. Yet, we find a narrative embedded in the midst of the book in chapters eight through ten.

In some cases, a change in genre will be announced by the writer. Luke 14:7, for example, says, "And He began speaking a parable to the invited guests ..." On the other hand, The Prodigal Son[100] and The Rich Man and Lazarus[101] are not introduced as parables, which require us to study and meditate to determine whether they are parables or some other literary genre.

The Bible contains several different literary genres, depending on how they are categorized. The genres include: narratives, parables, epistles (i.e. letters), poetry, wisdom and proverbs, laws, rules, exhortations, and prophecy. Hermeneutic Principle #5 teaches us that Scripture passages must be evaluated in light of their literary genre. One of the Scriptural literary genres that is frequently misunderstood is wisdom literature, when people try to interpret proverbs as promises. For example, should Proverbs 22:6, "Train up a child in the way he should go, even when he is old he will not depart from it..." be understood with the same weight as Matthew 28:20, "I am with you always, even to the end of the age?" The wise student of the Word

---

[100] Luke 15:11-32
[101] Luke 16:19-31

will consider the literary genre of the passage at hand as he or she explores possible interpretations.

Proceed with Care!

As we study our passage, we must make great effort to read and study with the greatest of care, observing words, punctuation, sentences, and capitalization. Careful reading goes all the way back to your elementary school days, but every one of us is still fallible and capable of making mistakes… otherwise, I would not be writing this paragraph! I've read things incorrectly more times than I'd like to admit, so I usually add the small step of scrutinizing every jot and tittle of my passage at hand, just to make sure that I'm seeing it correctly. The Analytical reading step is the perfect time to add this little check for accuracy into your study discipline!

There is another extremely important aspect of our analytical reading that I have not, yet, mentioned. Our speech and literature are filled with tiny, sometimes subtle devices that speakers and writers use to skillfully convey their message and direct our understanding. It would make sense to call them logic indicators, since they direct our thoughts in a powerful, subtle way. But at the risk of clouding the issue, I will refer to them by their common name, which is *conjunctions*.

Yes, it's true—the simple conjunctions that we use in our everyday speech deserve special attention in our meditation on the Word. As they connect phrases, clauses, and sentences, they also enable us to understand the flow and anticipate the direction of the writer or speaker's message. For, and, nor, but, or, yet, and so, are just the tip of the conjunction iceberg. I am emphasizing conjunctions at this point, because they are a key part of reading basics, and having a strong grasp of their implications can pave the way to greatly increased understanding of your passage of study.

FAN BOYS

Hey – now we're ready for a good time – the FAN BOYS are here! Yes, the well-known words that join our phrases, clauses, and sentences[102] together. We could call them coordinating conjunctions, but let's dispense with formalities for now. The Seven FANBOYS of English are listed in Table 12 - The Seven FANBOYS.

F	For
A	And
N	Nor
B	But
O	Or
Y	Yet
S	So

Table 12 - The Seven FANBOYS

What do the FANBOYS do for us? As they join words, phrases, clauses, and sentences they trigger thoughts in our minds about how the parts relate to each other. For example, if we encounter "for" at the beginning of a sentence,[103] we understand that it is a logical continuation or inference from the previous phrase, clause, sentence, paragraph or section. Consider the following examples in Table 13:

---

[102] A phrase is a group of words that **cannot** stand alone as a complete thought, whereas a clause is a group of words that **can** stand alone as a complete thought. Consider Matthew 2:3, for example, "When Herod the king heard this, he was troubled, and all Jerusalem with him." "He was troubled" is a clause and "and all Jerusalem with him" is a phrase. The difference is the ability of the words to convey a complete thought by itself or not.

[103] Beginning a sentence with a coordinating conjunction is generally considered to be incorrect grammar. **But** many grammarians feel that it should be permissible, including the translators of the ASV, ESV, NAS, and the NKJV. Although it may be discouraged in academic circles, many great writers and grammarians have embraced the practice for centuries.

F	For	"Repent, **for** the kingdom of heaven is at hand." Matthew 3:2 "**For** I am not ashamed of the gospel, **for** it is the power of God for salvation to everyone who believes ..." Romans 1:16
A	And	"**And** we know that God causes all things to work together for good to those who love God ..." Romans 8:28 "**And** the tongue is a fire, the very world of iniquity; the tongue is set among our members as that which defiles the entire body, **and** sets on fire the course of our life, **and** is set on fire by hell." James 3:6
N	Nor	"**Nor** let us try the Lord, as some of them did, and were destroyed by the serpents." 1 Corinthians 10:9 "WHO COMMITTED NO SIN, **NOR** WAS ANY DECEIT FOUND IN HIS MOUTH;" 1 Peter 2:22
B	But	"**But** the free gift is not like the transgression. For if by the transgression of the one the many died, much more did the grace of God and the gift by the grace of the one Man, Jesus Christ ..." Romans 5:15 "**But** of the Son He says, 'YOUR THRONE, O GOD, IS FOREVER AND EVER, AND THE RIGHTEOUS SCEPTER IS THE SCEPTER OF HIS KINGDOM.'" Hebrews 1:8

O	Or	"**Or** do you not know that your body is a temple of the Holy Spirit who is in you, whom you have from God, and that you are not your own?" 1 Corinthians 6:19 "that you not be quickly shaken from your composure **or** be disturbed either by a spirit **or** a message **or** a letter as if from us ..." 2 Thessalonians 2:2
Y	Yet	"**Yet** for this reason I found mercy, so that in me as the foremost, Jesus Christ might demonstrate His perfect patience as an example for those who would believe in Him for eternal life." I Timothy 3:16 "**Yet** you do not know what your life will be like tomorrow. You are just a vapor that appears for a little while and then vanishes away." James 4:14
S	So	"**So** then it does not depend on the man who wills or the man who runs, but on God who has mercy." Romans 9:16 "**So** also Christ did not glorify Himself so as to become a high priest, but He who said to Him, 'YOU ARE MY SON, TODAY I HAVE BEGOTTEN YOU'" Hebrews 5:5

Table 13 - Examples of FANBOYS (The Seven Coordinating Conjunctions)

As you considered the Scriptural examples of the FANBOYS (i.e. the seven coordinating conjunctions) in Table 13, did you notice how each one determined the direction of your thoughts as you read it? They not only enable us to anticipate the direction of the writer or speakers thought, but they give us insights about whether a thought is to be continued, contrasted, negated or extended and how it relates to previous thoughts. As you read the Scriptures or any other text, you can gain valuable insights from the selection and placement of these key words, to better understand the writer or speaker's intended meaning.

We have another reason, however, for mentioning the FANBOYS. Recall that, in Appendix F – Juxtaposing Matthew 18:1–14, we divided the passage by punctuation, to isolate each phrase, clause, and sentence. But it is also possible and sometimes helpful to divide the text at each conjunction – that is, divide it wherever you encounter one of the FANBOYS. This technique can sometimes be useful for revealing different aspects of the logic of the text. The technique is not always helpful, and it may not be as effective in certain literary genres, but it sometimes gives valuable insights into the writer or speaker's meaning.

Before we leave the subject of conjunctions, I should mention that the FANBOYS are the *coordinating* conjunctions. There are, however, other types of conjunctions that also give insight into how we should understand a phrase, clause, sentence, or paragraph; that is, the logic or logical flow of the message. The conjunctions also include *subordinating* and *correlative* conjunctions and *conjunctive adverbs*. But don't worry, this is not going to evolve into a lesson in English grammar – our purpose is to encourage you view these words and phrases, not as elements of grammar, but as indicators of the logical flow of the writer or speaker's message.

We will, however, look at a very common, yet important, category of conjunctions, which is the *conjunctive adverb.* You are most certainly familiar with these, but perhaps you have not looked at them as indicators of the logical flow of the message. Please review the list of the most common conjunctive adverbs in Table 14—Conjunctive Adverbs and consider how each one would affect your understanding of the relationship of the components it connects if you were to encounter it in a sentence.

after all	in addition	next
also	in fact	nonetheless
as a result	in other words	on the contrary
besides	incidentally	on the other hand
consequently	indeed	otherwise
finally	instead	still
for example	likewise	then
furthermore	meanwhile	therefore
hence	moreover	thus
however	nevertheless	

Table 14—Conjunctive Adverbs

These common words can give us great insight into the logical direction of the writer or speaker, so we should always be on the lookout for them. When you encounter one, take a moment to consider why it's there. If you find an unfamiliar conjunction in the course of your studies, research the word to get a feel for its usage and meaning in other contexts.

Reading Basics Summary

The ability to read well is one of the basic requirements of study. We can view the different types of reading, *skimming* or *inspectional*, *perusal*, and *analytic* or *meditative*, as tools for increasing our understanding. We will alternate between these different types of reading as we endeavor to understand the message of our contextual section.

Although there are many aspects of our study that deserve careful attention, focusing on the conjunctions can greatly increase our insights into the intended meaning of the writer or speaker. They offer tips for understanding the meaning and anticipating the direction. We should give special attention to conjunctions whenever we encounter them in our studies.

15
Worthy of Note

Notes as a Tool

In general, most people would not consider *notes* to be a tool. In our case, however, all of the notes and little scribbles and lines that you make on your printed contextual section will be used to build and shape your learning, especially in the final phase when you will *articulate* your learning, as we will explain in Chapter 20. In a sense, taking notes is pre-articulation—recording your  *intermediate* understanding so you can organize and transform it into a more comprehensive understanding.

In some of the earlier chapters, we demonstrated how to take notes at various points of your study. Rather than repeating those comments, we have chosen to reference the sections along with their page numbers so you can review it as it was originally presented. We will, however, briefly list examples of noteworthy information that you should record in your study notes.

Some of your notes will be written on your printed contextual section; others will be recorded in a separate journal, notebook, or paper, whichever is most convenient for you. You may also make notes in electronic form, whether on a computer or some other type of electronic device.

As you make your notes, it is important that you are specific, recording the details and references. Most of us have had the experience of trying to make sense of some of our own notes that left us wondering what we were trying to say. We are not saying that perfect form, spelling, and grammar are necessary – just that you make your notes thorough and clear enough for you and others to easily understand. You should record references, names, places, figures of speech, points, arguments, questions, inferences, and anything else that will help you retrieve your full thought at a later time. When you get to the articulation phase in Chapter 20, you will refer to these notes and bring them together to complete your study.

Worthy of Notes

What information should you note in your notes? Obviously, you would want to make notes about the direct points within a passage, the explicit and inferred, your observations, questions, application thoughts, prayer insights, and etcetera. But it is especially important to make notes about the less obvious inferences since they are not as easily discerned and would probably take more time to relearn. Some points are expected, while others are unexpected, especially those which are inferred.

Flashes of Insight

We also want to be sure to immediately record some of the flashes of insight that come to mind as we study – possibly the leading of the Holy Spirit. It is important to write them immediately, since they tend to be forgotten as quickly as they entered your mind. These brief moments of insight and illumination can bring deep joy to your study, and you certainly do not want to lose them forever!

As you muse on these insights, you should explore them via prayerful meditation and compare them with other truths that you know. If they do not stand the test of truth, then you should record the insight and note the reasons that it cannot be truth. It is quite possible that the Spirit led you down this path to strengthen your overall understanding – it is still an excellent part of the journey!

Create a Heading for Your Study in Your Notes
When you begin your study, it's a good idea to start with a new page or new document, with a heading line that has the **date, descriptive name for your study**, and the Bible **reference** of the passage. Refer to Figure 4—Study Notes Heading on page 136

Contextual Section and Boundaries
When you determine the beginning and ending boundaries of the context of your passage, you should make a note of them and explain your reasons for believing they are contextual boundaries. If your decision is ever questioned, these notes will help you remember the reasoning behind your decision. Refer to Figure 6 on page 149.

The Author and Book
Record the biographical information about the author of the book that contains your passage, along with information about the book, itself. Refer to Figure 8—Background Research Notes on page 156 for an example of how to record this information in your notes.

Big-6 Background Information
You should record the Big-6 environmental information that might have a bearing on your passage. Refer to Figure 10—Big-6 Influences Notes on page 167 for an example of how this might be recorded in your notes.

Notes about Clarifying the Terms
A portion of your study time may be spent researching the meanings of words as they were used in the original languages. It would be valuable to make notes about your findings, even if the research does not reveal anything unusual or insightful – at least you will be

confident that you understand the word correctly and you will not have to re-research it again in future studies!

If you have enough space on your printed contextual section, then that is an excellent place for recording notes about your word studies. The illustration in **Figure 16—Clarifying the Terms** on page 280, depicts making notes on your printed contextual section. If you require additional space, simply write the information on your note pages and reference the location on your printed contextual section.

As always, be sure to indicate your confidence level in your understanding of the words. If you are not certain, then you should place a star or "*" beside the word to indicate that you need to research it further. If you learned something about a word that gives insight into the meaning of a passage, then you should record that information in your notes.

Figures of Speech

As you explore figures of speech, you should make notes about their possible meanings. For example, which aspect of a metaphor is being referenced by the writer or speaker? Could it be more than one aspect? Which aspects are the most likely? How does it affect the point of the message? Should all of these questions about figures be noted? Perhaps, but our goal is not to create cluttered or excessive notes. It is probably enough that you record the things that you have learned regarding the essence and meaning of the figure as it brings out the intended meaning of the writer or speaker. It is also wise to note how the figure should *not* be interpreted and applied!

FANBOYS and Friends

Recall that writers and speakers use conjunctions, FANBOYS and Friends, to guide your mind to receive their message as they desire. In some cases, a conjunction will play an important or unexpected part in the meaning, and we should give special attention and *take note*.

For example, in 2 Timothy 3:14, Paul says, "You, *however*, continue in the things you have learned …" As we read this, we would, of course, muse on how "however" affects the flow of thought, but we should also make note of its meaning in our study notes.

Notes about Questions
In Chapter 16 – Exploring Through Questioning, we will continue our exploration of seeking understanding through questioning. In general, it is not necessary to write all of your questions and answers as you study. On the other hand, your note-taking becomes very important when you encounter questions that are difficult to answer.

If you have difficulty answering a question, it is wise to write the question, along with the possible answers. Be sure to also make note of the reason for the difficulty. We refer to these difficult questions as *pressure points*, since they make it very obvious where more attention is needed in your study. You should place a star beside the pressure points in your notes so you can easily return to them later.

Although it is not necessary to record all of your questions and answers, it is certainly helpful to record questions and answers that reveal points and insights. You should make note of the questions and question sequences that

+ lead to key truths within the passage
+ have multiple possible answers – include the possible answers in your notes, along with the questions and implications that follow
+ reveal profound or hidden insights
+ lead to an important clue or key to understanding the passage

Weaving

Chapter 18 – Follow the Weaver, explains how to follow the message of the writer or speaker so we can be certain that we understand the message as it was intended. As we follow the weaver and identify the threads and clues of the message, it is important to make notes that will trace the flow, since it provides context for our interpretation. Documenting this information will help us remember our reasons for interpreting the text as we determine best.

Notes about Future Studies

As you make notes during your studies, you will occasionally find that some thoughts and questions should actually become a completely separate study. For example, one such question might be *"What is the Kingdom of Heaven?"* Or *"What did Jesus mean by '... in My name?'"* In these cases, we could simply note that it would require more study and then continue on with our current study. But we should also maintain an on-going list of ideas for future Bible studies. This will assure that you have plenty of ideas for studies that interest you. Refer to Figure 15 below for an example of such a list.

Bible Study Ideas

1) The *Kingdom of Heaven* and the *Kingdom of God*:
   I encountered the *Kingdom of Heaven* term in Matthew 18:1 and realized the need for deeper understanding of the entire subject. It would be a good idea to begin with a word study of both terms. (*November 30*)

2) "In My Name":
   I encountered this term in Matthew 18:5 and have heard it most of my life, but I'm really not sure of Jesus' meaning in this passage and others... it's frequently used as a closing to prayer, but I'd like to really understand it. (*November 30*)

Figure 15 - Bible Study Ideas

16
Exploring Through Questioning

In Chapter 6, we introduced Reflective
Questioning, explaining how we can use
questioning to prayerfully interact with the Holy
Spirit during our studies and how we can pose
questions to ourselves to sharpen our
understanding. In this chapter, we will take the
concept of questioning to another level and explain how it can be
used as a *power tool* for exploring the Word of God.

Why Ask Questions?

At one point in my professional career, I worked under a vice
president who was very successful in leading our organization. As a
group of my peers were discussing his success, several people
commented that he always seemed to know how to ask the right
questions. Everyone who met with him had to be fully prepared,
because even though he was not an expert in every area, he was able
to skillfully question and probe, exposing the strengths and
weaknesses of presenters' cases as they spoke.

The ability to ask the right questions can place a person in a position
of great power. Knowing how to ask probing questions enables us to
reveal truths and lies and
strengths and weaknesses. It is a
powerful tool for clarifying the
things we know and is also able
to shine a light on the void of
things we do not know. Through
the use of well-crafted
questions, we are able to connect our new learning to the truths that
we have already established. By assuming the role of a humble
questioner, we can more readily learn from our Master, which is

> We are not questioning
> the Master – We are
> questioning to clarify our
> understanding.

exactly what we are seeking as we study the Bible. It is essential to understand that we are not questioning or challenging the Master – we are, rather, questioning to clarify our own understanding.

Socratic Style Questioning

The style of questioning that we'll be exploring can be traced back 2,500 years to the city of Athens in ancient Greece. It was during the short-lived, mini-renaissance of that time that styles of thought originated, developed, and were refined, profoundly influencing the world of the New Testament and the modern western world.

Socrates (circa 470 BC) is credited with developing a style of questioning that is characterized by exposing unsupportable ideas so they could be discarded, and then working to rebuild the concept at hand with supportable facts. Although Socrates is known as a philosopher, he really didn't philosophize as most philosophers do. Instead, he simply claimed to be on a quest to know truth and his method of seeking truth was through asking questions. His students, Plato and Xenophon, were faithful in recording many of his discussions with others. It is from their accounts and comments that we learn how he honed and mastered the skill of exploratory questioning. Socratic style questioning and its variants continue to be heavily used in modern times in law, science, and psychotherapy.

Socratic style questioning is not a matter of simply asking random questions about a subject and it is not conducted in the form of an adversarial debate, where the objective is to outwit and defeat your opponent. Conversely, Socratic style questioning is systematic in its approach and is typically used in a cooperative effort between the questioner and the person being questioned with the hope of finding the truth for the benefit of all parties. Whether we study alone or with others, the goal of our questioning is to arrive at the truth by solidifying our understanding of the things that we know and do not know.

Another interesting fact about Socratic style questioning is that the questioner assumes the role of the student, while the person being questioned assumes the role of the teacher. This is the perfect arrangement for our study of the Word, since we will be asking questions of our teacher, the Holy Spirit, as He leads us to His truth. We will pose questions to ourselves and seek the leading of God's Spirit as we attempt to formulate and answer questions.

There is an enormous difference between our questioning and that of Socrates. Since Socrates sought truth through questioning people, he was unable to arrive at a solid confidence in the answers that he received. It came to the point that Plato recorded Socrates' sad lament, "I neither know nor think that I know."[104] On the other hand, believers have the Word of God as their bedrock of truth, which is God's *declaration* of truth. Since this declaration was given by the Designer, Himself, we are able to arrive at solid, reliable answers to our questions, answers from God, having full confidence in our resulting knowledge and understanding.

Questioning: The Tool of Tools
We will be using *Questioning* as a tool throughout our study in conjunction with our other tools. For example, as we use the *Clarify Terms* tool, we will use questioning to explore how the meaning of a passage would change if we replace one term with another. We will also ask questions about how the context might dictate our selection of a term from the *semantic range*. We will also use questioning with the *Follow the Weaver* tool, to explore how the writer or speaker wove his or her thoughts through our contextual section. As we arrive at conclusions throughout our study, both intermediate and final conclusions, we will ask questions to verify their validity. In general,

---

[104] (Plato, 399 B.C.)

we will ask questions in every aspect of our study, since they are able to refine and sharpen our understanding of a passage.

Four Categories of Questions

Questions generally fall into the following four categories:

Closed Ended—Questions that result in limited responses, such as *yes* or *no*.

Limiting—Questions that limit the answers (multiple choice)

Leading—Questions that bias or lead the response

Open Ended—Questions that allow freeform responses

In most cases, open ended questions will result in the greatest amount of thought and creativity in responses. But in reality, all types of questions are useful for exploring and arriving at conclusions. It is often more fruitful, however, to freely use open ended questions and sparingly use closed ended, limiting, and leading questions.

How Can I Compose Effective Questions?

That's a good question. One of the easiest ways to compose effective questions is by posing ideas about the meaning of a passage and then composing questions to determine its validity. The ideas may be your own or they may be statements of others. We refer to these ideas or possible solutions as *hypotheses,* which probably takes you back to your days in middle-school science class. But the concept is the same: we develop a possible answer or solution (i.e. hypothesis) and explore it with questions to determine if it is consistent or within the bounds of the text.

In some cases, the answers to your hypotheses will be very clear, allowing you to confirm the hypothesis or discard it. On the other hand, we often find that there is some latitude in the teaching of the Scriptures when they do not address a subject directly. In these cases, we may say that they *infer* an answer, but that is not necessarily the same as the clear teaching of the text. Recall the teaching of Hermeneutic Principle #11: "Only the explicit teaching of a passage may be understood as having the full authority of the Scriptures." We must be careful about how much authority we give to our inferred conclusions!

If your hypothesis is important or could have significant bearing on the meaning of your passage or on other teachings, then it would be wise to record it and the associated questions in your study notes, along with your conclusions. This will help you understand how you arrived at a certain conclusion.

In order to give a better idea of how to compose questions as part of a Bible study, we have provided some sample questions in Appendix D – Sample Questions that will give you an idea about the nature of exploratory questions. We have grouped the questions into categories that you can reference as you study. You do not need to memorize the questions, but you should carefully read them to become familiar with exploratory questions and understand them, as they will give you a flavor for how to compose your own insightful questions. The lists of questions that we have provided are by no means exhaustive; you will create your own questions, as needed, as you explore your passage.

The *Question* categories that we have created are:

1. **Clarifying terminology**
2. **Exploring the Weaving**
3. **Exploring the substance of a passage**
4. **Exploring my conclusions**
5. **Applying my learning**
6. **Validating the effectiveness of my questions**

- **Please turn to Appendix D – Sample Questions and take time to peruse the questions.**

Answers about Questions

As you study your passage and carefully compose and pose questions to yourself, you should try to answer them with thoughtful, thorough answers. Typical Socratic style questioning usually follows an answer with another question to assure that you fully explore the issue. We can also gain insight by responding to a question with further questioning, since it gives a broader panorama of the issues at hand.

When you encounter a question that you are unable to answer, you should ask yourself why it is difficult.

- Do I need to use another tool to help answer this question? Perhaps *Clarify the Terms* or *Meditate and Reflect*?

- Am I unable to answer the question because the answer contradicts something that I already know? Perhaps you're dealing with a paradox of the Scriptures or perhaps you're having difficulty accepting the truth that you've encountered.

- Is it possible that the answer lies elsewhere within this contextual section? Perhaps it is to be found in the previous paragraphs using the *Follow the Weaver* tool, or perhaps it will be uncovered in the following paragraphs as you continue to study them in order.

- Could this question be answered by revisiting the background of the book, the author, or the Big-6 contexts?

- Would it be helpful to use the *Juxtapose* tool to see if other translation teams understood this passage differently?

- What question could I ask that would yield further insight into this portion of the passage?

It is wise to make notes about *insightful* questions that you composed along with series of questions that yielded special insights. Perhaps you were able to answer them, but perhaps not. Sometimes they spawn great discussions with other believers that can be explored together through questioning. The resulting learning can be rich and enjoyable! In some cases, you will want to make note of the questions and reasoning that led you to a certain point, so you can become well acquainted with the deeper aspects of God's Word.

Questions with Multiple Possible Answers

In cases where there is more than one possible answer to your question, it would be wise to record the question along with the possible answers. In these cases, you should use questioning to determine the most likely answer, and record your reasoning for your decision. For example, if you were exploring the following verse,

"Then the Jews, because it was the day of preparation, so that the bodies would not remain on the cross on the Sabbath (for that Sabbath was a high day), asked Pilate that their legs might be broken, and that they might be taken away." John 19:31

You might ask questions similar to the following:

Q: What is meant by "that Sabbath was a **high** day?"
A: This Sabbath was the first day of the Feast of Unleavened Bread
Q: If it is not necessarily the 7th day of the week, what does it imply about the day of Jesus' crucifixion?
A: Perhaps Jesus' crucifixion was on a weekday other than Friday (the 6th day).
Q: If the Sabbath Day was the first day of the Feast of Unleavened Bread, was it necessarily the 7th day of the

week?
A: No
A: The weekly Sabbath Day, in general, was a great day
Q: If it is the 7th day of the week, what does it imply about the day of Jesus' crucifixion?   **A:** Jesus was crucified on a Friday (the 6th day).

Recording the different possible answers will give you assurance that you have fully explored all possibilities for understanding your passage. In most cases, your questioning will reveal the correct answer as you explore the context. In general, this is not a time consuming task, and it leads to greater confidence in your final conclusions. It is always a good idea to make notes about your reasoning and final answers to your questions.

The Advantage of Asking

Learning through questioning gives much deeper insight than learning by having information spoon-fed to you. There are many benefits to this type of learning. Besides being enriching to the soul and giving a taste of deeper understanding, it will enable you to articulate both sides of arguments and discern which side is closer to the truth. Since you will explore the Scriptures—the facts and the questions—from a firsthand perspective, you will sense an ownership in your understanding and increase your confidence as you discuss and defend God's Word.

As followers of Christ, our part is to seek the truth with honest and good hearts. We are able to seek the truth through questioning with the assistance of the Holy Spirit, and our search is fully able to lead us to reliable knowledge and understanding. Unlike Socrates, our search for certainty can come to rest when it comes face to face with the absolute truth of God's Word.

17
Clarifying the Terms

Clarifying the Terms

It is common knowledge that researching a word requires us to don our spectacles, unclasp an ancient, leather-bound book, and pore through mysterious words until we unlock the hidden meaning that has been eluding us. What was that? You just clicked on a word and found its semantic range? Okay – we will explore that method of clarifying the terms. In reality, clarifying

the terms or the meanings of words is a rather simple process. Rather than making it sound complicated by referring to it as a process, we'll just call it a tool ... one of the tools in our Bible study toolset.

The formal term for clarifying the terms in is *lexical analysis*. It is a term from the ivory towers, but fortunately, we have some tricks up our sleeve that will greatly simplify this effort for those who are not scholars of the original Biblical languages. Our purpose is to help non-scholars leverage the learning and tools of Bible scholars to gain a deeper understanding of God's Word. Clarifying terms is not adequate in itself for producing understanding—it is not the end-game of Bible study, although it is an indispensable part of it. Clarifying terms is just one of the common tasks of the process.

The Terms

One of the basic principles of communication is that all participants in a discussion must share a common understanding of the words that are being used. As we apply this principle to Bible study, we must strive to understand the meaning of words as they were used by the original writer or speaker. For our purposes, we may not have to research every word, but in general, we should research those that are ambiguous or unclear in our minds or may be pivotal in our interpretation decisions. It is only after we have an accurate understanding of the possible meanings of a word that we can expect to correctly interpret a passage.

The first term we will clarify is *term*. *Term* and *word* are not synonymous. A term is a *concept* that is referred to by one or more words. For example, the word *baptize* is a word, but it has different meanings in different contexts. In some passages it refers to immersion in water, in others it refers to a mighty act of the Holy Spirit, in others it refers to a resolve to repent, while in others it refers to identification or association with someone, such as Moses. In our discussions and studies we must understand the context in which a word is used, as that will provide clues about the concept or term that the writer or speaker is trying to convey. It would be very short-sighted to assume that the word *baptize*, for example, always refers to the same concept without considering its context.

Semantic Range
It seems that we're dealing with semantics, doesn't it? Indeed we are – the study of the meanings of words is referred to as *semantics*. Thus, the different possible meanings of a word are referred to as the **semantic range**. As we seek to understand all of the possible meanings of a word in the Bible, we are really seeking its semantic range as it was understood during the time of the writing.

For example, the Bible commonly uses the word *saved,* which is translated from the Greek word *sozo*. We find, however, that this word is used to relay many different concepts or terms, one of which is the concept of salvation from the judgment of our sin (Acts 2:47). Other uses of the word include being saved from some sort of danger, such as a stormy sea (Matthew 8:25), or salvation from sickness (i.e. healing—Matthew 9:22, James 5:15), or rescuing from a bad situation, such as the Israelites being saved out of Egypt (Jude 5). So, once again, we see that a word refers to a different term or concept, depending on how it is used in its context. We could say that *sozo* has a broad semantic range.

As an example, let's consider the New Testament's usage of *world*. In most cases, our English word *world* is based on the Greek word *kosmos*.[105] But a little investigation shows us that *kosmos* has at least seven different meanings in its semantic range, as shown in Table 15.

universe
earth
world system
people
adorning
adornment
tremendous amount[106]

Table 15—Semantic Range for *World* or *Kosmos*

It is of great importance that we consider the various options from the semantic range as we study. For example, which of the options in Table 15 would be the best fit for *world* in John 3:16 ("For God so loved the world …")? When Jesus made this statement, was he referring to the universe, the earth, the world system, the people, or did he have another meaning in mind? When we read the following verses, it becomes clear that He was referring to individuals, so the correct understanding of this passage is, no doubt, that "God so loved

---

[105] Κόσμος, from which the English word *cosmos* is derived.
[106] (Louw & Nida 1996, 146)

people ..." Therefore, our choice of words from the semantic range must be based on the context in which it is used.

This brings us to another very important principle of Bible study:

> ## Principle:
> ✦ *The meaning of a word must be determined by its context.*

Once again, we see the important role that context plays within communication. Since the meaning of a word is determined by its context, we must reserve our final judgment about its meaning until we are able to consider it within its context. This is the essence of Hermeneutic Principle #10, which instructs us to clarify the terms *as* we explore the substance of a passage, since the context provides clues about how a word is being used.

Do You Love Me?
Let's bring the concept of *term* down to a deeper level with another example. Suppose we are reading from the gospel of John and encounter Jesus' dialog with Peter in John 21:15–17. Three times in this passage, Jesus asked Peter if he loved him, and three times Peter responded, "You know that I love You." The third time, Peter was grieved because Jesus questioned his love for Him.

When we read this section from an English Bible, we scratch our heads and wonder what we missed in their conversation. But if we were to spend time clarifying the terms in this passage, we would see a completely new dimension that illuminates our understanding. The term we need to explore in this passage is found in the word "love." Those of us who are English speakers understand the concept of a wholesome, tender, charitable love. We also understand the concept of love between brothers; the concept of love within a family; and the concept of passionate, erotic love. The ancient Greeks also understood these concepts, but they had a different *word* for each, so they were able to be more precise in their communication. Specifically, the Greek words were *agape, phileo, storge,*[107] *and eros,* all of which are translated as *love* in English.

Let's return to the term *love* in the discussion between Jesus and Peter. If we were to substitute the actual Greek words in place of *love,* the dialog would look something like this:

Jesus:	"Peter, do you **agape** Me more than these?"
Peter:	"Yes, Lord; You know that I **phileo** You."
Jesus:	"Peter, do you **agape** Me?"
Peter:	"Yes, Lord; You know that I **phileo** You."
Jesus:	"Peter, do you **phileo** Me?"
Peter:	"Lord, You know all things; You know that I **phileo** You."

With this improved understanding of the terms in this passage, we find ourselves better equipped to explore its meaning through meditation. Hopefully these examples illustrate the value of making the effort to clarify the terms within your passage—it is not only valuable, it is essential for understanding the intended meaning of the writer or speaker.

Which Words to Research?

Many years ago, my wife and I were part of a group of young married couples who were considering Paul's words in 1 Corinthians 7:14:

---

[107] The Greek word *storge* does not appear in the New Testament—it is found in extra-Biblical literature.

> "For the unbelieving husband is **sanctified** through his wife, and the unbelieving wife is **sanctified** through her believing husband; for otherwise your children are unclean, but now they are **holy**."
>
> 1 Corinthians 7:14

As you can imagine, many people in the class were quite perplexed about the meaning of this passage, asking many questions and proposing some strange interpretations. The discussion could have been easily brought under control, however, if the leader had simply said, *"Let's step back for a moment and try to clarify some of the terms in this verse …"*

Now, we all know that a good discussion leader would begin by asking for input from the group, rather than simply defining the terms for them, and one of the first questions that he or she should ask would be something like, *"Are all of the terms in this passage clear in your minds?"* or *"Which words need clarification?"* As it turned out, much of the confusion resulted from a misunderstanding of the words *sanctified* and *holy*. If everyone had understood these two terms, then the group could have explored the *substance* of the passage much more confidently and arrived at a healthy understanding of it.

In a similar manner, as you study, you should pose the same questions to yourself, *"Are all of the possible terms in this passage clear in my mind? Which words need clarification? "* This is one of the first steps of questioning your understanding in an effort to sharpen the image of the passage.

Is it necessary to research all of the words in the passage? It certainly would be if you were one of the scholars responsible for translating the text from the original language to English. For the most part, however, we can probably trust the translation decisions for the very common words. In some cases, however, we will want to second-guess the translators' decisions to see if another rendering might support something you found in the context.

If you suspect another rendering of a word might be more fitting, then you should certainly investigate further. One of the easiest ways to do this is by comparing your Bible version with other literal Bible translations to see how other teams of scholars rendered the words. The technique for comparing Bible versions will be discussed in Chapter 19 – Dare to Juxtapose! A simple word comparison is illustrated in Figure 24 on page 364. In some cases, it may be best to confer with someone who is experienced with the original languages of the Bible.

Let's Do It
Using the contextual section that you printed in the **Print It** section of the Context Concepts chapter, carefully read through the paragraph that you are currently studying and highlight words or phrases that may be vague in your understanding.

After you've highlighted all of your *uncertain* words, take time to research them and make notes of possible meanings in the margin of your printout. Refer to Figure 16 below for an example of verifying words for our Matthew 17:24 – 18:35 contextual section.

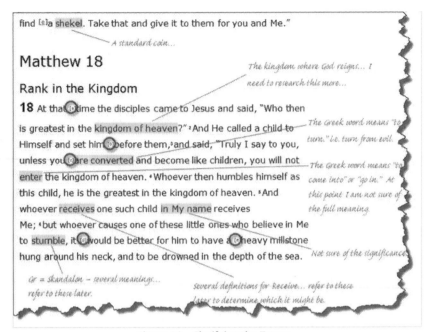

find [s]a shekel. Take that and give it to them for you and Me."

A standard coin...

Matthew 18

The kingdom where God reigns... I need to research this more...

Rank in the Kingdom

18 At that time the disciples came to Jesus and said, "Who then is greatest in the kingdom of heaven?" 2And He called a child to Himself and set him before them, 3and said, "Truly I say to you, unless you are converted and become like children, you will not enter the kingdom of heaven. 4Whoever then humbles himself as this child, he is the greatest in the kingdom of heaven. 5And whoever receives one such child in My name receives Me; 6but whoever causes one of these little ones who believe in Me to stumble, it would be better for him to have a heavy millstone hung around his neck, and to be drowned in the depth of the sea.

The Greek word means "to turn." i.e. turn from evil.

The Greek word means "to come into" or "go in." At this point I am not sure of the full meaning.

Not sure of the significance.

Gr = skandalon – several meanings... refer to these later.

Several definitions for Receive... refer to these later to determine which it might be.

Figure 16—Clarifying the Terms

Notes about markings in Figure 16:

Low-Hanging Fruit

Let's begin with the easy answers about these terms—the low-hanging fruit in the orchard of Bible words. Notice in Figure 16 that we've circled some of the references. These references, which are usually letters or numbers that are found beside words in some versions of the Bible (the New American Standard Version in this case), reveal the *literal* meaning of the underlying word in the original language. As we refer to these references, we can quickly see the literal meaning of the word in its original language, which can be very helpful for our understanding.

Why didn't they simply use the literal meaning in the English version? It's because the translators felt another rendering would make more sense to the English reader, but they also included the literal word(s) to make their meaning available to shed light on interpretation decisions. These little notations sometimes produce special insights in our studies, so be sure to consider them as you study!

If you feel that one of the literal meanings might be relevant to your understanding, you should make a note of it on your printed text or in your study journal. In our example passage in Figure 16, I circled five letters and have provided their meanings in Table 16. Just for practice, refer to Table 16, read the English rendering, and consider how the literal meaning might be substituted in its place.

Note	English Rendering	Literal Meaning
[a]	At that [a]time the ...	hour
[b]	... and set him [b]before them ...	in their midst
[c]	... unless you [c]are converted ...	are turned
[d]	... it [d]would be better ...	is better
[e]	... have a [e]heavy millstone ...	millstone turned by a donkey

Table 16—Literal Meanings of Words

Depending on the format of your Bible, you may find other types of low-hanging fruit in the form of italicized words or phrases, bracketed words or sections, or other indicators within the text. It is important to familiarize yourself with the format of your Bible, as you will gain insight by understanding these little keys. Most Bible publishers explain their formatting keys in their introductory information, in the foreword.

Reaching the Not-So-Low-Hanging Fruit
You may be wondering where we found the information about our *uncertain* words, especially the meanings of the Greek words and, once again, you have asked another excellent question!

As we've mentioned before, God raised up scholars who have dedicated their lives to becoming intimately familiar with the Biblical languages and have created tools for the sole purpose of assisting others in better understanding His Word. Furthermore, many of these works were created by people whose native language was English, making many of them readily usable for you and me. We must emphasize that we are not referring to Bible commentaries – we are referring to books that describe how words were used in different ways in the Bible and in other ancient texts, and how you can locate them throughout your Bible.

We generally have three options for researching the words of the Bible. They are:

1) Hardcopy Books
2) Software
3) Internet Resources

Although we would like to provide an exhaustive list of study resources, we have decided to limit our list to those which are easily accessible and relatively inexpensive. We have also sought to highlight those which are relatively easy to use, not requiring training in the Biblical languages. More advanced resources certainly exist, but we have chosen those which provide an easy entryway into the realm of Biblical languages. As you become comfortable with these tools, you may desire to advance to more complex tools.

Our selections also include resources that are ingenious and very useful, to the extent that their concepts are still in widespread use today, having been refined and improved over the years. Examples of these resources include Vine's *Expository Dictionary of Old and New Testament Words* and *Strong's Exhaustive Concordance of the Bible*.

Both of these works were based on the King James Version (KJV) of the Bible, which means that you may have to do a little extra work if you are using a more recent version of the Bible. Scholars and organizations have since produced similar tools that continue to use these methods with more recent versions of the Bible.

> *Be sure to read the information about Vine's and Strong's works in the section below, since they provide keys and techniques in many modern and advanced Bible study tools!*

Hardcopy Books:

- William Edwy Vine's *Expository Dictionary of Old and New Testament Words* (*Affectionately known as "Vine's"*). This book should be in the library of every student of the Word. It provides a comprehensive listing of the ancient Greek and Hebrew root words of the Bible *as they were used in that day*, which is our desire in researching Bible words! We want to know how the writers, speakers, and audiences would have used and understood words, rather than how they are understood in our modern world.

- *Strong's Exhaustive Concordance of the Bible*, by James Strong, DD. A concordance is an index of the words of the Bible; an *exhaustive* concordance lists every word in the Bible. We have listed Strong's concordance because it was the first of its kind and was developed specifically for the King James Version of the Bible. Since concordances have been developed for other versions of the Bible, we recommend that you purchase a concordance for your preferred version or use an electronic means of searching. Many modern Bibles contain a non-exhaustive concordance.

***Strong's Numbers*—**One of the ingenious outcomes of Strong's work was that he assigned a number to every unique word of the Bible in their original languages (i.e. Hebrew, Aramaic, and Greek). These numbers are still in use today, allowing us to refer to specific words *without ambiguity*. Strong's numbering system is still widely used today, although another numbering system, the *Goodrick-Kohlenberger* system (i.e. "GK"), was developed later, which is more complete. Don't let these numbers intimidate you—their purpose will become very clear when you see them in use as we demonstrate searching.

- ***Mounce's Complete Expository Dictionary of Old and New Testament Words*,** by William D. Mounce. This book is captioned as "Vine's for the 21st Century," which is quite a claim! This book uses both the Strong's and GK numbering systems, which increases its reach to more words. It also includes both New and Old Testament words for each English word, rather than requiring the reader to turn to another section of the book. Similar to Vine's, this book is *not* exhaustive, since that would make it unwieldy. It contains all Greek words that occur ten-times or more and all Hebrew words that occur fifty-times or more. Additionally, it contains words that are theologically or exegetically significant, even though they may not occur as often.

Bible Software

There are some excellent Bible programs available in the form of computer programs or apps for mobile devices. Software searches have some enormous advantages over manually searching hardcopy books. As we mentioned in Chapter 7 – Selecting a Bible, perhaps the greatest advantage is realized when searching for multiple words at the same time. For example, if you want to find all verses that contain "Abraham" and "Isaac" in a hardcopy book, it would be necessary to search for one of the terms and then manually look at each verse to see if it contains the other. It becomes far more complex if more than two search terms are added. When searching via software, you would simply enter all of the desired terms and let the system do the work.

Some of the more popular Bible software packages are:

Software Name	Website
e-Sword	www.e-sword.net
Logos	www.Logos.com
OliveTree	www.OliveTree.com

One of the best ways to research Bible software is to do an internet search for "Bible software reviews," which will return many different websites and some good information about these tools.

Internet Resources
There are several websites that offer excellent Bible study tools, including those which allow us to research the meaning of a word in its original language. These websites include those listed in Table 17.

Web Site Name	Web Address
Bible Gateway	www.BibleGatway.com
Blue Letter Bible	www.BlueLetterBible.org

Table 17 - Web Sites with Bible Research Tools

In Appendix E—Researching a Word, we have provided a detailed example of how to research a word using the Blue Letter Bible web site. Since researching a word of the Bible is a very important skill for every student of the Word, this is a good opportunity for you to try it! After you follow the example in this appendix, try to research a Bible word of your own to assure that you are able to find its semantic range.

At this time, please turn to Appendix E and follow the tutorial for researching a word.

After you've finished, return here and continue reading.

As you follow the example in Appendix E, you will learn how to research a word to see how it was used and understood in the era and culture in which it was written. Is there more to know beyond this? Yes, there is. Knowing the meaning of a word may not reveal aspects that do not easily translate from language to language. For example, we may not be able to see the tense, aspect, mood, voice, person, gender or plurality in which a word is used, or be able to observe the wordplay of the original authors. In most cases, however, the Bible translation teams have taken care of these tasks for us, but understanding the meanings of words opens new horizons for those who are not Biblical language scholars.

Christianized Words

As you consider the words of the Bible, you should be aware that some words were initially used in a *general* sense, but developed a *Christianized* meaning over time. Examples of these words include *amen, apostle, baptize, cross, sanctified,* and *saved.* As we mentioned earlier, *saved* or the Greek *sozo*, had similar meanings to our modern English usage, such as saved from drowning, saved from a bad situation (e.g. saved by the bell), or saved for later. The word also developed a Christianized meaning of *saved from God's judgment or punishment* of sin, so we must be careful when assessing the use of the word to make sure we're interpreting it as the writer or speaker intended. We should not immediately assume the Christianized meaning.

Things to Look For

As you research the words of your contextual section, you should look for the characteristics of words that are listed below. The most important is, of course, how the word is used in its context, but you should also:

Seek to understand how the words were used:
- By the writer/speaker
- By his or her contemporaries

As we've mentioned before, our goal is not to learn the meaning of our modern words as they may have originated from the Biblical languages—our goal is to understand how the words were used in Bible times, by the original writer or speaker.

Ask yourself if it is used figuratively:
- How does it apply to the subject or point?
- What is its suggested or implied meaning in the context?
- What aspect(s) of the figure is/are applicable to the writer/speaker's point?

> *Figures of speech and Proverbs*
> *contain highly compacted*
> *insights and tidbits of wisdom.*
> *Meditation is the tool*
> *that transforms them into understanding.*

Consider whether any of the Big-6 contexts influence the meaning of a word or term:
- For example, was it spoken in a military context, an agricultural context, religious, or some other context?

Research names that are mentioned in the text:

- Are you familiar with the people, places, times, and things? For example, Asher, Ashdod, Aviv, and Asherah:
    - *People:* Asher is one of the sons of Jacob and a tribe of Israel
    - *Place:* Ashdod is a city of the Philistines
    - *Time:* Aviv is the first month of the Hebrew lunar calendar for religious events.
    - *Thing:* An Asherah or Astarte is a Canaanite deity
- The OT uses alternate names for kings ... we really need to know **who's who!**

Alternate Names of Kings in the Old Testament
Jehoiakim = Eliakim
Jehoiachin = Jeconiah = Coniah
Jehoahaz = Jehoaz = Shallum
Zedekiah = Mattaniah

Finding the kings and prophets on the *Kings and Prophets Chart* can greatly increase your understanding of the era in which they lived, along with providing other Big-6 insights. The Kings and Prophets Chart is available through the www.AncientWords.us web site.

- Some people in the New Testament have different names:

Alternate Names in the New Testament
Matthew = Levi
Peter = Simon = Cephas
Saul = Paul
Barnabas = Joseph

As you research the terms, be sure to update your notes. This will enable you to revisit the information at a later time, but it will also help you remember it more effectively.

18
Follow the Weaver

The *Follow the Weaver* tool? Why would we give such a strange name to a Bible study tool? My wife asked the same question. One reason is to make the name easier to remember, but more importantly, it is to help you remember the concept behind it. Recall that the origin of the word *context* carries the idea of weaving, referring to weaving a message through speech or text. It is also interesting that the word *thread* can refer to a theme or subject that runs throughout a 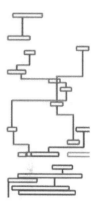 literary work. In this chapter, we will explore techniques for following the threads that a writer or speaker uses to interconnect thoughts to create the overall message.

As you study your contextual section, looking for the threads that are woven throughout, you should not always expect to see explicit hints that indicate the flow of the message. Instead, the indicators are sometimes subtle and muted and the threads of the tapestry are not discernable until the message is actually understood. On other occasions, however, you will see very clear indications of the weaving as the writer or speaker constructs the message, such as "First of all ..." or "Secondly ..."

An example of a muted thread can be seen in the relationship between the first two paragraphs of our example contextual section, (Matthew 17:24–27 and 18:1–6). At a first look, it appears as if 18:1 might be a contextual boundary that began with the disciples' question, "*Who then is the greatest in the kingdom of heaven?*" But when we recognize that Jesus subtly alluded to the kingdom of heaven in the first paragraph (17:26 & 27), in His words, *"Then the sons are exempt. However, so that we do not offend them ..."*, His inference becomes quite clear. It was this inference to the kingdom that spawned the disciples' question in the next paragraph about who is the greatest, the thread or the weaving that we are seeking.

Why Is It Important to Follow the Weaver?
Following the weaver gives us great insights about a writer or speaker's thoughts within their context, in the spirit of how they were intended. Recognizing the clues in the text is a key to answering one of our most important questions for understanding a message. That is, *what was the reason for this statement, question, response, or event?* When we are able to answer that question, then the intended meaning usually becomes evident.

For example, we often hear Matthew 18:20, "For *where two or three are gathered in My name, I am there in their midst."* quoted without regard for its intended meaning. But when we follow the weaver, we realize that Jesus' words are referring to heaven's support of decisions of the church on earth, rather than Christ's presence with us. Believers can be confident that Christ is always present with every Christian, whether in a lonely prison cell or in a mighty gathering of worshipers. Our goal is to understand the intended meaning, and tracing the threads of the weaver is an excellent tool for finding these keys.

Figure 17 contains an illustration of the threads that flow through our example contextual section. Although you will probably not be able to read the text of on the left side, it illustrates how you can use highlighters and pens to circle the key words and thoughts that are woven throughout. You should make similar markings and notes that will clarify the threads and the weave of your passage. Take a moment to inspect our attempt to understand the flow in Figure 17.

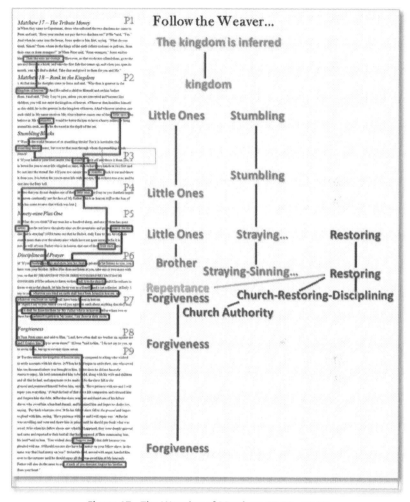

Figure 17 - The Weaving of Matthew 17:24 - 18:35

Notice in Figure 17 that the threads are not necessarily apparent through words that are repeated, even though repeated words can greatly simplify our task when they are present. In general, we are seeking the flow of a *thought* or an *idea* as it is woven through the paragraphs. Notice in Figure 17, for example, that the idea of *little ones* is also expressed as *brother*, and the idea of *stumbling* is revealed as *straying* and *sinning*. Jesus also conveyed the concept of repentance as *listens to* you (v15), which expressed the same idea. He continued with the concept and related it to the level of the church, rather than at an individual level. The linkages between the ideas are woven through the paragraphs of the passage.

Is weaving a complicated concept? Certainly not! You create threads and weaving in your everyday conversations in the same way that the writer and speakers of the Bible did. It would actually be very strange to write or speak in unrelated sentences and thoughts. Ideas and thoughts that are conveyed outside of a context tend to be cryptic and mysterious, and your friends would wonder where the words came from and where they were headed. You can be quite comfortable with the idea of following the weaver—it simply describes a concept that is very familiar to you.

So how do we follow the weaver's threads from thought to thought and paragraph to paragraph? How do we recognize the indicators of connecting threads? Should we expect a thread to appear in every paragraph of a contextual section or might it come and go and reappear in various places? Is it possible for multiple themes to be woven concurrently throughout a contextual section? Once again, following the weaver is not difficult, but we will take a look at some hints that can help us clarify the message of the weaver.

The Obvious Weaving Clues
Let's begin by looking at some of the more obvious weaving clues:

✦ **Repeated words, thoughts, and themes.**
These clues can be seen in Figure 17, with *little ones* being repeated three times (18:6, 10, and 14). The words *stumbling* and *stumbling block* were emphasized by repeating them many times. These are indications that we should look for similar thoughts that appear in other parts of our passage, but perhaps with different words. As mentioned earlier, the concept of *stumbling* was mentioned metaphorically through the lost sheep going *astray* (v12), and the brother sinning (v15).

As you explore a passage, make sure that you do not limit your search to the same word— writers and speakers frequently emphasize their points by using synonyms and figures of speech. If we limit our search to repeated words, then it is likely that we will miss a key connection of the weaving.

At the beginning of His sermon on the mount, Jesus repeated the phrase *"Blessed are the ..."* As we study these words, we must try to seek a common theme within these differing conditions of people. There is a common theme and connection – seek it!

✦ **An indication of related points ... i.e. bullet points or lists**
When a writer or speaker presents a list of items, we can gain a better understanding of the message by seeking the theme that is common to them. This is usually an indication of the thread that was woven into the message.

Examples of lists in the Scriptures:
- The fruit of the Spirit[108]
- *"There are six things which the LORD hates, yes, seven which are an abomination to Him..."*[109]
- The Ten Commandments[110]
- Justice, mercy, faithfulness (Matt 23:23)
- Micah 6:8 Justice, love kindness, walk humbly with your God

We can group the characteristics (perfections) of God and observe how they recur in the Scriptures to gain a better understanding of Him (Love, Lovingkindness, Holiness, Mercy, Justice, etc.)

✦ **Cyclical Events** in the Scriptures
Having an understanding of significant lists or events in the Bible can give insight to the meanings of passages when least expected. For example, having an understanding of the Appointed Times in Leviticus 23, can explain the feast days that Jesus and others observed in the New Testament.

- The Appointed Times—Leviticus 23 include:
    - The weekly Sabbath
    - Passover
    - The Feast of Unleavened Bread
    - The day of First Fruits
    - The Feast of Weeks
    - The Day of Trumpets
    - The Day of Atonement
    - The Feast of Tabernacles

---

[108] Galatians 5:22–23
[109] Proverbs 6:16–19
[110] Exodus 20:1–17

- The cycle of sin, oppression, crying to God, and deliverance in the book of Judges (refer to Judges 2:11-23) provides insight into the relationships of the events and the meaning behind them, as woven together by the writer.
- The lists of heavenly symbols that indicate related prophetic events:
    - The book with seven seals—Revelation 5:1
    - The seven trumpets—Revelation 8:2
    - The seven bowls—Revelation 15:7

Logical Indicators

Once again, the FANBOYS and friends are able to help us identify a connection between thoughts in a contextual section and reveal the threads of the message. When the writer or speaker uses one of the FANBOYS or coordinating conjunctions, we should give attention and follow them as indications of the logic that lead us to information, questions, and conclusions.

- An excellent example of this is found in Luke 19:11: "... Jesus went on to tell a parable, **because** ..." This gives us a strong indication of the point of the parable.
- Romans 12:1 is a classic example of **therefore**. It tells us that the following points are based on the previous points.
- Hebrews 9:7 says, "... nor was it that He would offer Himself often, as the high priest enters the holy place year by year with blood that is not his own. **Otherwise**, He would have needed to suffer often since the foundation of the world ..." The conjunction **otherwise** indicates that this sentence is logically connected (i.e. woven) with the previous text. In order to understand it correctly, we must study and understand the previous point.

Principles

Principles are usually accompanied by one or more specific examples, which reveal a thread that is woven into the text. Look at the following principles and observe how the example(s) are related to them.

- Cannot serve two masters—Matthew 6:24
- Love your enemies—Matthew 5:44
- The Golden Rule—Matthew 7:12
- The greatest commandment—Deuteronomy 6:5

Clues

How do we find weaving clues in our contextual section? The first step is to read your passage and become familiar with it. Once you have a feel for its themes, you should identify the words that describe them and make note of them. You may then take advantage of technology and search for the words within your contextual section and follow the linkages to reveal the threads. Remember, however, that the writer or speaker may not reuse the same word, which means that searching for the same word would be fruitless. The best way to find the common thoughts and ideas is to carefully read your passage, simply being watchful for restatements of the idea.

We also highly recommend that you seek clues by asking probing questions about the text. That is, using the *Exploring Through Questioning* tool that was explained in Chapter 16. You may refer to the questions for weaving in Appendix D – Sample Questions, to help you get started. Asking questions will help you explore and assure that you are zeroing in on the message.

References to OT Passages
Another tip for finding the threads in your passage is by noting quotes from the Old Testament. Some translators indicate Old Testament references with some form of font or case difference or setting it apart by indentation. The NASB, for example, uses small upper case letters to denote an OT reference Matthew 13:14 is rendered as:

"In their case the prophecy of Isaiah is being fulfilled, which says, 'YOU WILL KEEP ON HEARING, BUT WILL NOT UNDERSTAND; YOU WILL KEEP ON SEEING, BUT WILL NOT PERCEIVE;'"

As always, care is required when reading the Bible, since not every OT reference was indicated by the translators. With some references, we will recognize them because of our own familiarity with the OT. In other cases, we will need to increase our familiarity with the OT so we can recognize references to it in the NT. The purpose is so we can consider how the writer or speaker used them in his or her message.

Hebrews 9:7 also provides an excellent example as it refers to the Day of Atonement. The writer did not mention the appointed time by name, but it becomes clear from the description, "… enters the holy place once per year, not without taking blood …" that it is referring to the Day of Atonement as described in the entire chapter of Leviticus 16. With this knowledge, it becomes evident that the thread of the passage is about atonement and that the Day of Atonement in the Law of Moses taught of Christ's perfect atonement.

Times, Dates, Feasts, and Sabbaths
Developing your understanding of how Israel tracked time can give insights into the message of the Bible. For example, simply knowing that the Jewish day ended and began at sundown can explain the events of certain passages. Consider Mark 1:32, "When evening came, after the sun had set, they began bringing to Him all who were

ill and those who were demon-possessed." Why does it make a difference that the sun had set? Since the prior events took place on the Sabbath, the people were not allowed to walk a distance to where Jesus was staying, nor were they able to bring or carry those who were ill or demon possessed. But the setting of the sun signaled the end of the Sabbath and they were then able to do the laborious tasks that were forbidden on the Sabbath per the Law. Thus we see how this little statement weaves a thread to the previous comment about the Sabbath day.

Other important time indicators of the Bible include hours (e.g. the third hour, sixth hour, ninth hour), watches (e.g. the morning watch), months, the lunar calendar, the new moon, and the Appointed Times.

Which Came First? Cause and Effect

Where your treasure is, there will your heart be also ... or is it where your heart is, there will your treasure be, also?[111] One man told me that my question is irrelevant, because both the heart and treasure will be in the same place in the end. But his reasoning overlooked the key to Jesus' point that our hearts will follow our treasure and gravitate to it. Jesus' point is that, if we choose to accumulate wealth on earth, then our hearts will be obsessed with guarding and being with our earthly treasure. On the other hand, if we choose to focus on accumulating heavenly wealth, then we will be free from worry over them, since they cannot be taken from us. Being the owner of heavenly treasure will shape a person's entire outlook in this world. Thus, the *cause and effect* or *which came first* can be of great importance as we follow the weaving and reasoning of the writer or speaker.

---

[111] Matthew 6:21 "for where your treasure is, there your heart will be also."

Sequences that Build upon Each Other

Some Scripture passages teach us through lists of items that are related to other items. Musing on each item with the intent of understanding how items relate to each other, can give insight into the overall meaning and direction of the passage. Consider the following lists:

- 2 Corinthians 4:8–11 "... we are afflicted in every way, but not crushed; perplexed, but not despairing; persecuted, but not forsaken; struck down, but not destroyed; always carrying about in the body the dying of Jesus, so that the life of Jesus also may be manifested in our body. For we who live are constantly being delivered over to death for Jesus' sake, so that the life of Jesus also may be manifested in our mortal flesh."

- James 1:14–15 "But each one is tempted when he is carried away and enticed by his own lust. Then when lust has conceived, it gives birth to sin; and when sin is accomplished, it brings forth death."

- James 4:1–3 "What is the source of quarrels and conflicts among you? Is not the source your pleasures that wage war in your members? You lust and do not have; so you commit murder. You are envious and cannot obtain; so you fight and quarrel. You do not have because you do not ask. You ask and do not receive, because you ask with wrong motives, so that you may spend it on your pleasures."

- 2 Peter 1:5–8 "Now for this very reason also, applying all diligence, in your faith supply moral excellence, and in your moral excellence, knowledge, and in your knowledge, self-control, and in your self-control, perseverance, and in your perseverance, godliness, and in your godliness, brotherly kindness, and in your brotherly kindness, love."

Look Within the Same Paragraph!

Make sure you study the other thoughts within the same paragraph to see how they relate to each other. John 3:16, for example, is not a standalone verse about salvation. We are all familiar with this verse, which is about God's loving salvation, but we need to understand His loving salvation in light of the related thoughts and ideas of the paragraph. It is by following the thoughts of the weaver and the threads throughout the contextual section that we gain a comprehensive understanding of the message.

✦ Take a moment to study the paragraph from **John 3** (below) to see how its message was woven into the paragraph:

John 3:16–21

"For God so loved the world, that He gave His only begotten Son, that whoever believes in Him shall not perish, but have eternal life. For God did not send the Son into the world to judge the world, but that the world might be saved through Him. He who believes in Him is not judged; he who does not believe has been judged already, because he has not believed in the name of the only begotten Son of God. This is the judgment, that the Light has come into the world, and men loved the darkness rather than the Light, for their deeds were evil. For everyone who does evil hates the Light, and does not come to the Light for fear that his deeds will be exposed. But he who practices the truth comes to the Light, so that his deeds may be manifested as having been wrought in God."

✦ Did you get a fuller sense of Jesus' message when you viewed it as a unit that was woven together?

19
Dare to Juxtapose!

We have juxtaposed the ESV and NAS renderings of Matthew 17:24–19:35, but don't worry—the ancient manuscripts are still intact. If you're not familiar with juxtaposing, you may find it to be a very useful tool. Juxtapose simply means to position two or more things side-by-side so they can be compared.

How can juxtaposing be used as a tool for our studies? Recall from Chapter 7 that the English language has been blessed with some excellent versions of the Bible that are based on faithful translation philosophies. Because of this, we are able to do a side-by-side comparison (i.e. juxtaposition) of the same passage from different Bible versions. This enables us to see how they are similar and more importantly, how they differ from each other.

In other words, we are relying on the expertise and honest and good intentions of the translation teams as they translated the original languages into English to the best of their abilities. Since translation work is not an exact science, the Bible versions contain some minor differences that can give insight about where there may be some latitude for understanding a passage differently. These differences may hold a key to answering a question about your passage or contextual section.

For example, Appendix F contains a portion of our contextual section that has been juxtaposed in the ESV and NAS. Each line is divided at the *punctuation* of each version. In other words, whenever we encountered a punctuation mark (. , ; ! ? etc.), we inserted a blank line so the thoughts would be aligned between versions. It would also be useful to divide the passage by verses or by conjunctions (i.e.

FANBOYS and Friends), depending on what you are seeking as you compare the Bible versions.

A close inspection of these juxtaposed texts will reveal:
- Different selections of words
- An omission of an entire verse (Matthew 18:11 was omitted from the ESV),
- Different section headings
- Perhaps a slightly different tone in certain places

We are not suggesting that you create such a comparison table for your contextual section as a normal part of your study, even though you would probably gain some insights by doing so. But you should consider *juxtaposing* as one of your tools of Bible study that you can use whenever the need arises. For example, if you are questioning a word in the text or the structure of a sentence or paragraph, juxtaposing may reveal a key that will help you put some pieces of the puzzle together.

Give it a Try!
For practice, turn to Appendix F – Juxtaposing Matthew 18:1–14 and highlight or circle each difference that you observe between the two Bible versions.

❖ In addition to observing and noting the differences, you should consider each difference and ask yourself how it might affect the overall interpretation and your understanding.

❖ Consider if the differences may indicate latitude for a different interpretation of your passage.

❖ Consider how identical or very similar translations may confirm that the meaning of the original language is very clear.

❖ You may want to write a brief note beside the differences that seem most significant to you.

Since both the ESV and the NASB were translated by teams of scholars who were seeking a pure interpretation of the Word, you will, no doubt, be on solid ground by considering either rendering as you make your interpretation decisions. As you study your passage, you may want to use juxtaposition to compare other literal Bible versions, as well – other literal versions are shown in Figure 1 - Bible Version Comparison on page 120.

Juxtaposing and You

So how do all of these factors affect your personal approach to Bible study? Having easy access to some excellent *literal* translations of the Bible gives you an excellent opportunity to compare and observe where and how teams of scholars differed in their final decisions about the resulting English translation. Comparing literal Bible versions will allow you to see different word selections from the original language to the English, different phrasing of the sentences, and different beginnings and endings of thoughts in sentences and paragraphs. If you are struggling with a rendering in one version, you can easily consult the same passage in another literal version for insights from a different team of scholars to see if it sheds light on your passage.

Notice that we have stipulated literal versions of the Bible for comparison purposes. Literal versions are well suited for this purpose, since the goal of literal translations is to reproduce the meaning of words and the grammatical structure of the original text. If you were to attempt a similar comparison of paraphrased versions, your final product would be of little value, since such translations intentionally depart from the original words and phrasing for the purpose of enhanced readability. It is, therefore, of great importance that you apply your comparison efforts to literal versions of the Bible.

Juxtaposing Online

One of the easiest ways to juxtapose is by using online Bible study tools. For example, the BlueLetterBible.org web site allows you to view a single verse in multiple Bible versions simultaneously, which can greatly simplify the task. Juxtaposing is a powerful tool in our set of Bible study tools. We highly recommend that you use it regularly, especially since the online study tools greatly simplify the task!

Juxtapose Test Drive

Using the BlueLetterBible.org web site, compare Genesis 49:12 in the NASB, ESV, and NIV, to compare the renderings of the translation teams. Which do you think captures the meaning of Jacob as he spoke the words? In this case I would choose the rendering of the NIV.

20
Articulating Your Learning

CONGRATULATIONS! You have arrived at the final step of your study: the articulation phase. What do we mean by articulate? Articulating is the act of organizing your thoughts into a clear, crisp manner and putting them into words so you and others can understand them and learn from them. This is your opportunity to make a record of your journey through facts, teachings, insights, answers, questions, threads, and themes—to make notes of how the Holy Spirit sharpened your understanding of concepts from another realm.

There are many benefits to the mind when we write information, not the least of which is greatly increasing your ability to remember it! Another important reason for transferring our learning to writing is because the things that we actually know and **do not** know become evident as we try to express them. For example, if you think you understand a concept, but have difficulty articulating it, then it's likely that you do not understand it as well as you thought – perhaps you need to apply some further thought to the subject. You may not necessarily need to re-study it immediately, but you can make a comment in your notes that says, "I don't have a solid understanding of this concept—more thought and info needed!"

The steps for articulating are easy. Begin by rereading your entire contextual section. You should then spend time musing on the notes from your study and summarize them as conclusions in bullet form beneath each paragraph of your printed contextual section. Write them as if one of your friends will be reading them. Try to make them clear, concise, and easy for him or her to understand. Be sure to include the key questions and answers that you composed during your study, along with insights about points, facts, figures of speech, the connections within the weave, and areas that will require additional study.

As you write, pieces should fall into place and your understanding should become refined. Now, you are the weaver. You will re-weave the message of the contextual section into your notes. Your notes will clarify the message. This is your opportunity to bring a greater element of precision and certainty to your learning. Rather than simply rewriting your notes, you should record them as conclusions about the message. Be sure to separate the direct teaching of the Scriptures from your own inferences, per Hermeneutic Principle #11.

Now that you have studied the passage on your own, it is time to consider it in light of other passages in the Bible. You should consider the words and teachings of other Scripture passages as they may relate to your passage of study. Do they add additional light? Do they add ideas that extend the teaching or perhaps temper it in a different way? You should record these musings in your articulation notes, as well.

Hopefully, you can see that we are not asking you to write a term paper or thesis. If you can organize your thoughts clearly and thoroughly enough to explain the concepts to someone else, then you are on your way toward understanding.

After you have written your articulated notes, it would be wise to write a summary of your study—one or more paragraphs about the things you've learned in summary form. You should also include a paragraph about how you will respond to this study.

Example of Articulating
Rather than giving a detailed explanation of articulating, I've provided my articulation notes from our example study of The Parable of the Lost Sheep. Recall that our contextual section was Matthew 17:24–18:35. Please read through my notes in the remaining pages of this chapter to get a feel for articulating your learning.

> *Matthew 17—The Tribute Money*
>
> **24** When they came to Capernaum, those who collected the two-drachma tax came to Peter and said, "Does your teacher not pay the two-drachma *tax?*"
>
> 25 He *said, "Yes." And when he came into the house, Jesus spoke to him first, saying, "What do you think, Simon? From whom do the kings of the earth collect customs or poll-tax, from their sons or from strangers?"
>
> 26 When Peter said, "From strangers," Jesus said to him, "Then the sons are exempt.
>
> 27 "However, so that we do not offend them, go to the sea and throw in a hook, and take the first fish that comes up; and when you open its mouth, you will find a shekel. Take that and give it to them for you and Me."

Matthew 17:24–27 Notes:

- The events and dialog of this entire chapter took place inside a house in Capernaum (except for Peter's conversation with the tax collectors).
- Jesus initiated the conversation with Peter, probably as a lesson for Peter and all the disciples that were in the house (per 18:1).
- Jesus did not mention the Kingdom of Heaven, but He implied that He and Peter are sons of a king in v27, with "<u>However</u>, so that we do not offend them …" Are Jesus and Peter sons of a "king of the earth?" No, sons of God—the Kingdom of Heaven.
- Jesus implied that the reason they would pay the tax was so the tax collectors would not be offended. What is implied by this? It speaks to the reality and presence of the Kingdom of Heaven—it **is** here!
- Does this mean that we do not have to pay taxes or conform to our world's system? No, although we are truly exempt, our Master taught us to live among the world in a non-offensive way, unless it results in a conflict with His ways

- Are sons of the kingdom supposed to pay taxes in this world? Yes.
- We also learn of Jesus' miraculous powers through the fish and shekel.
- What are the main points of this paragraph? That Peter and Jesus, etc. are sons of the King, citizens of the kingdom, living as aliens on earth.
- Is this paragraph about paying taxes? It's a secondary theme.

Matthew 18 – Rank in the Kingdom

1   At that time the disciples came to Jesus and said, "Who then is greatest in the kingdom of heaven?"

2   And He called a child to Himself and set him before them,

3   and said, "Truly I say to you, unless you are converted and become like children, you will not enter the kingdom of heaven.

4   "Whoever then humbles himself as this child, he is the greatest in the kingdom of heaven.

5   "And whoever receives one such child in My name receives Me;

6   but whoever causes one of these little ones who believe in Me to stumble, it would be better for him to have a heavy millstone hung around his neck, and to be drowned in the depth of the sea.

Matthew 18:1–6 Notes:

- Multiple disciples were present in this conversation.
- What prompted their question, "Who then is the greatest in the kingdom of heaven?" It seems it was prompted by Jesus' words of the previous paragraph, regarding being sons of a king. This is the linkage—the thread that weaves these paragraphs and thoughts together.
- Does their question seem to be motivated from ego or self-exaltation? Not necessarily—it could be a natural response to kings, sons, and strangers.

- Jesus presented a living metaphor of a child to illustrate His point. What aspect of this metaphor is He applying to being great? It is obviously humility, based on verse 4.
- Jesus shifted the flow of the conversation in v5 with "And whoever receives one …" Why did He do this? The only reason I could come up with is that He wanted to teach them about His concern for little ones.
- Receiving one such child *in His name,* shows that we also receive Jesus.
- Causing a little one to stumble is extremely hurtful to Jesus and the one who does so will receive very severe punishment—it would be better for him to die than to have to endure the punishment for it!
- Who is the "little one?" Based on what I learned from my study of the following paragraphs, I realize that a little one is a) someone who 'believes in Me," per v6 b) is also allegorized as a *lost sheep* in the parable of vv12–14, c) has heavenly angels that watch over them, per v10, d) not necessarily a child, per v15, e) can fall into sin and should be restored and protected by other believers, per vv15–16, f) may need to be shunned by the church if unrepentant, per v17.

Matthew 18 – Stumbling Blocks

7 "Woe to the world because of its stumbling blocks! For it is inevitable that stumbling blocks come; but woe to that man through whom the stumbling block comes!

Matthew 18:7 Notes:

- What prompted this warning? It is clearly a response to the statement in v6, which emphasized Jesus deep love and concern for little ones.
- This warning is directed toward **anyone** who might cause a little one to stumble—it is directed at the person who might become a stumbling block.
- The word for *man* is anthrōpos (ἄνθρωπος), which means mankind or people, rather than the male gender in particular. Thus, men, women, and children can cause someone to stumble—the warning is not directed only to men.
- The word for *stumble* is skandalon (σκάνδαλον). The most likely term of the semantic range is: "any person or thing by which one is (entrapped) drawn into error or sin"
- This is a dire warning that I need to heed, because there are many ways to cause a person to sin … even sins that may not be excessive, such as gossip or causing someone to lust.
- Stumbling blocks are inevitable in this world, and the people who become a stumbling block will face some sort of severe punishment. Whatever it is, they will definitely wish they had not done so!

Matthew 18

8   "If your hand or your foot causes you to stumble, cut it off and throw it from you; it is better for you to enter life crippled or lame, than to have two hands or two feet and be cast into the eternal fire.

9   "If your eye causes you to stumble, pluck it out and throw it from you. It is better for you to enter life with one eye, than to have two eyes and be cast into the fiery hell.

10   "See that you do not despise one of these little ones, for I say to you that their angels in heaven continually see the face of My Father who is in heaven.

11   ["For the Son of Man has come to save that which was lost.]

Matthew 18:8–11 Notes:

- I tend to believe that Jesus' extreme statements were spoken as a sort of hyperbole to seize our attention. On the other hand, He is speaking **very** literally when He gives the reason: "It is better to enter life crippled or lame, than … be cast into eternal fire." Also "It is better for you to enter life with one eye than … be cast into the fiery hell."
- It seems clear that He is not telling us that such self-mutilation will atone for such sins, if we commit them. The point is "Don't do it!"
- V8 warns us not to stumble, whereas v7 warns people who would cause others to stumble. It is possible, however, that He is referring to the sin of causing someone to stumble.
- V10 has another reference to the "little ones," which is also found in vv6 and 14. They provide a clear linkage about the identity of the little ones, which is also the same as the straying sheep and the brother who is in sin.
- In v10, the word for *despise* is kataphroneō (καταφρονέω), which is often translated as "think little of," although it can carry the idea of disdain. In that light, it seems like Jesus may be telling us that there is a very significant person in your midst (i.e. a little one), because they have angels who stand in the presence of the Almighty God. Thus, we should esteem any and every believer as being very important—He sees how you treat or esteem them!
- This also implies that angels (guardians?) are assigned to every believer (i.e. v6 "who believes in Me …"). I had always heard that angels guarded children, but since I am a *little one,* it follows that an angel is watching over me—I hope to meet him someday.
- V11 has brackets around it, which are the translators' indication that this verse is not contained in the earliest manuscripts. It was probably added by an overly zealous scribe who thought it fit here. The verse does contain a truth, "The Son of Man has come to save that which was lost," because the verse is also found in Luke 19:10, where it is legit and spoken in a different context. It may be fitting here—it may be a principle that describes Jesus' ministry.

Matthew 18 – Ninety-nine Plus One

12 "What do you think? If any man has a hundred sheep, and one of them has gone astray, does he not leave the ninety-nine on the mountains and go and search for the one that is straying?

13 "If it turns out that he finds it, truly I say to you, he rejoices over it more than over the ninety-nine which have not gone astray.

14 "So it is not *the* will of your Father who is in heaven that one of these little ones perish.

Matthew 18:12–14 Notes:

- This is my original passage of interest. A similar parable is in Luke 15:4–7, but it was presented in a different context.
- The story of the parable is clear: something of great value was lost, someone earnestly desired it and searched for it, and there was great rejoicing and celebration when it was found. The same three themes of all three Luke 15 parables. It is about a *little one*.
- What prompted Jesus to tell the parable? How does it fit with the message that He wove in this contextual section? What is the linkage that connects the parable to the preceding and following paragraphs?
- One of the linkages is the term *little ones* in v14, the same term from vv6 and 10. We've learned that the little ones are believers in Christ, and the parable implies that they can and do stray, although the *man* deeply desires their return.
- Jesus' words continue into v15, without any transition, or pause. It seems that vv15–18, which talk about restoring a brother who is in sin, are an explanation of the parable. From it, we can surmise that the lost sheep is actually a believer who has strayed into sin (per v15). In this context, the lost sheep does not

represent an unbeliever and the searching efforts of the man do not seem to represent evangelism.

- The point of the parable is that Jesus wants all of His children to be free from sin, and He will search to rescue them.
- What is meant by the word *perish* in v14? It is in reference to these little ones, whom we've determined are straying believers. In what way would they perish? Physically? Spiritually? Other? When we combine it with the concept that a little one is a brother in sin (v15)—*I need to give this continued thought!*

Matthew 18 – Discipline and Prayer

15 "If your brother sins, go and show him his fault in private; if he listens to you, you have won your brother.
16 "But if he does not listen to you, take one or two more with you, so that BY THE MOUTH OF TWO OR THREE WITNESSES EVERY FACT MAY BE CONFIRMED.
17 "If he refuses to listen to them, tell it to the church; and if he refuses to listen even to the church, let him be to you as a Gentile and a tax collector.
18 "Truly I say to you, whatever you bind on earth shall have been bound in heaven; and whatever you loose on earth shall have been loosed in heaven.

Matthew 18:15–18 Notes:
- What prompted Jesus to begin talking about a brother who sins? I believe the idea of a sinning brother has been woven through this message since v6, when He spoke of stumbling. In other words, the idea of a brother stumbling, is in the same vein of causing a brother to stumble (i.e. sin), which is in the same vein as His warning not to stumble, which is allegorized by a straying sheep. He now continues with His message very literally, as restoring a brother who sins.
- It becomes very clear in vv15–17, that the sinning brother is a believer in Jesus, a little one, represented by the straying sheep.

313

- Jesus told the disciples how to restore someone, in a tender and loving way, allowing him or her to save face and to keep the church from public disgrace. First meet privately and discuss the sin, *encouraging* him or her to repent. "If he listens to you, you have won your brother." It is in listening to you that I am inferring the need to repent—it is certainly more than giving ear to the concerned person. From what I can tell, it looks like the matter does not need to go any farther if the person repents. Neither the church nor others need to be informed.

- The second part of the restoration process only occurs if the person does not listen. When that happens, the person is to meet with the sinning brother with two or three others. The purpose is to "act as witnesses and confirm the facts," but there is apparently the intent of convincing the brother to repent, because v17 again speaks of *refusing to listen*.

- The third part of the restoration process only occurs if the person does not listen—the matter is to be told to the church. Once again, there is a third opportunity for the person to listen (i.e. repent) and remain in the church.

- There are actually three attempts to restore the sinning brother. It seems that the section-heading in my Bible "Discipline and Prayer," missed Jesus' tender, loving attempts to restore the brother. The heading infers that this is a process of discipline, whereas it is characterized by loving restoration.

- The discipline aspect is invoked only after three attempts have been made to restore the brother.

- The discipline that is handed down is a matter of shunning the individual—not allowing them to be a part of the community of believers. To some, this may seem harsh, but the objective is to maintain the purity and reputation of the church. I gathered this from Paul's writings, in 1 Corinthians 5:9–13.

- Jesus did not say that this discipline need be permanent—we do not need to enact the discipline as if it is permanent. If the person repents, then the church should forgive and receive him or her back into the body. This comes from 2 Corinthians 2:5–11.

- When v18 is read within the context of v17 ("let him be to you as a Gentile and a tax collector"), it appears that heaven (i.e. the head of the church in heaven?), is honoring and supporting the discipline decision that was made within the church on earth, both binding the punishment on the brother and loosening it as the church on earth agrees. Something or Someone that we cannot see, behind the supernatural spiritual veil, is supporting the decisions of the church.

Matthew 18:19-20

19 "Again I say to you, that if two of you agree on earth about anything that they may ask, it shall be done for them by My Father who is in heaven.
20 "For where two or three have gathered together in My name, I am there in their midst."

Matthew 18:19–20 Notes:
- V19 is clearly a continuation of Jesus' teaching in v18, since it begins with "Again I say to you ..."
- V19 is clearly an affirmation of His words in v18, teaching that if "you"—i.e. the church—agree on earth about anything they may ask, it shall be done for them by My Father who is in heaven." When this verse is considered in its context, it would be consistent to say that the purpose of their asking is regarding the discipline of a sinning brother. It would be inconsistent with the context to suggest that Jesus is telling them they can have whatever they desire, such as a new automobile or the wealth of the world.
- The implications are the same for v20—they should be understood in the context of church discipline. When the church gathers together and agrees on a decision, "I am there in their midst."
- What does He mean by "I am there in their midst?" This statement could be taken in two ways: 1) That Jesus is in their

midst, guiding them as they make the decision or 2) that He is supporting them from the spiritual realm, which is heaven (v18).

Matthew 18 – Forgiveness

21   Then Peter came and said to Him, "Lord, how often shall my brother sin against me and I forgive him? Up to seven times?"

22   Jesus *said to him, "I do not say to you, up to seven times, but up to seventy times seven.

Matthew 18:21–22 Notes:

- Why did Peter ask this question about his brother sinning *against him*? Was the preceding section only about a sin against another person or was it about a brother sinning, in general? One possible reason for his question is because later manuscripts have additional text in v15. Rather than simply saying "If your brother sins," the text was changed to say "If your brother sins *against you.*"
- The reason Peter asked this question confirms that Jesus message in the previous paragraphs is about a brother sinning—all the way from a little one stumbling, through v17.
- Then how do we know how to interpret the passage and the parable of the unforgiving slave (vv23–34)? I really don't think it poses a conflict or contradiction. The teaching can be applied in either case, for the most part.
- What did Jesus mean by "seventy times seven?" It seems like He's teaching us to not count offenses—we should **always** forgive when someone sins against us. It should be our way and lifestyle as followers of Christ.
- The requirement of forgiving others is the reason for the following parable of the unforgiving slave.
- Does it make a difference in our response that Jesus said, "And if he sins against you seven times a day, and returns to you seven

times, saying, '**I repent**,' forgive him." (Luke 17:4)? I think it means that we should still forgive willingly, but it implies that repentance is an integral part of the forgiveness equation.

Matthew 18:23–35

23   "For this reason the kingdom of heaven may be compared to a king who wished to settle accounts with his slaves.

:

34   "And his lord, moved with anger, handed him over to the torturers until he should repay all that was owed him.

35   "My heavenly Father will also do the same to you, if each of you does not forgive his brother from your heart."

Matthew 18:23–35 Notes:

- Jesus responded to Peter's question with this parable of the unforgiving slave. The point of the parable is clearly that we must forgive and are expected to do so.
- We learn that the offenses of others toward us are miniscule, when compared to our offenses against God. We **must** forgive others if we want to be forgiven!
- Jesus made it very clear that our forgiveness must be more than just phrasing the words, "I forgive you." We must forgive **from the heart.** These are difficult words, but He emphasized the point even more by saying, "My heavenly Father **will also do the same to you …**"
- It's tempting to dismiss this fearsome teaching by saying that all of our sins will be forgiven through our faith. But we must ask why Jesus would give this warning when He already understands that. It's a warning that I will take to heart and learn to practice.

- We learn from Hebrews 10:31 that it's a terrifying thing to fall into the hands of the living God. It's best that we heed Jesus' warning, rather than test the rules of forgiveness by living unforgiving lives.

Summary

During your study, you have undoubtedly encountered many facts and items of interest—some you may have already known, while others may have been new to you. Some of your learning may have been through connecting the dots between things that you already knew, which can add great insight and significance to simple facts. Regardless of how much you've learned or the richness of it, you will find that your learning will be lost unless you articulate and write it.

Articulating your understanding is a very important phase of study. Your learning will become crystalized in your mind as you review your journey and transfer the experience into writing. You will then be able to review the information later and share it with others.

As you store the final notes from your study, be sure to save your printed contextual section, along with all of your notes and scribblings. You may want to place your articulation notes immediately after your printed contextual section, followed by any other notes or articles that were meaningful in your study. Whether you are saving your notes in hard copy or in electronic form, it is convenient to save them in a folder that is named for your study, such as "The Lost Sheep of Matthew 18."

Since you have articulated your learning, you should be equipped to engage in a healthy discussion about the passage with other people. Perhaps you can even teach the passage if you give it some more thought!

21
Onward!

We've been through a lot together ...

I am honored that you have given your time and attention to the concepts of this book. As closing words, I remind you of my opening words in the preface, "Reading this book and learning its principles will not help you improve your life unless you actually engage in Bible study." So do it for the glory of God and prepare yourself to joyfully meet Him on that great day to come!

May the Lord richly bless you!

Teach a boy to fish and he will eat for a lifetime;

Teach a believer to study God's Word and ...

He will be like a tree firmly planted by streams of water,
Which yields its fruit in its season
And its leaf does not wither;
And in whatever he does, he prospers.
Psalm 1:3

Appendix A
Progressive Revelation Examples

The following table contains texts of Scripture that illustrate the concept of Progressive Revelation. Notice how some of the passages seem to be obscure and not in the context of a prophetic message, but when they are understood together, they progressively form a picture of God's Anointed One.

Reference	Scripture Text	Notes
Gen 3:15	And I will put enmity between you and the woman, and between your seed and her seed; He shall bruise you on the head, and you shall bruise him on the heel.	This verse contains the first hint about the Messiah, although it can most easily be seen in retrospect.
Gen 12:3	And I will bless those who bless you, and the one who curses you I will curse and in you all the families of the earth will be blessed.	God's promise of a son to Abram
Exo 12:46	It is to be eaten in a single house; you are not to bring forth any of the flesh outside of the house, nor are you to break any bone of it.	Moses' instructions about the Passover lamb which foretold the coming Messiah (see John 19:36)

Deut 18:15	The LORD your God will raise up for you a prophet like me from among you, from your countrymen, you shall listen to him.	Moses foretold about a great prophet who would be an Israelite.
Isa 9:6	For a child will be born to us, a son will be given to us; and the government will rest on His shoulders; and His name will be called Wonderful Counselor, Mighty God, Eternal Father, Prince of Peace.	Isaiah's very enlightening prophecy about the essence of the coming Messiah.
Psa 110:1	The LORD says to my Lord: "Sit at My right hand until I make Your enemies a footstool for Your feet."	David's revelation that the Messiah, who would be his descendant, is greater than he. (Ref Matt 22:44)
Isa 53:5	But He was pierced through for our trans-gressions, He was crushed for our iniquities; the chastening for our well-being fell upon Him, and by His scourging we are healed.	Isaiah's prophecy that part of the Messiah's work would be to bear our punishment so we could be healed.

Isa 61:1-2a	The Spirit of the Lord GOD is upon me, because the LORD has anointed me to bring good news to the afflicted; He has sent me to bind up the brokenhearted, to proclaim liberty to captives and freedom to prisoners; to proclaim the favorable year of the LORD	Isaiah's prophecy that Jesus fulfilled in Luke 4:17-19 (see below)
Mic 5:2	But as for you, Bethlehem Ephrathah, too little to be among the clans of Judah, from you One will go forth for Me to be ruler in Israel. His goings forth are from long ago, from the days of eternity.	Micah's prophecy that the Messiah would come from Bethleham.
Zech 12:10	I will pour out on the house of David and on the inhabitants of Jerusalem, the Spirit of grace and of supplication, so that they will look on Me whom they have pierced; and they will mourn for Him, as one mourns for an only son, and they will weep bitterly over Him like the bitter weeping over a firstborn.	Zechariah's prophecy, indicating that God, Himself, was the one who was pierced

Matt 16:15-17	He said to them, "But who do you say that I am?" Simon Peter answered, "You are the Christ, the Son of the living God." And Jesus said to him, "Blessed are you, Simon Barjona, because flesh and blood did not reveal this to you, but My Father who is in heaven."	Jesus affirmed that His Father in heaven revealed that He is the Christ.
Luke 4:17-19	And the book of the prophet Isaiah was handed to Him. And He opened the book and found the place where it was written, "THE SPIRIT OF THE LORD IS UPON ME, BECAUSE HE ANOINTED ME TO PREACH THE GOSPEL TO THE POOR. HE HAS SENT ME TO PROCLAIM RELEASE TO THE CAPTIVES, AND RECOVERY OF SIGHT TO THE BLIND, TO SET FREE THOSE WHO ARE OPPRESSED, TO PROCLAIM THE FAVORABLE YEAR OF THE LORD."	Jesus confirmed that the prophecy from Isaiah 61:1-2a referred to Himself, as recorded in Luke 41:21 "And He began to say to them, 'Today this Scripture has been fulfilled in your hearing.'"
John 1:41	He found first his own brother Simon and said to him, "We have found the Messiah" (which translated means Christ).	Andrew's testimony that Jesus is the Messiah.

John 19:36	For these things came to pass to fulfill the Scripture, "NOT A BONE OF HIM SHALL BE BROKEN."	John indicates that the Passover lamb was a foreshadow of the Christ—specifically Jesus.
Acts 2:36	Therefore let all the house of Israel know for certain that God has made Him both Lord and Christ—this Jesus whom you crucified.	Peter's proclamation to the crowds on the day of Pentecost.

Table 18—Examples of Progressive Revelation

Appendix B
Common Idioms in the Bible

"Able," when applied to God or Christ, denotes both *willingness* and *ability*. Romans 4:21, 11:23, 14:4, 16:25, Hebrews 2:18
"All" often denotes the greater part. 1 Corinthians 8:1
"All" often means the greatest degree or quality of that to which it is applied. 1 Corinthians 13:2, 2 Timothy 1:15, James 1:2
"All" signifies some of every kind. Matthew 4:23, Acts 10:12
"Doctrine" or **"Teaching"** (διδαχή, *didachee*) refers to the content that is taught; **but it is *also* used idiomatically for the discourse in which it is taught**, having to do with the *style* of teaching; the *manner* as well as the *content*. See Matthew 7:28, 29. **Mark 4:2** "And He was teaching them many things in parables, and was saying to them in His *teaching*,": *i.e.*, his teaching or discourse. Also, Mark 11:18, 12:38. **Acts 2:42** "They were continually devoting themselves to the apostles' *teaching* and to fellowship, to the breaking of bread and to prayer." **1 Corinthians 14:26** "... each one has a psalm, has a *teaching*, etc.": *i.e.*, a discourse to give.
"To eat or drink" As the Hebrews used the nouns *meat* and *drink* of knowledge, so they naturally used the verbs *eating* and *drinking* to denote the operation of the mind in receiving, understanding, and applying doctrine or instruction of any kind, as we speak of "digesting" what is said, or of "inwardly digesting" it. It thus marks a very intimate and real partaking of the benefits of that which we receive through our minds.

Jeremiah 15:16 "Your words were found *and* I ate them," The rest of the verse explains the figure.

Ezekiel 3:1 "... Son of man, *eat* what you find; *eat* this scroll, and go, speak to the house of Israel.": *i.e.*, consider it, and get the contents of this roll by heart, and then go and speak it to the house of Israel, as is clear from verse 4: "Speak with my words unto them."

1 Corinthians 12:13 "... and we were all made to *drink* of one Spirit.": *i.e.*, receive. Compare Luke 13:15.

"**Not to be**" or "**not**" is a Hebraism for *to be wretched* and *vile, to be nothing*; while on the other hand, "**To be**" or "**are**" means to be in high esteem, or of great value

2 Samuel 19:6 (7) "... princes and servants are *nothing* to you"

1 Corinthians 1:28 "... and the base things of the world and the despised God has chosen, the things that are *not*, so that He may nullify the things that *are*,"

"**To permit**," *i.e.*, if God so orders it, and gives the needed grace and strength.

Hebrews 6:3: "And this we will do, if God permits.":

"**To seek**," *i.e.*, they put them in the first place, and are over-anxious, with excessive anxiety.

Matthew 6:32 "For the Gentiles eagerly seek all these things;"

Luke 12:30 "For all these things the nations of the world eagerly seek;"

"**To touch**"—to hurt or to do any harm to.

Genesis 26:29, Ruth 2:9, Job 1:11, Job 2:5, Psalm 105:15, Zechariah 2:8, Hebrews 11:28, 1 John 5:18

"**To *face* or *meet* another**" is used for making war with him, or of meeting him in battle.

2 Kings 14:8, 11; 23:29, etc.

"**To walk**" is used to describe a person's lifestyle and character.

Genesis 17:1, 5:24, 6:9, 17:1, Exodus 16:4, Leviticus 18:3, 26:3, Deuteronomy 5:33, 19:9, Judges 2:17, 1 Kings 6:12, 8:23, Psalm 1:1,

26:1, 119:35, Romans 6:4, 8:4, 1 Corinthians 3:3, 2 Corinthians 4:2, 5:7, Ephesians 2:10, 5:8, etc.
"To hear" is used of understanding and obeying. John 8:47, Luke 8:15
"To eat and drink" is a Hebraism used not merely for chewing food or swallowing any liquid, but for good living and normal life; Matthew 11:18, 19, Luke 7:33, 34, 17:27, 28
"To do" for to bring to pass, do a very great deal, do all. Psalm 37:5, Daniel 9:19 (*i.e. "take action"*)
"To work" is used of seeking to gain salvation by human merit. Romans 4:4, 5, as opposed to grace (chap. 11:6).
"To give account" means not simply to render a mere account, but to suffer all the consequences of unrighteousness. Matthew 12:36, Luke 16:2, Romans 3:19, Hebrews 13:17, 1 Peter 4:5
"To hide one's face"—to ignore, overlook, or pay no attention to someone or something Deuteronomy 31:17-18; 33:20, Job 13:20, 24, Psalm 13:1, 27:9, 44:24, 102:2, Isiah 8:17, Micah 3:4
"To hide one's eyes"—to ignore, overlook, or pay no attention to someone or something Isaiah 1:15, Ezekiel 22:26
"To look" or **"to see"** is often used (*a*) implying the *delight* or *pleasure* felt by the beholder (whether it be sinful or innocent): Psalm 22:17 (18); 35:21; 59:10 (11), Matthew 5:28 (*b*) Sometimes also as implying *sorrow and grief:* Genesis 21:16; 44:34. John 19:37 (compare Zechariah 12:10–14, Revelation 1:7). (*c*) And sometimes implying *attention and provision:* Matthew 7:5, 1 Corinthians 10:12 (where the figure is well translated "take heed," as it is also in Colossians 4:17).
"To hear" The verb ἀκούειν (*akouein*), *to hear*, is used

idiomatically, not only to hear the voice of the person speaking, but to *understand, to receive, to believe*, etc., what is said, having regard, not to the speaker, but to the subject-matter.

John 8:43 "Why do you not understand what I am saying? *It is* because you cannot **hear** My word."

John 9:27 "He answered them, 'I told you already and you did not **listen**; why do you want to **hear** it again? You do not want to become His disciples too, do you?'" *In the latter clause it is used in its ordinary sense; in the former idiomatically.*

Galatians 4:21 "Tell me, you who want to be under law, do you not **listen** (*i.e.*, understand) to the law?"

"**Called**." *To be called* is used of being *acknowledged, accounted*, or simply of *being*.

1 John 3:1 "See how great a love the Father has bestowed on us, that we would be **called** children of God;"

"**Living**" was used by the Hebrews to express the *excellency* of the thing to which it is applied.

John 4:10, 11 "Living water."

Acts 7:38 "Living oracles."

Hebrews 10:20 "Living way."

1 Peter 2:4, 5 "Living stones."

Revelation 7:17 "Living fountains."

"**To make the hand heavy**"—severe chastisement
1 Samuel 5:6, Job 23:2, Psalm 32:4

"**To put forth the hand**"—to inflict punishment
Exodus 9:15, 1 Samuel 22:17, Job 1:11, Psalm 55:20, 125:3, 138:7

"**Riches**" denotes not merely money, but an *abundance* of that to which it is applied; as our English word "wealth" is used of things other than money.

Romans 2:4 "Or do you think lightly of the **riches** (i.e. the greatness) of His kindness and tolerance and patience, not knowing that the kindness of God leads you to repentance?" *i.e.*, His abounding goodness, or wealth of goodness.

Ephesians 1:7 "Him we have redemption through His blood, the forgiveness of our trespasses, according to the **riches** (*i.e.*, the great abundance or wealth) of His grace."

Ephesians 3:8 "... to preach to the Gentiles the unfathomable **riches** of Christ," (*i.e.*, wealth or greatness)

Colossians 1:27 "... what is the **riches** of the glory of this mystery ..." (*i.e.*, the great abundance)

"**To sanctify**" often means to make *ceremonially clean: i.e.*, to cleanse a thing from those defilements which made it unfit for sacred uses. Hence, it means simply *to set apart, fit*, or *prepare* for a particular purpose.

1 Corinthians 7:14 "For the unbelieving husband is **sanctified** through his wife, and the unbelieving wife is sanctified through her believing husband ..." (*The presence of a believing husband or wife in a family is able to 'set apart' their children to God*)

1 Peter 3:15 "but **sanctify** Christ as Lord in your hearts ..."

How can we "sanctify God," as in, except by setting Him high above and apart from every other object of respect and veneration?

The word "**son of**" or "**children of**" means "*the essence of*" or "*the nature of*". It is an idiomatic usage and not according to Greek usage. It does not necessarily refer to a person's immediate offspring, since the Scriptures often refer to a grandson or many generations hence as a *son*.

"**Son of death**"—"He must surely die" (i.e. he is or will be the essence of death... i.e. dead)

Recall King David's response to Nathan's allegory? The Hebrew reads, "the man ... is a **son of death**."—2 Samuel 12:1

See also: 1 Samuel 20:31, 26:16, and Psalm 102:20 (21) (*the underlying Hebrew is "son(s) of death"*

"**Son of God**"—Matthew 8:29: "What business do we have with each other, **Son of God**?" *Jesus is the essence of God!*

"**Son of the living God**"—Matthew 16:16: "Simon Peter answered, 'You are the Christ, the **Son of the living God**.'" *Jesus is the essence* *of the living God!*

"Son of hell" Matthew 23:15—the essence or nature of hell …

"Sons of the evil one" Matthew 13:38—the nature of the evil one (i.e. the devil)

"Son of the devil"—the nature of the devil

Acts 13:10

"Sons of disobedience"

Ephesians 2:2, 5:6

This is very much stronger than the mere tame expression disobedient children. It means that they pertain to and belong to Satan in a special manner; are those in whom he works.

 "Sons of wrath"—those deserving of God's wrath

Ephesians 2:3

"The son of perdition"—one who will suffer eternal damnation.

John 17:12

"Sons of light" or **"Children of light"**—*i.e. Children of God*

Luke 16:8, John 12:36. 1 Thess. 5:5. Ephesians 5:8

"Children of the devil" (1 John 3:10. Acts 13:10).

"Children of this age" *i.e., men who are characterized by living for this present age or life.*

Luke 20:34

"Sons of the resurrection" *i.e. those who will be raised from the dead to life.*

Luke 20:36

The word **"son"** is not necessarily a reference to a person's immediate offspring, since the Scriptures often refer to a grandson or many generations hence as a *son*. Once again, this is an idiomatic usage.

Exodus 1:7 "But the **sons of Israel** were fruitful and increased greatly, and multiplied"—*These people were the 'descendants' of Israel' (i.e. Jacob), who lived hundreds of years after him, yet they're called sons.*

2 Samuel 19:24—Mephibosheth is called the "son of Saul." Recall

that he was Saul's grandson. **Numbers 18:21**—the "sons of Levi"—actually his descendants, since Levi generations earlier   **Matthew 1:1** "Jesus the Messiah, the *son of David*, the *son of Abraham* ..."
"**To spare with the eyes**"—to have mercy   Ezekiel 20:17
"**To spread out the hand**"—To pray or appeal   2 Chronicles 6:12-13; 29, Job 11:13, Psalm 88:9, Isaiah 1:15; 65:2
"**To withdraw the hand**"—to take away punishment   Joshua 8:26, 1 Samuel 14:19, Psalm 74:11

Table 19—Appendix B—Common Idioms in the Bible

Note: Much of the information in Table 19—Appendix B—Common Idioms in the Bible *was gleaned from* E.W. Bullinger's book, *Figures of Speech Used in the Bible.*

Appendix C
Guidance for Identifying Contextual Boundaries

General Guidelines for Identifying Contextual Boundaries
❖ **Do not rely on chapter divisions as indicator of contextual boundaries:**
Example: John 16:1 "These things I have spoken to you so that you may be kept from stumbling."

John 16:1 is clearly a continuation of Jesus' words from the previous chapters, so it could result in erroneous interpretations to assume that this verse begins a new contextual section.

Example: 1 Corinthians 8:1–11:1 are a *contextual section.* This means that 1 Corinthians 9:1 and 10:1 cannot be contextual boundaries.

❖ **Do not rely on paragraph divisions as indicators of contextual boundaries:**
Example: The contextual section in 1 Corinthians 8:1–11:1 contains many paragraphs, but they are all part of the larger context and should not be viewed as contextual boundaries. It is quite common for a contextual section to contain multiple paragraphs.

Contextual Boundaries in Narrative Literature
Narrative literature is one of the easiest literary genres for finding the contextual boundaries. As the name suggests, narrative literature *narrates* stories. Old Testament, books that are predominately narrative in style include Genesis, Exodus, Numbers, Deuteronomy, Joshua, Judges, Ruth, 1 & 2 Samuel, 1 & 2 Kings, 1 & 2 Chronicles, Ezra, Nehemiah, and Esther. Narrative literature is also found in both the Major and Minor Prophets and a small part of Leviticus. New

Testament books that are predominately narrative in nature include Matthew, Mark, Luke, John, and Acts.

In narrative literature, a contextual boundary *might* be indicated by:

❖ **A change of location or scene**
Example: Matthew 19:1 "When Jesus had finished these words, He departed from Galilee and came into the region of Judea beyond the Jordan ..."

Notice that the location and scene changed, and the text indicates a clear shift in the conversation and dialog. This is a very clear indication of a change of context—i.e. a contextual boundary.

Example: "Now there was a man of the Pharisees, named Nicodemus, a ruler of the Jews; this man came to Jesus by night and said to Him, 'Rabbi, we know that You have come from God as a teacher...'"[112]

Notice that the scene changed and the flow of the narrative changed from public settings to the private dialog between Jesus and Nicodemus, which is a strong indication of a change of context—i.e. a contextual boundary.

But not always: Matthew 26:35-36 "Peter said to Him, 'Even if I have to die with You, I will not deny You.' All the disciples said the same thing too. Then Jesus came with them to a place called Gethsemane, and said to His disciples, 'Sit here while I go over there and pray.'"

Notice that the scene and location changed from "reclining at the table" (Matthew 26:20) to the place called Gethsemane, but, the

---

[112] John 3:1–2

mood and conversation seemed to continue, so this is probably not a change of context.

A similar occurrence of a change of location or scene is found in Matthew 13:36 "Then He left the crowds and went into the house. And His disciples came to Him and said, 'Explain to us the parable of the tares of the field.'"

Notice that the scene and location changed from telling parables by the sea. After telling the parables to the crowd, He went into the house and the disciples asked Him to explain one of the parables, so the conversation continued. So we cannot say that 13:36 is a contextual boundary, despite the change of location or scenery.

❖ **Change of Day or Time**
Example: Acts 2:1 "When the day of Pentecost had come, they were all together in one place."

Notice that the change to the "day of Pentecost" brings in a completely different context, which indicates a contextual boundary.

Example: Ezekiel 8:1 "It came about in the sixth year, on the fifth day of the sixth month, as I was sitting in my house with the elders of Judah sitting before me, that the hand of the Lord GOD fell on me there."

Notice that Ezekiel's mention of the new date introduces a new context.

But not always: Acts 20:30 "But on the next day, wishing to know for certain why he had been accused by the Jews, he released him and ordered the chief priests and all the Council to assemble, and brought Paul down and set him before them."

Notice that the text indicates a change of day, but the context is clearly a continuation from Paul's arrest on the previous day, which indicates that the flow of the context is continuing, and it would not be wise to consider Acts 20:30 as a contextual boundary.

❖ **Change of conversation participants may indicate a contextual boundary:**
Example: Matthew 10:1 "<u>Jesus summoned His twelve disciples</u> and gave them authority over unclean spirits, to cast them out, and to heal every kind of disease and every kind of sickness."

Chapter 9 of Matthew records some of Jesus' magnificent miracles of raising the dead, healing the sick, and casting out demons. There is no indication of a change of location or scenery, but the conversation shifts to Jesus summoning His twelve disciples and giving them instructions. This begins a flow that is very different from that of chapter 9 and clearly indicates a contextual boundary.

But not always: Matthew 20:20-21 "<u>Then the mother of the sons of Zebedee came to Jesus with her sons</u>, bowing down and making a request of Him. And He said to her, 'What do you wish?' She said to Him, 'Command that in Your kingdom these two sons of mine may sit one on Your right and one on Your left.'"

Notice that the flow of the conversation completely shifted from Jesus forewarning his disciples of His immanent death to a request from the mother of the sons of Zebedee. The dialog between Jesus and the three immediately followed His words about His death. Although the conversations are of a very different nature and the original topic is not resumed afterward, it is probably necessary to study the two conversations (i.e. Matthew 20:17–19 and 20:20–28) as part of the same context.

❖ **Be aware of parenthetical events or conversations:**
The Scriptures, like other excellent literature, record parenthetical events or thoughts within its stories and teaching (similar to parentheses in a sentence). Even though the parenthetical events or thoughts may take us to a different time, place, or conversation, we must be careful that we do not quickly judge them as a contextual boundary. They may simply be a story within a story or a subplot within the drama, and should be studied within their larger context.

Is it ever legitimate to study a parenthetical story or message on its own? Absolutely! But we must make sure we have first studied them within the larger context and looked to see if there might be some interplay between them.

Example: Matthew 9:18–26 records the story of Jesus raising the daughter of a synagogue official from the dead. But shortly after the story begins, we are presented with a *parenthetical* story of a woman who had been suffering from a hemorrhage for twelve years seeking healing from Jesus. Immediately after her healing, the larger story resumes, telling about Jesus raising the little girl from the dead. The story of the woman was recorded as a *parenthetical* event within the story of the raising of the little girl.

The point is that we must look for the overall flow of the context before assuming that we've encountered a contextual boundary. In the case of the ninth chapter of Matthew, the same context records many different stories—even parenthetical stories, but the overall theme of the contextual section is to relay Jesus' many miracles among the people.

❖ **A change of events may indicate a contextual boundary:**
Example: Exodus 3:1 "Now Moses was pasturing the flock of Jethro his father-in-law, the priest of Midian; and he led the flock to the west side of the wilderness and came to Horeb, the mountain of God."

Notice that this passage is part of the much larger narrative about Moses' calling to lead the nation of Israel out of Egypt. Nonetheless, it is a legitimate beginning contextual boundary and could be studied somewhat independently, as long as the larger context is considered in the process.

Example: Daniel 3:1 "Nebuchadnezzar the king made an image of gold, the height of which was sixty cubits and its width six cubits; he set it up on the plain of Dura in the province of Babylon."

It is tempting to rely on chapter divisions as indicators of contextual boundaries, but we should only consider it as a coincidence if a chapter division happens to coincide with a contextual boundary. This is the case with Daniel 3:1. The actual indicator of the contextual boundary is the very different scenario between the ending of chapter 2 and the beginning of chapter 3. It is because of this that we can safely conclude the Daniel 3:1 indicates a contextual boundary.

❖ **In the book of Judges, an ending contextual boundary is frequently indicated by a summary of a judge's work with a phrase that describes the land having rest or being undisturbed:**
Example: Judges 3:11 "Then the land had rest forty years. And Othniel the son of Kenaz died."

Example: Judges 3:20 "So Moab was subdued that day under the hand of Israel. And the land was undisturbed for eighty years."

Example: Judges 5:31 "Thus let all Your enemies perish, O LORD; But let those who love Him be like the rising of the sun in its might. And <u>the land was undisturbed</u> for forty years."

But not always: Judges 8:28 "So Midian was subdued before the sons of Israel, and they did not lift up their heads anymore. And <u>the land was undisturbed</u> for forty years in the days of Gideon."

Notice that Judges 8:28 may appear to be a contextual boundary, but the story of Gideon continues. Once again, we have an indication of a possible contextual boundary, but a change in the flow of the context is the factor that determines a boundary.

Contextual Boundaries in the Pentateuch

Contextual boundaries in the Pentateuch are generally the same as those in other genres, including a change of time, events, conversation participants, etc. The following contextual boundary indicator, however, is somewhat unique to the Pentateuch.

❖ *In the Pentateuch, an <u>ending</u> contextual boundary is sometimes indicated by a genealogy:*
   Example: Genesis 5:1–32 lists the genealogy of Adam through Noah's sons, indicating the *ending* contextual boundary of the section.

   Example: Genesis 10:1–32 lists the genealogy of Noah and his sons, indicating an *ending* contextual boundary of the section.

   Example: Exodus 6:14–27 lists the leaders of the tribes of Israel during the exodus from Egypt, indicating a contextual boundary.

Genealogies are not the only indicators of contextual boundaries in the Pentateuch! Be watchful for the other indicators that we've described.

Contextual Boundaries in Poetic and Wisdom Literature

❖ *In general, each Psalm can be viewed as a complete contextual section, although some seem to be closely linked together:*
Example: Psalm 1 and 2—these Psalms were linked in the Hebrew Bible
Example: Psalm 104 and 105

Although the contextual sections are different, it may be possible to gain some additional insights by comparing the Psalms for similarities.

❖ *We must consider that Psalms are abundant with prophecies, so they cannot be considered in isolation:*
Example: The following Psalms clearly contain prophecies of the Messiah and the writers of the New Testament confirm that Jesus fulfilled them:

New Testament	Psalm	Psalm Text
Matthew 13:35	78:2	"I will open my mouth in a parable; I will utter dark sayings of old..."
Luke 20:42	110:1	"The LORD says to my Lord: "Sit at My right hand until I make Your enemies a footstool for Your feet."
John 19:24	22:18	"They divide my garments among them, and for my clothing they cast lots."
Acts 4:11	118:22	"The stone which the builders rejected has become the chief corner stone."

Hebrews 1:8–9	45:6–7	"Your throne, O God, is forever and ever; a scepter of uprightness is the scepter of Your kingdom. You have loved righteousness and hated wickedness; therefore God, Your God, has anointed You With the oil of joy above Your fellows."

Since many of the Psalms are prophecies that are confirmed in the New Testament, it may be insightful to consider the New Testament passages as a secondary part of the contextual section.

❖ **The captions above certain Psalms relate them to events in the historical books:**
Example: Psalm 34 was written about the events in 1 Samuel 21:10-22:2
Example: Psalm 51 was written about the events in 2 Samuel 12:1-15
Example: Psalm 52 was written about the events in 1 Samuel 22:9
Example: Psalm 56 was written about the events in 1 Samuel 21:10-15
Example: Psalm 59 was written about the events in 1 Samuel 19:11

Although the captions in the Scriptures are not inspired, the tone of the above Psalms clearly relate to the associated events.

❖ **In the Psalms and Wisdom literature, a contextual boundary is usually indicated by a change in authorship.**
Example: The Psalms were authored by multiple individuals, including David, Moses, Asaph, the descendants of Korah, and Solomon

Example: The Proverbs were authored by Solomon, Agar, and Lemuel

Although the captions in the Scriptures are not inspired, in the case of contextual boundaries, it is probably safe to assume that we've encountered a change of context when a new author is introduced.

❖ **The book of Job is characterized by alternating speakers.**
   Example: Job 4:1 "Then Eliphaz the Temanite answered …"
   Job 6:1 "Then Job answered …"
   Job 8:1"Then Bildad the Shuhite answered …"
   Job 9:1 "Then Job answered …"
   Job 11:1 "Then Zophar the Naamathite answered …"

Although it may be reasonable to assume the existence of a contextual boundary, it is important to realize that the comments are usually a response to the previous speaker, so they must also be considered in light of the previous contextual section.

❖ **The presence of a new writer or speaker may indicate a contextual boundary:**
   Example: Proverbs 10:1"The proverbs of Solomon. A wise son makes a father glad, but a foolish son is a grief to his mother."

The introduction of "The proverbs of Solomon" is probably introducing a new set of proverbs that may be studied as a contextual section.

❖ **Contextual boundaries may be difficult to identify in Ecclesiastes and Proverbs due to the nature of Wisdom literature. It is helpful, however, to look for a change of subject or overall theme, which may indicate the existence of a new contextual section:**
   Example: Proverbs 8:1 "Does not wisdom call, and understanding lift up her voice?"

In the above example, the speaker changes from a father to the voice of Wisdom. Wisdom becomes the new speaker and although the nature of the subject is similar, it is likely that we have a change of context. Even though the change of speaker is obvious, the change of subject matter tenor is equally obvious, which may indicate a new contextual section.

❖ *It is usually legitimate to quote proverbs as stand-alone pearls of wisdom. But as you study the wisdom literature of the Bible carefully, you will find that much of it forms a beautiful tapestry of understanding when considered as a whole. You should, therefore, seek to find the common thread or themes in wisdom literature that will increase your overall understanding. Once again, this is a product of context!*

Contextual Boundaries in Epistles

❖ An epistle is simply a name for a personal letter. If you were to receive a long personal letter from a close friend, you would probably find that it addresses multiple subjects, each of which is mentioned within its own context. In the same way, the epistles of the Bible are written in a very logical and sequential style with multiple contexts. The best way to identify the contextual boundaries in an epistle is by becoming very familiar with it. But until you get to that point, you should be watchful for changes in theme and subject matter as you read the text.

❖ *In 1 Corinthians, Paul sometimes introduces a new context with the words, "Now concerning ..."*
Example: 1 Corinthians 7:1 "<u>Now concerning</u> the things about which you wrote, it is good for a man not to touch a woman."
Example: 1 Corinthians 8:1 "<u>Now concerning</u> things sacrificed to idols, we know that we all have knowledge. Knowledge makes arrogant, but love edifies."

Example: 1 Corinthians 12:1 "<u>Now concerning</u> spiritual gifts, brethren, I do not want you to be unaware."
Example: 1 Corinthians 16:1 "<u>Now concerning</u> the collection for the saints, as I directed the churches of Galatia, so do you also."

❖ *An indicator of a contextual boundary in Paul's epistles is sometimes indicated when a paragraph begins with "Finally".*
Example: Ephesians 6:10 "<u>Finally</u>, be strong in the Lord and in the strength of His might."
Example: Philippians 3:1 "<u>Finally</u>, my brethren, rejoice in the Lord. To write the same things again is no trouble to me ..."
Example: Philippians 4:8 "<u>Finally</u>, brethren, whatever is true, whatever is honorable, whatever is right ..."
Example: 1 Thessalonians 4:1 "<u>Finally</u> then, brethren, we request and exhort you in the Lord Jesus ..."

Contextual Boundaries in the Prophets
❖ *In the Prophetic books, contextual boundaries may be indicated by phases that indicate a new prophecy:*
Example: Isaiah 13:1 "<u>The oracle concerning Babylon</u> which Isaiah the son of Amoz saw."

A new contextual boundary is indicated by the pronouncement of an oracle.

Example: Jeremiah 30:1–2 "<u>The word which came to Jeremiah from the LORD</u>, saying, 'Thus says the LORD, the God of Israel, "Write all the words which I have spoken to you in a book."'"

A new contextual boundary is indicated by the pronouncement of the word from the Lord.

Example: Zechariah 7:1 "In the fourth year of King Darius, the word of <u>the LORD came to Zechariah</u> on the fourth day of the ninth month, which is Chislev."

A new contextual boundary is indicated by the declaration of a prophecy.

Example: Ezekiel 16:1 "<u>Then the word of the LORD came to me,</u> saying ..."

Once again, a new contextual boundary is indicated by the word of the Lord being given to a prophet.

But not always: Isaiah 7:10–11 "Then the LORD spoke again to Ahaz, saying, 'Ask a sign for yourself from the LORD your God; make it deep as Sheol or high as heaven.'"

The above verse is not actually a contextual boundary, since the passage is a continuation of the context that began in Isaiah 7:1. Remember—it's all about context, so make sure you include all of it but not more!

❖ ***The prophetic books contain a significant amount of narrative literature. The contextual boundary indicators are the same as in other narrative literature.***

Once again, these are indications that a contextual boundary may be present, so it is your responsibility to study the context before and after the statement to make sure.

Appendix D—Sample Questions

Questions for Clarifying Terminology

- Do I understand the meaning of every word or figure of speech as they are used in this passage?
- What is the meaning of this word or phrase?
  - Is it literal or a figure of speech?
  - How can we tell?
- What are the possible non-literal meanings of this word or figure of speech?
- Which usage seems most appropriate for this passage?
- What is the semantic range for this word?
- How would the meaning of the passage change if a different term was selected for this word from the semantic range?
- Which usage is most likely in the spirit of the context?
- Which usage is most consistent with other uses of the word in the Bible?
- How is this word used in other passages with similar teaching?
- How is this word used in other passages with different teachings?
- Is this word being used in a general sense or in a specific *Christianized* sense?
- In what way does the context reveal how this word should be understood?
- How is the *original* word used in other passages?
  - In this book
  - In this testament (i.e. Old Testament or New Testament)
  - In the entire Bible
  - In extra-Biblical literature
- If a word is interpreted differently than the norm, how would it affect the meaning or teaching of this passage?
- Should the words of this phrase be interpreted individually or together—perhaps as an idiom or figure of speech?

Questions for Weaving

- What prompted this statement, question, discourse, event, response, or action?
- Can I explain the events, words, or situation that prompted each statement in this paragraph?
- Why did he or she choose to open the subject this way?
- Are there repeated words, thoughts, or themes in this paragraph that are found in previous paragraphs?
- If so, do they give insight to the meaning of words or the intended meaning of the writer/speaker?
- What can you infer from the repeated words, thoughts, or themes?
- What is implied by the repetition?
- Do they reveal or reinforce a known teaching? Which teaching?
- Does the feeling, mood, or mindset from the previous paragraphs effect the dialog or events of this paragraph?
- How would I trace the flow of thoughts or events through this contextual section?
- What are the relationships or linkages between the thoughts within this paragraph and with other paragraphs?
- What was the purpose of the writer/speaker in taking us on this journey?
- What was the reason the writer/speaker used a particular conjunction (i.e. FANBOYS and friends)?
- How did it affect his or her message?
- Did this paragraph begin with a conjunction (i.e. FANBOYS and friends)? If so, did it expose a connection between paragraphs?
- Have I studied the paragraphs in their given order?
- Have I studied the paragraphs within the spirit of their context?

Questions for Exploring the Substance of a Passage

- Have I been faithful to ask questions about the direct facts that are stated in the text?
- Am I studying the Scriptures with an honest and good heart?
- Do I need to compare wording and sentence structure to that in another literal version of the Bible?
- What is the main point of this paragraph?
- What are the sub-points or lessons within the lesson? What can we learn from them?
- Have I been faithful to explore the main point of this paragraph along with the sub-points?
- Does the main point of this paragraph relate to another point or theme in the contextual section or in this book?
- Is something being inferred, implied, or intimated by this statement or question in the text? If so, how would I articulate it?
- Have I identified a logical progression of thought in the passage?
- If so, what is the beginning point (*Point A*) and what is the ending point (*Point B*)? What are the points in between?
- Does this statement contain a universal principle that I should record?
- Have I confidently answered all of my own questions? If not, what additional information do I need? Where do I need to search?
- Can we trust the words of the writer/speaker? (e.g. are the words of Job's friends truth?)
- How can I determine if my doubts are valid or not?
- Does this paragraph present multiple points of view (e.g. Jesus' and the Pharisees?)
- Am I able to articulate the different viewpoints and the reasoning behind them?
- What is the writer/speaker's intent in using this particular conjunction (i.e. FANBOYS & Friends)?

Questions for Exploring the Substance of a Passage—Cont'd

- Why did the writer/speaker use a list to make a point (e.g. Galatians 5:19-21 & 22-23)?
- Does the message make sense? Can I explain it to others?
- Does this paragraph reveal a paradox? What are the paradoxical perspectives?
- How can I determine if my own facts, terms, and logic are correct?
- How would I describe the significance of this passage?
- Is the message of the passage difficult to understand?
- Is the message of the passage difficult to accept?
- What was the writer/speaker assuming the reader already knew or understood when he or she made this statement?
- Have I adequately explored all of the *main* teachings, implications, and inferences of this passage?

Questions for Exploring My Conclusions

- Have I articulated my *intermediate* conclusions about what this passage is teaching?
- What are the conclusion(s) most clearly reflect **the entire** message of this passage?
- Do I have any doubts or reservations about my conclusions?
- If so, have I noted them and explained my reasoning?
- Are the principles that I've found universal or do they have contingencies?
- How would I articulate my conclusion and resulting understanding?
- Can I give a specific example or illustration of how this my interpretation would be followed?
- Can I give a specific example or illustration of someone not following this interpretation?
- Can I articulate exactly how I reached this conclusion from the Scriptures?
- What are the *smaller* lessons taught in this passage?
- Have I accounted for how they should affect my understanding of the Scriptures?
- How would I describe the specific details of my interpretation of this passage? (*Note: if you cannot articulate it, then you may not truly understand it!*)
- Were your conclusions influenced by your experience, emotions, or assumptions, rather than by the message of the passage? (*Remember the honest and good heart!*)
- How will this interpretation influence your understanding of the overall teaching of the Scriptures?
- What specific doctrines or teachings of the Bible can be affected or influenced by the interpretation of this passage?
- Were my conclusions softened or tempered or diluted because of my preference to hold to a more comfortable or familiar interpretation?
- How might I reconcile the paradoxical issues raised by this conclusion?

Questions for Applying my Learning

- What is the message that I need to learn from this passage?
- How does this teaching affect my life and circumstances?
- Is my attitude and behavior in alignment with this teaching?
- If not, what adjustments should I make?
- Do I need to seek reconciliation with someone?
- Do I need to ask forgiveness of someone?
- Do I need to make restitution to someone?
- Do I need to change my way of life?
- What are the implications of this teaching?
- How does this teaching differ from my culture and the teaching of the world?
- Should I tolerate the differences or do I need to act?
- Can I formulate a Scriptural response and take a stand?
- How can I explain this teaching to others?
- How can I explain my resulting Scriptural lifestyle to those who do not believe?
- Have I adequately sought the Spirit's leading with my understanding and subsequent response?
- Have I *made notes about* how I will understand, reject, dismiss, embrace, or flag this teaching?
- Is my intended application consistent with the teaching of Jesus and the fruit of the Spirit (Galatians 5:22-23)?
- How will my new understanding affect my actions? (*Give specific examples*)
- How will my new understanding affect my beliefs? (*Give specific examples*)
- What are the implications of holding this belief and lifestyle?
- What would be the likely responses of others if I take this action?
- Can I give a specific example of someone who has followed such an interpretation?
- Do I feel this interpretation aligns with the whole, combined teaching of Scripture?

Questions for Validating My Questions

- Are my questions focusing on the portions of this text that are difficult or pivotal (i.e. the pressure points)?
- Are my questions focusing on the aspects of the text of which I am uncertain?
- Have I thoroughly explored the obvious message of this passage?
- Are my questions and exploration focusing on the main point(s) of the writer/speaker or on the peripheral?
- Are my questions exploring points of conflict or difficulty?
  - Paradoxical points ("God is love" versus "Jacob I loved, but Esau I hated")
  - Unexplained responses, events, or questions (e.g. Jesus' response to Philip in John 12:23)
  - Difficult answers
- Have I been faithful to ask questions that probe deeper? (i.e. questions that are spawned by other questions)
- Am I honestly exploring this passage as the author intended?
- Am I truly allowing it to speak for itself or am I making it fit my assumptions and the things I already believe?
- Am I studying to learn or am I studying to prove something?
- Does this question represent an objective, unbiased perspective?
- Does this question assume an answer to another question that should have been asked first?
- Does this question demonstrate logical reasoning?
- Have I been faithful to ask questions about simple facts that are stated in the text?
- How does my question relate to the main thrust of the passage?
- Am I resistant to directly addressing the teaching of this passage?
- Should this question be flagged (i.e. put on hold) with the hope that it will be answered later in the context?
- What am I assuming when I asked this question?
- What other questions could I ask that would help clarify the

Appendix E
Researching a Word

We will use the **Blue Letter Bible**[113] web-site to illustrate the procedure for researching a word in its original language. Since our example *contextual section (Matthew 17:24–18:35)* contains some interesting words, **we will use Matthew 18:6 to illustrate the procedure**. Use a web-browser and follow as we demonstrate.

❖ From a web browser, navigate to: www.blueletterbible.org

Figure 18—Enter the web-site name in your browser

❖ Go to the "Search" option within the BlueLetterBible.org web site. As with all web sites, the look and feel may change over time, but the procedure for researching a word should remain generally the same. *Be flexible and operate on principles, rather than exact instructions.*

---

[113] The Blue Letter Bible website: www.BlueLetterBible.org ***Note:*** *All web-page images in Appendix E are from The Blue Letter Bible website.*

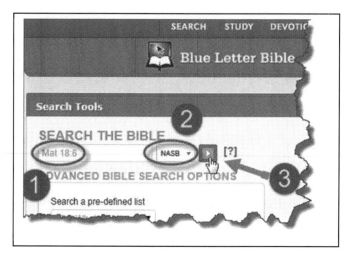

Figure 19- Enter your search information

In the *Search Tools* window, **we have selected the following options** (refer Figure 19).

1) **Matthew 18:6** as the verse to research. *It is also possible to select an entire chapter by not specifying a verse in this field.*

2) **NASB** as the Bible version. *Remember, we want to use a* <u>*literal*</u> *translation of the Bible, such as* **NASB, ESV, NKJV, or ASV.**

3) Press the "**Enter**" key or click the *right arrow* button to run the search.

❖ Refer to Figure 20 to see an example of how the Blue Letter Bible displays the results of the search. Notice that it lists our selected verse at the top and then displays the verses through the end of the chapter.

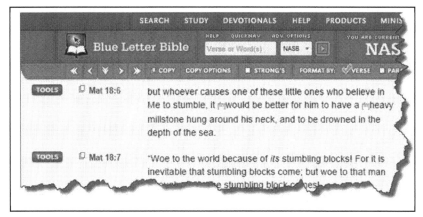

Figure 20—Search Results for Matthew 18:6 in the NASB

❖ Notice the "**TOOLS**" button to the left of each verse in Figure 21. Click on the TOOLS button ❶ that is beside "Mat 18:6", as indicated in Figure 21.

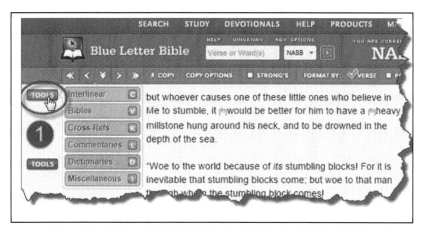

Figure 21—Click on the "TOOLS" button that is beside "Mat 18:6"

Clicking the TOOLS button results in an *Interlinear* display of the words, as shown in Figure 22 (*Notice that the "Interlinear" tab is automatically selected*). "Interlinear" simply means that the words of the original language are *interspersed*, line-by-line (i.e. linear), with the English words. *Take note of the other tabs across the top of this screen, as we will be referring to these later.*

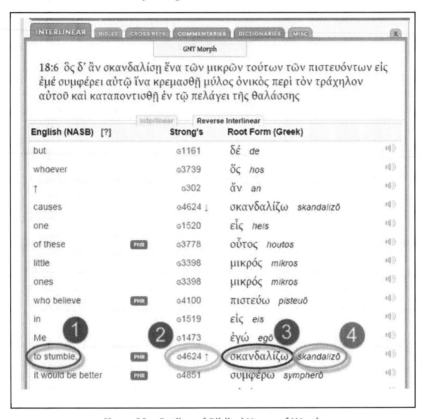

Figure 22—Outline of Biblical Usage of Words

Referring to the highlighted items in Figure 22, we will continue with our example passage and research the word *stumble* in this verse.

❶ Our English word of interest is displayed as: "*to stumble*".

❷ The **G4624** is the **Strong's number** that we introduced under the *Hardcopy Books* section of this chapter. Recall that Dr. Strong assigned a number to every unique word of the Bible. Since this is a Greek word, the number is prefixed with a "G". In similar manner, Hebrew words are prefixed with "H". We will be referring to this number in our next step.

❸ The actual Greek word, σκανδαλίζω, is displayed in Greek characters, **which is the word that we want to research.** To learn more about this word, continue with item 4 ...

❹ The English phonetic spelling of the word, *skandalizō,* is displayed to the right of the Greek word. Knowing this will help you pronounce the word when you discuss it with others.

  o Notice the little *speaker* icon on the right side... Click on it if you would like to hear an audible pronunciation of the word—Go ahead—try it!

❖ Now we are going to see the information that we've been seeking, which is the *Semantic Range* of the word *skandalizō.*

⇨ **Click on the "G3624" Strong's number as indicated by the ② in Figure 22.**

The Blue Letter Bible web site displays an Outline of the Biblical Usage of our word *skandalizō* as it was used during the era of the writing—**this is the Semantic Range!** Refer to Figure 23 and consider the possible meanings of the word. Once again, it is of great importance to understand words as they were used by the writers and speakers of the original texts, and here, we have found what we were seeking!

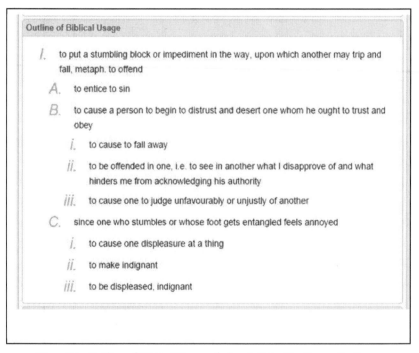

Outline of Biblical Usage

I.   to put a stumbling block or impediment in the way, upon which another may trip and fall, metaph. to offend

  A.   to entice to sin

  B.   to cause a person to begin to distrust and desert one whom he ought to trust and obey

    i.   to cause to fall away

    ii.   to be offended in one, i.e. to see in another what I disapprove of and what hinders me from acknowledging his authority

    iii.   to cause one to judge unfavourably or unjustly of another

  C.   since one who stumbles or whose foot gets entangled feels annoyed

    i.   to cause one displeasure at a thing

    ii.   to make indignant

    iii.   to be displeased, indignant

Figure 23—Outline of Biblical Usage of *skandalizō—The Semantic Range*

❖ Now that you have learned the possible meanings about your word, you should note make notes in your study journal, especially if you have found something unexpected. Keep in mind that we are *not* making our final determination about *which* meaning should be used—that will be determined as we spend time meditating on the passage in its context.

❖ **One final note**—this would be a good time to see how other literal Bible versions interpret the word. We began our study with the **NASB**, so let's take a look at how the **ESV, NKJV,** and **ASV** render the word. *You are only one click away from getting this information!* Recall that we suggested that you take note of the tabs in Figure 22. In order to see how other Bible versions rendered our word *skandalizō,* simply click on the "Bibles" tab as indicated in Figure 24.

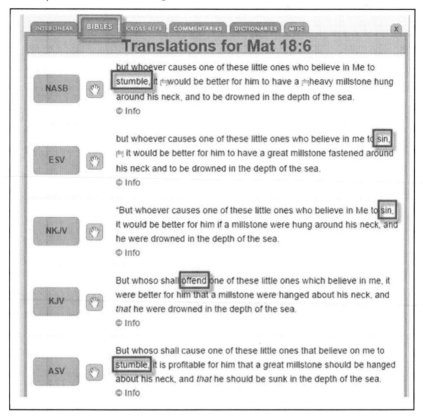

Figure 24—Bible Version Comparisons

You can make the display even more useful by moving the verses up or down so your desired versions will be adjacent to each other. To do this, simply click on the little *hand* icon beside the version name to *grab* it, and move it where you desire.

Notice that our word *skandalizō* is translated as *sin* and *offend* in other versions. What is the value of seeing how other versions rendered this word? The answer is that it allows us to see the interpretation decisions of various scholars, giving us insight into legitimate understandings of the word. Once again, this exercise is most meaningful when comparing *literal* Bible translations.

Appendix F
Juxtaposing Matthew 18:1–14

Matthew 18 New American Standard Bible (NASB)	Matthew 18 English Standard Version (ESV)
18 [1]At that [a]time the disciples came to Jesus and said,	**18** [1]At that time the disciples came to Jesus,
	saying,
"Who then is greatest in the kingdom of heaven?"	"Who is the greatest in the kingdom of heaven?"
[2]And He called a child to Himself and set him [b]before them,[3]	[2]And calling to him a child,
and said,	he put him in the midst of them [3]and said,
"Truly I say to you,	"Truly,
	I say to you,
	unless you turn and become like children,
unless you [c]are converted and become like children,	
you will not enter the kingdom of heaven.	you will never enter the kingdom of heaven.
[4]Whoever then humbles himself as this child,	[4]Whoever humbles himself like this child is the greatest in the kingdom of heaven.
he is the greatest in the	

kingdom of heaven. ⁵ And whoever receives one such child in My name receives Me; ⁶ but whoever causes one of these little ones who believe in Me to stumble, it [d]would be better for him to have a [e]heavy millstone hung around his neck, and to be drowned in the depth of the sea. **Stumbling Blocks** ⁷ "Woe to the world because of *its* stumbling blocks! For it is inevitable that stumbling blocks come; but woe to that man through whom the stumbling block comes! ⁸ "If your hand or your foot causes you to stumble, cut it off and throw it from you; it is better for you to enter life	⁵ "Whoever receives one such child in my name receives me, ⁶ but whoever causes one of these little ones who believe in me to sin, [a] it would be better for him to have a great millstone fastened around his neck and to be drowned in the depth of the sea. **Temptations to Sin** ⁷ "Woe to the world for temptations to sin! [b] For it is necessary that temptations come, but woe to the one by whom the temptation comes! ⁸ And if your hand or your foot causes you to sin, cut it off and throw it away. It is better for you to enter life crippled or lame than with two hands or two feet to be thrown into the eternal fire.

crippled or lame, than [f]to have two hands or two feet and be cast into the eternal fire. ⁹ If your eye causes you to stumble, pluck it out and throw it from you. It is better for you to enter life with one eye, than [g]to have two eyes and be cast into the [h]fiery hell.	⁹ And if your eye causes you to sin, tear it out and throw it away. It is better for you to enter life with one eye than with two eyes to be thrown into the hell[c] of fire.
¹⁰ "See that you do not despise one of these little ones, for I say to you that their angels in heaven continually see the face of My Father who is in heaven. **¹¹** [[i]For the Son of Man has come to save that which was lost.] **Ninety-nine Plus One** **¹²** "What do you think?	**The Parable of the Lost Sheep** **¹⁰** "See that you do not despise one of these little ones. For I tell you that in heaven their angels always see the face of my Father who is in heaven. [d] **¹²** What do you think? If a man has a hundred sheep, and one of them has gone

If any man has a hundred sheep, and one of them has gone astray, does he not leave the ninety-nine on the mountains and go and search for the one that is straying? [13] If it turns out that he finds it, truly I say to you, he rejoices over it more than over the ninety-nine which have not gone astray. [14] So it is not *the* will [i]of your Father who is in heaven that one of these little ones perish.	astray, does he not leave the ninety-nine on the mountains and go in search of the one that went astray? [13] And if he finds it, truly, I say to you, he rejoices over it more than over the ninety-nine that never went astray. [14] So it is not the will of my[e] Father who is in heaven that one of these little ones should perish.

Glossary

Allegory	A representation of an abstract or spiritual meaning through concrete or material forms; figurative treatment of one subject under the guise of another. (Dictionary.com)
Analogy Analogous	A similarity between like features of two things, on which a comparison may be based: "the analogy between the heart and a pump." (Dictionary.com)
Axiom	1. A self-evident truth that requires no proof. (Dictionary.com) 2. A universally accepted principle or rule. (Dictionary.com)
Autograph	A manuscript that was written by the original author—i.e. not a copy.
Bible	The message that was transmitted from God's Spirit, as He inspired His prophets and apostles to record it without error, eventually becoming the canonized books of the Old and New Testaments.
Big-6 Context	The set of circumstances in which a statement was made or an event took place. The Big-6 environmental contexts include the following environments: ❖ Historical ❖ Cultural/Social ❖ Geographical ❖ Political/Governmental ❖ Religious ❖ Military

Colloquial	Familiar conversational speech or writing, rather than formal.
Colloquialism	A common word or phrase that is characteristic of colloquial speech or writing.
Command	An order or directive to take a specific action. Compare to Principle and Exhortation.
Context	1. the parts of a written or spoken statement that precede or follow a specific word or passage, usually influencing its meaning or effect: "You have misinterpreted my remark because you took it out of context." (Dictionary.com) 2. the set of circumstances or facts that surround a particular event, situation, etc. (Dictionary.com)
Contextual Section	The text that lies between the beginning and ending contextual boundaries. Sometimes referred to as a *section*.
Convict	When a person is convinced in his or her heart or conscience of a truth or application (i.e. a change or new behavior)
Conviction	When a person is convinced of a certain interpretation or application of a Scripture passage.
Declarative Prophecy	A message from God that states or *declares* a truth. Compare to *predictive* prophecy, which foretells or *predicts* a future event.

Deity or Deities	Divine character or nature, especially that of the Supreme Being; divinity. (Dictionary.com) Deity can refer to the God of the Bible or to false gods or goddesses, such as idols or mythological beings. Most deities share the common characteristic of immortality.
Didactic	Words or a message intended for instruction; teaching.
Discourse	A formal discussion of a subject in speech or writing, as a dissertation, treatise, sermon, etc. (*noun*) (Dictionary.com)
Doctrine	Something that is taught; teachings collectively: *religious doctrine.* (Dictionary.com) A formalized concept or *teaching.*
Dual Fulfillment	Dual Fulfillment refers to the possibility that a single, predictive prophecy can be fulfilled in two separate and *apparently* unrelated events. For example, the prophecy of the *abomination of desolation* in Daniel 11:31 seems to have been fulfilled during the Inter-testamental period, but Jesus indicated a yet, future fulfillment of Daniel's prophecy in Matthew 24:15.
Eisegesis	An interpretation, especially of Scripture, that expresses the interpreter's own ideas, bias, or the like, rather than the meaning of the text. (Dictionary.com)
Ellipsis *abbreviated* as "..."	Ellipsis means "omission." When "..." is encountered in text, it means that some of the text has been omitted.

Epistle	A letter, especially a formal or didactic one; written communication. (Dictionary.com)
Exegesis	An interpretation style that seeks to allow the text to *lead out* or speak for itself. Compare to *eisegesis, which* interjects the interpreter's ideas or bias into the text.
Exhortation	A message that conveys urgent advice or recommendations. (*Compare to principle and command*)
Extra-Biblical	Information or content that is found outside of the Bible, usually in ancient documents, such as historical or religious texts.
Figure of Speech	A word or phrase that is used in a non-literal sense for the purpose of increasing emphasis.
General Revelation	The message from creation that leads mankind to the conscious awareness of the work and existence of the Creator. Compare to *Special Revelation*.
Heart	The component of the intellect that holds our values and affections, and determines our character. "The heart does not simply guide us, rather, the heart is actually who we are."

Hebrew Poetry	Poetry used by the ancient Hebrews is characterized by patterns of repeated or contrasting thought, rather than by the rhyme of modern Western poetry. "Hebrew poetry is artistic, concentrated language. It compresses a maximum of thought into a minimum of words. Content and need to be unpacked if it is to be appreciated and understood."[114]
Hyperbole	A figure of speech that intentionally exaggerates a point for the purpose of emphasizing its gravity.
HypoCat or Hypocatastasis	A figure of speech that compares two things, while explicitly identifying only one of them. It is the responsibility of the reader or listener to identify the unidentified object and discern the similarities.
Idiom	A language or dialect that is peculiar to a group of people, as compared to the languages or dialects of others.
Illumination	To enlighten with understanding or knowledge.
Implication	Something that is suggest without being explicitly stated.
Inerrant	Free from error; infallible. (Dictionary.com) "The original autographs of the Scriptures are inerrant."
Inerrantist	An individual who holds the Scriptures to be inerrant.
Infer	To draw a conclusion, as by reasoning. (Dictionary.com)

---

[114] (Bandstra, 1999)

Inference	A conclusion that is reached by reasoning.
Inspiration	The concept that "God breathed" His message into the hearts of certain men to record it exactly as He desired, resulting in the Holy Scriptures, which is our Bible.
Intertestamental Period	The historical period of approximately 400 years that began with the close of the book of Malachi until the opening of the New Testament.
Knowledge	1. Facts, truths, or principles, including *perceived* facts, truths, or principles, which are not necessarily true. 2. Acquaintance with facts, truths, or principles, as from study, investigation, or meditation.
Lexical	Pertaining to the words or vocabulary of a language, especially as distinguished from its grammatical and syntactical aspects.
Lexicon	1. A dictionary, esp one of an ancient language such as Greek or Hebrew 2. A list of terms relating to a particular subject 3. The vocabulary of a language or of an individual (Dictionary.com)
Literal (word)	The usage of a word in its primary, lexical meaning.
Literal (translation)	A version of the Bible that *attempts* to translate with word-for-word accuracy.
Logic	The intellectual process of reasoning or thinking about something.

Meditation	Continued or extended thought; reflection; contemplation. (Dictionary.com)
Metaphor	A figure of speech that represents one thing by another thing.
Metonymy	A figure of speech that uses one name or noun instead of another, having some sort of relationship between the two. For example, "The Crown" is often used to refer to the authority of a monarchy, and "The White House" is often used to refer to the president and administration. Metonymy exchanges two related nouns. (Also see Synecdoche)
Narrative Literature	Literature that provides and account of stories, events, experiences, or dialogues, as if the writer is narrating the account.
Papyrus (*plural: Papyri*)	A material on which to write, prepared from thin strips of the pith of this plant laid together, soaked, pressed, and dried, used by the ancient Egyptians, Greeks, and Romans. (Dictionary.com)
Parable	An illustration that *likens* one set of circumstances to another by the use of an extended figure of comparison.
Paradox	A statement or proposition that seems self-contradictory or absurd but in reality expresses a possible truth. (Dictionary.com) Religious truths are often expressed in paradox.
Passage	A section of Scripture, such as a phrase, verse, paragraph or chapter.

Personification	A figure by which things are represented or spoken of as persons; or, by which we attribute intelligence, by words or actions, to inanimate objects or abstract ideas … when anything is addressed as a person.[115]
Poetry	*See Hebrew Poetry*
Poetical Books	In the Old Testament, the books Job, Psalms, Proverbs, Ecclesiastes, and Song of Solomon, are categorized as the Poetical Books.
Predictive Prophesy	A message from God that foretells or *predicts* a future event. Compare to *declarative* prophecy, which states or *declares* a truth.
Pressure Point	A question or uncertainty in your own understanding that is revealed as you explore a passage.
Principle	A general and fundamental truth that may be used in deciding conduct or choice: "to adhere to principle." (Dictionary.com) A principle is generally universal in nature and abstract as compared to the rules that are based on it.

---

[115] (Bullinger, 2012—First Published in 1898)

Progressive Revelation	As the Scriptures were given by God throughout the centuries, new information and insights were revealed that shed light on His previous revelations. The newer revelations provide additional information about matters that were previously revealed, which enlarge the picture and our understanding. Thus the message was revealed in a gradual or progressive manner.
Proof Text	A passage that is extracted from its context and used to develop or prove a point that does not reflect the original intent of the writer or speaker. Synonymous with contextomy.
Proverb	A short, memorable, and often highly condensed saying embodying, esp with bold imagery, some commonplace fact or experience.[116]
Revelation	1. A message that is *revealed* by God. 2. The last book of the New Testament.
Rite	A religious observance, ceremony, or custom.
Sanctification	Being set apart, to be used for a specific purpose. Those who have faith in Christ have been set apart from the world to be used for God's purposes.

---

[116] (William Collins Sons & Co. Ltd, 1979, 1986, 1998, 2000, 2003, 2005, 2006, 2007, 2009, 2012)

Scriptures	The Bible: The message that was transmitted from God's Spirit, as He inspired His prophets and apostles to record it without error, eventually becoming the canonized books of the Old and New Testaments.
Section	The text that lies between the beginning and ending contextual boundaries. Also called a *contextual section*.
Simile	A figure of speech that compares objects or concepts. A simile is always denoted by a word that indicates a comparison, such as *like* or *as*.
Special Revelation	The message or *revelation* from God that was given through inspiration by His Spirit in the Scriptures or by messages from God through angels, dreams, visions, and prophecy. The Bible is the chief example of special revelation, while other special revelation includes the message to Moses through the burning bush and Jesus' revelation to Saul on the road to Damascus. Compare to *General Revelation*.
Synecdoche	A figure of speech that connects two ideas, by using a part of a concept, object, or person to refer to its entirety. Synecdoche exchanges two associated ideas. For example, an automobile is sometimes referred to as "wheels." (Also see Metonymy)

Synoptic Gospels	The first three gospel accounts in the New Testament, Matthew, Mark, and Luke. They are referred to as *synoptic* because they *look alike* or *similar,* in their content and style, whereas the fourth gospel, John, conveys a different feel and perspective.
Thread	A theme that recurs throughout the Bible or a literary work. For example, the concept of a Redeemer is a thread that weaves throughout the Bible, from Genesis to Revelation.
Understanding	The state of a person's heart after considering the truths of God and aligning his or her ways accordingly . Understanding should not be confused with knowledge, as understanding is much deeper than knowledge, which is generally cognizance of information. The Scriptures speak of understanding as agreeing with and being aligned with God's righteous declaration.
Wisdom	The intellectual process that compares information with existing information (knowledge) and values, resulting in understanding. If a person's information or knowledge are incorrect or not aligned with truth, then their resulting understanding will also become skewed.
Wisdom Literature	A literary genre that teaches about the ways of God, virtue, and prudence. The wisdom literature of the Bible has characteristics of other wisdom literature of the ancient near east.

Word of God—God's Word	The Bible: The message that was transmitted from God's Spirit, as He inspired His prophets and apostles to record it without error, eventually becoming the canonized books of the Old and New Testaments.
Worldview or World View	A comprehensive perspective of everything in life. A worldview includes a perspective of God, life, the origin of the cosmos and life, society, the material world, emotions, ethics, philosophy, and generally, anything that could shape their perspective of life and the world around them. A world view attempts to explain the condition and events of the world in a meaningful way. The validity of a worldview can be judged by its ability to truly explain the good, the bad, and the difficulties of all aspects of life.

Bibliography

Bandstra, B. L. (1999). *Reading the Old Testament.* Belmont: Wadsworth Publishing.

Biblica, Inc. (2011). *New International Version.* Nashville, Tennesee, USA: Harper Collins Christian Publishing.

Bullinger, E. W. (2012—First Published in 1898). *Figures of Speech Used in the Bible.* New York, New York, USA: Cosimo Classics.

Crossway - a publishing ministry of Good News Publishers. (2006). *The English-Greek Reverse Interlinear New Testament: English Standard Version.* (J. Schwandt, & C. J. Collins, Eds.) USA: Crossway - a publishing ministry of Good News Publishers.

Dictionary.com. (n.d.). *Dictionary.com Unabridged.* Retrieved October 27, 2014, from Dictionary.com: http://www.Dictionary.com

Elder, L., & Paul, R. (1998, May/June). The Role of Socratic Questioning in Thinking, Teaching, and Learning. *71, Issue 5.* Rohnert Park, California, USA: Heldref Publications.

Howard G. Hendricks, W. D. (2007). *Living by the Book.* Chicago, IL, USA: Moody Publishers.

Jensen, I. L. (1978). *Jensen's Survey of the Old Testament.* Chicago, Illinois, USA: Moody Publishers.

Josephus, T. F. (n.d.). *Antiquities of the Jews.* (W. Whiston, Trans.)

MacDonald, W. (1962). *True Dicipleship.* Kansas City, Kansas, USA: Walterick Publishers.

Maxwell, M. (2014). *How to Use the Socratic Method.* Retrieved June 2015, from www.SocraticMethod.net: http://www.socraticmethod.net/how_to_use_the_socratic_method/using_the_socratic_method.html

Mortimer J. Adler, C. V. (1940). *How to Read a Book.* New York, New York, USA: Simon & Schuster, Inc.

Norman L. Geisler, W. E. (1974). *From God to Us.* Chicago, Illinois, USA: Moody Press.

Plato. (399 B.C.). *Apology.* (B. Jowett, Trans.) Athens, Greece: Public Domain - The Project Gutenberg.

Rhodes, R. (2009). *The Complete Guide to Bible Translations.* Eugene, Oregon, USA: Harvest House Publishers.

Richards, I. A. (1936). *The Philosophy of Rhetoric.* New York, New York, USA: Oxford University Press.

Roberts, E. V. (2012). *Writing About Literature.* Upper Saddle River, New Jersey, USA: Pearson Education, Inc.

Spurgeon, C. H. (2010). *Lectures to My Students Kindle Edition* (Vol. Volume 4). Amazon Digial Services, Inc.

Tenney, M. C. (1961). *New Testament Survey.* Grand Rapids, Michigan, USA: Wm. B. Eerdmans Publishing Co.

The Institute for New Testament Textual Research. (2012). *Novum Testamentum Graece* (28 Rev Mul edition ed.). (T. I. Research, Ed.) Munster, Germany: German Bible Society.

Thiessen, H. C. (1949). *Lectures in Systematic Theology.* Grand Rapds, Michigan, USA: Wm. B. Eerdmans Publishing Company.

Travers, M. E. (2003). *Encountering God in the Psalms.* Grand Rapids, MI, USA: Kregel Publications.

Ussher, J. (1658). *Annals of the World.*

William Collins Sons & Co. Ltd. (1979, 1986, 1998, 2000, 2003, 2005, 2006, 2007, 2009, 2012). *Collins English Dictionary - Complete & Unabridged 2012 Digital Edition.* William Collins Sons & Co. Ltd., HarperCollins Publishers.

Bible Version	Publisher Notes
American Standard Version	1901 – Public Domain
Complete Jewish Bible	1998 – Lederer Messianic Publications
Contemporary English Version	2000 – American Bible Society
Douay-Rheims	1609 – Public Domain
English Standard Version	2001 – Crossway Bibles
God's Word Translation	1995 – God's Word to the Nations
Good News Bible	2001 – American Bible Society
Holman Christian Standard Bible	2004 – Holman Bible Publishers
King James Version	1611 – Public Domain
Modern Language Bible	1969 – Zondervan Publishing House
New American Bible	1970 – Salsbury
New American Standard Bible	1960, 1962, 1963, 1968, 1971, 1972, 1973, 1975, 1977, 1995 – the Lockman Foundation
New English Bible	1970 – Oxford University Press
New English Translation	2005 – Biblical Studies Press, L.L.C.
New International Version	1973, 1978, 1984, 2011 – Biblica
New Jerusalem Bible	1985 – Doubleday
New King James Version	1979, 1980, 1982 – HarperCollins Publishers
New Living Translation	2006 – Tyndale House Publishers
New Revised Standard Version	1989 – The Division of Christian Education of the National Council of the Churches of Christ in the USA
Revised English Bible	1989 = Oxford University Press
Revised Standard Version	1946, 1952, 1971 – The Division of Christian Education of the National Council of the Churches of Christ in the USA
The Living Bible	1971 – Tyndale House Publishers
The Message	2002 – Eugene H. Peterson
Today's New International Version	2005 – Biblica

Index of Illustrations

Figure 1–Bible Version Comparison.................................120

Figure 2–Ephesians 1:13–14 123

Figure 3–A portion of Papyrus 46. 124

Figure 4–Study Notes Heading.......................................136

Figure 5–Contextual Boundaries and Section......................137

Figure 6–Example of Recording Contextual Boundaries in Study Notes 149

Figure 7–Printout of Contextual Section............................149

Figure 8–Background Research Notes 156

Figure 9–The Big-6 Contexts 158

Figure 10–Big-6 Influences Notes 167

Figure 11–Common Figures of Speech in the Bible 181

Figure 12–PxP Study Flow 235

Figure 13–PxP in Concise Terms 236

Figure 14–Meditation 240

Figure 15–Bible Study Ideas...264

Figure 16–Clarifying the Terms 280

Figure 17–The Weaving of Matthew 17:24 - 18:35 291

Figure 18–Enter the web-site name in your browser 357

Figure 19–Enter your search information.............................358

Figure 20–Search Results for Matthew 18:6 in the NASB..........359

Figure 21–Click on the "TOOLS" button that is beside "Mat 18:6"...359

Figure 22–Outline of Biblical Usage of Words 360

Figure 23–Outline of Biblical Usage of *skandalizō—The Semantic Range* 362

Figure 24–Bible Version Comparisons 364

Made in the USA
Columbia, SC
03 July 2018